Additional Praise for *If at Birth You Don't Succeed*

"Zach makes you want to be a better person, with his humor and his heart and everything he's had to deal with from the time he was born. I've never met anyone like him, and I've met a lot of people."   —Oprah Winfrey

"Cerebral palsy couldn't stop Anner from becoming a celeb, traveling the world, and friending Oprah (for starters)."
                                                    —*Cosmopolitan*

"A laugh-a-minute read . . . *If at Birth You Don't Succeed* recounts his journey from being what he calls a 'crappy baby' [with cerebral palsy] to the host of his own travel show and an improbable workout guru. If there was ever a book that showed the importance of laughing at yourself, this is probably it."
                    —*Mental Floss* (#1 Best New Book for Spring)

"Zach Anner is a truly inspiring and hysterical human being with a warped sense of humor (and body). He's also an exceptional writer and his memoir is an absolute joy."
                                                    —Rainn Wilson

"I love Zach Anner and I love his memoir. If everyone were a little more like Zach, the world may not be a *better* place, but it would be funnier place, which is a great step forward."
                            —Alexis Ohanian, cofounder of Reddit

"I think I speak for everybody when I say . . . I want to see more of Zach."   —John Mayer

"Comedian Zach Anner takes readers on his wild wheelchair ride through thirty years of dealing with cerebral palsy—'the sexiest of the palsies,' as he likes to say. He rides a Mars Rover, wins an Oprah contest to create his own travel series, and discovers he's not only datable but desirable, too. Hilarious and inspiring, Anner has made a life filled with fans, love, and Internet fame—reminding us that disability is no match for dreams." —*People* (Book of the Week)

"Zach Anner is way more than an inspirational figure for anyone who has ever felt impossibly different: he's also a great f**king writer. Wise and funny, with unfailing insight into the booby trap known as the human mind, you will hang on every word as you watch him turn his considerable intellectual gifts into a life worth envying. I like that this book has no genre, and neither does this special man." —Lena Dunham

"A characteristically hilarious and candid book about growing up with cerebral palsy, winning a reality TV contest with Oprah's OWN channel, and becoming an unlikely-yet-inspiring fitness guru and YouTube celebrity with more than ten million views." —*What's Trending*

"Zach Anner is the living definition of 'giving better than he's gotten.' Life dealt him a difficult hand, but he managed to beat the house with humor, heart, and a fearless punk attitude. Required reading." —Patton Oswalt

"Wonderful . . . Anner's comedy is the peppy, uplifting sort you'd expect from someone who Oprah says 'makes [her] want to be a better person,' such as his elaborate Olive Garden metaphors for the nature of life. . . . Anner remarks wryly that being expected to act as an ambassador for the disabled 'is a tightrope walk, which is hard on four wheels.' Maybe so, but with this book, he makes it look easy."

—*Publishers Weekly* (starred review)

"Funny, empowering . . . An inspirational memoir with a seasoned, infectious sense of humor . . . [Anner's book chronicles] his three decades of life (so far) with cerebral palsy, a permanent condition that hasn't prevented him from living his dream as a comic, a media sensation, and a motivational speaker."

—*Kirkus Reviews*

"Forget the travel show, Oprah. Give him a sitcom."

—*The New York Times*

"Our favorite lovable, optimistic, and absolutely hilarious YouTube star in a wheelchair."

—*The Huffington Post*

"He's a unique, creative kid with a smart, edgy sense of humor."

—Arsenio Hall

"Meet Zach Anner . . . He's handsome, smart, and funny [and] has won . . . legions of online fans."

—Tara Parker-Pope,
The New York Times

"Zach Anner . . . Internet folk hero."

—*Vulture,*
New York magazine

If at Birth You Don't Succeed

MY ADVENTURES WITH DISASTER AND DESTINY

Zach Anner

Illustrations by Kevin Scarborough

 St. Martin's Griffin ☙ New York

www.stmartins.com

Designed by Meryl Sussman Levavi

The Library of Congress has cataloged the Henry Holt edition as follows:

Anner, Zach, 1984–
    If at birth you don't succeed : my adventures with disaster and destiny / Zach Anner.
        p. cm.
    ISBN 978-1-62779-364-3 (hardback)
    ISBN 978-1-62779-365-0 (e-book)
    1. Anner, Zach, 1984–   2. Comedians—United States—Biography.
    3. Cerebral palsied—United States—Biography.   I. Title.
    PN2287.A645A3 2016
    791.4302'8092—dc23
    [B]   2015023841

ISBN 978-1-250-11654-3 (trade paperback)

Our books may be purchased in bulk for promotional, educational, or business use. Please contact your local bookseller or the Macmillan Corporate and Premium Sales Department at 1-800-221-7945, extension 5442, or by e-mail at MacmillanSpecialMarkets@macmillan.com.

First published by Henry Holt, an imprint of Henry Holt and Company, LLC

First St. Martin's Griffin Edition: March 2017

P1

For my mom and dad,

who gave me life

and a sense of humor about it

Contents

Part II: Friends in Search of Benefits

Part III: The Learning Curve of a Late Bloomer

If at Birth You Don't Succeed

. . . Well, Why Don't I Start?

It's 8:00 a.m. on a Sunday morning and I'm bouncing on a trampoline surrounded by a film crew, shouting jokes into a camera. Soon, the doors of the Jumpstreet trampoline park in Austin, Texas, will open to a flood of children on their way to the best birthday parties ever, but for now it's empty and cavernous as my friends struggle to steady their cameras and boom poles while catapulting me up into the air like a rag doll. I'm thirty years old and being professionally silly is what I do for a living—or at least part of it.

I've been a comedian, hosted travel shows, explored world religions, started improv troupes, given keynote speeches at conferences around the country, and had a milk shake named after me called the Handicappuccino. I was also briefly an Oprah protégé and the subject of a John Mayer song (sadly, it wasn't "Your Body Is a Wonderland"). Not bad for a guy in a wheelchair who almost flunked out of kindergarten and whose only degrees are a GED and an honorary "Ducktorate" from the Disney College Program.

But on this cold February morning, I'm a fitness guru and we're filming an episode of my YouTube series *Workout Wednesday*. The theme of this ridiculous installment is "Bouncing Back," and I'm shouting every random esoteric pop culture reference I can think of to sell my audience on the idea that the greatest failures can also be catalysts for triumph. For me, that's been true from the start.

When I was born, instead of waiting to become an angelic, full-term bouncing cherub, I showed up two months early to my own birthday party as a three-pound, seven-ounce screaming hairless mole rat of a boy, kept alive by a series of tubes that would later become known as the Internet. I take full responsibility for this kerfuffle. Even though my mother was involved in the process, she'd gone through the whole ordeal with my brother a year earlier and he'd turned out great. There's no denying it: I was a crappy baby who failed his way into this world and I've been making the best of it ever since.

As a result of my untimely birth, I have cerebral palsy, which I guess, if you wanna get technical about it, is a neurological condition that can affect motor skills, speech, and mobility to varying degrees. In my case, it means that my movements resemble that of a marionette whose puppeteer is having passionate maritals behind the little red curtain. I use an electric wheelchair because I have no sense of balance and muscle spasticity has arched my spine like a cat's, while my legs are really just for show. I also have a lazy eye, but I believe that has less to do with the CP and more to do with the fact that as a baby I was operated on by an ophthalmologist who'd previously performed surgery only on giraffes. With my eyes unable to track, I never read, and I can't type, so I never thought I'd write a book, yet here you are, reading the first pages of my memoir like a champ. As it turns out, I'm somebody who was born in the wrong month, but at the right time to tell his unlikely—though not unlucky—story.

My success is as much a product of the age we live in as anything else. I gained notoriety thanks to a viral video, I got to work for Oprah thanks to the format of reality TV, I traveled the country using suggestions from the Internet, hell, I even met my girlfriend on Twitter. We've worked together on this book over Skype and Google Docs, while she was living in Berlin and I was six to nine time zones away in the United States. If I had been born only a few decades earlier, I might have been some mysterious recluse confined to a decrepit mansion who writes poems about what grass must feel like. Instead, I've lived a vibrant life and get to share my story with you.

In the following pages you'll read about all my career peaks and my many romantic valleys. You'll get a behind-the-scenes look of what it's like to work at Disney World and also what it's like to narrowly avoid self-castration. I hope you'll find these stories relatable, humorous, and meaningful, because if not, there's just a lot of really embarrassing shit in here. Some of these stories would have been too personal and painful to share if I didn't think they had the potential to help other people feel a little more comfortable in their own skin. For better or worse, I have now published all the things that up until this point I was too ashamed to tell my mother.

My life didn't really make a whole lot of sense to me before I started writing this book. How on earth did I get my own TV show from the most powerful woman in the world before I had my first kiss from a girl? How did somebody who couldn't get a job cold-calling people for magazine subscriptions end up in the entertainment industry? How did a kid who was unable to legally obtain a driver's license blossom into a man who was trusted behind the wheel of the Mars Rover? And how did a guy who regularly falls off toilets make friends who would literally carry him up mountains? What I've learned from taking a bird's-eye view of my life so far is that the good fortune I've had has come from seizing not just my moments but my mistakes. I might not be able to tie my own shoelaces, but if there's one skill I've perfected, it's the art of finding the humor and the purpose in every failure. I've accepted that we've all got crap to deal with and problems that we're fighting not to be defined by. At the end of the day, we all want the same stuff: fulfillment, love, support, comfort, and a hot-air balloon with laser guns attached to it. The most important thing is that we appreciate the crazy ride we're on.

The "Bouncing Back" *Workout Wednesday* episode ended with my friends launching me into a trampoline wall in an epic wipeout. As I lay there, sweaty and bruised, the only thing I had energy left to do was nurse my whiplash and go get some breakfast tacos. But then my friend and cameraman Chris Demarais came up to me with a twinkle in his eye and said, "You know, this place has a mechanical bull. Would you be up for filming another one?"

I considered my exhaustion and the risk of injury, anticipated the impatient line of gawking eight-year-olds, and decided to grab the bull by the horns.

"Sure," I said. "Just let me catch my breath." Because I knew that no matter how this shook out, getting creamed on a trampoline and riding a mechanical bull is a pretty badass way to spend a Sunday morning.

Giddy-up!

I

Oprah to Nope-rah

CHAPTER 1

What's in a N4me?

I grew up watching a lot of plays because my mom worked for Buffalo's annual Shakespeare in the Park, so I can appreciate the Bard's work for the sword fights and the Reese's Peanut Butter Cups I'd get at intermission. I look back fondly on those summer nights spent sitting on a blanket, lathering up in bug spray, and crawling through the crowd to see if I could charm my way to even better snacks from strangers. Whenever the soliloquies bored us, my brother Brad and I would scamper off to the playground and stage duels with plastic dollar-store swords. No matter how vigorous the battle, we'd always try to make it back to the hill in time to catch the real fencing between the Montagues and Capulets onstage. I must have seen the "good parts" of *Romeo and Juliet* forty times as a five-year-old.

But when I was old enough to actually read and comprehend

the ill-fated tale of the two Italian teenagers, I took exception to some of Bill's poetic assertions, in particular his hypothesis that "a rose by any other name would smell as sweet." Even at twelve, I knew, in my heart of hearts, that this was absolute rubbish. If roses were known as "break-up-me-nows," a long-stemmed dozen delivered to your girlfriend's office on Valentine's Day would do a pretty decent job of killing the mood, and if you called a rose a "blooming colonoscopy," *nobody* would care how lovely it smelled and I guarantee you that Dame Maggie Smith would not attend your garden party.

Now, Shakespeare's poetry might be enough justification for two angsty teenagers to fall in love and kill themselves, but let's be honest—that's kind of like shooting fish in a barrel. I'm not saying who's the better writer here, me or Shakespeare (I'll leave that up to you to decide after you read my chapter on manscaping)—all I'm saying is that names matter. I know this because without my name, my life would have taken a completely different course. I would go so far as to say that if my name was anything else, no one would care who I was. This book would not exist. Whether you want to call it fate, destiny, or a coincidence of star-crossed letters, my name and my path were intertwined from the day I was born.

If my dad had had his way, I might've been known as Trondor. *Tron* was a very popular movie in the early '80s, but I'm glad I didn't wind up as a twenty-nine-year-old whose name-sake was a fictional DOS-based computer program on a scooter (although, on reflection, he would've gotten the scooter part right). The other name at the top of my dad's list was Benjamin. And Benjamin Anner doesn't sound half bad! You know, like the type of guy who might wear cardigans and Oxford shirts and cultivate a dry yet biting wit. But that wasn't what my dad had in mind. He wanted me to adopt the abbreviated "Ben," so that when paired with Anner my name would become Benanner. Yes, that's right, my own father wanted my name to be a play on the word "banana." I don't want to make assumptions, but I'm pretty darn sure that the only person willing to embrace the nickname "Be- nanner" wears Hawaiian shirts and tube socks with sandals, has a police scanner on his paddleboat, and goes to strip clubs for the buffet. I've had a plethora of nicknames in my life- time, but thankfully, none were as damning as that.

I grew up being called "Zachy" by my grandma. The kids at school called me "Zach Attack," except for one of my fellow oc- cupational therapy patients who had Down syndrome and would excitedly exclaim "Zach Morris!" every time I rolled into a room, and then, upon learning that I was not the popular character from *Saved by the Bell*, was repeatedly disappointed. There were other nicknames too. My brother and I interchange- ably called each other "Fuckface." After my parents' divorce, my mom's boyfriend Greg joined in with my family's crude but loving sense of humor and decided to call me by the endearing nickname "Dickless," whereas my best friend, Andrew, chose to go with the affirmative, often just referring to me as "Dick."

Then there were the names that I gave myself: "Sergio" and "Eduardo" (when I went through my Latin lover phase), and, when forced to shuffle down the street with my walker, I would occasionally even adopt a female persona, donning my mother's barrettes and shifting my already ultra-girly prepubescent voice up an octave to become "Zacharina." Since walking was a tedious activity that only served to remind me that I couldn't move like other kids, I had to spruce it up with something fun that normal boys would do—like cross-dressing!

Of course, there were also the names that invariably come with being born with cerebral palsy and using a wheelchair. Cripple, retard, spaz, gimp, and a whole bunch of other things whispered under somebody's breath in the hallway or shouted in the heat of a floor hockey match in gym class. Thankfully, the only name that stuck was the one I was given at birth.

I came to be known as Zach Anner through tumultuous circumstances. When my mother went into labor with me two months ahead of schedule, the time my parents had to think of baby names was cut short. So my mom, who had always liked the name Zachary, named me after a US president no one really knows or cares about, Zachary Taylor. The most notable and only thing I ever learned about him was from the dictionary with all the presidential portraits in my dad's house. He was the one president in that book wearing a sword in his painting, which to my six-year-old mind made him cool enough to be my namesake.

My parents' reasoning was not sword-based; they felt Zachary suited me because of President Taylor's nickname: "Old Rough and Ready." This didn't seem to fit with my premature arrival at three pounds, seven ounces, and my five-week stay in an intensive care nursery; the name was just wishful thinking that someday, no matter how rough things were, I would be ready. But the only thing I was ready for when I was born was not dying. And then not dying progressed to living. At the time of my birth, living *well* was nothing more than a hope. It would take a long time for me to make good on the promise of "Old Rough and Ready," but in some ways, I owe both my identity and my career to my name.

For the first quarter century of my life, my birth name was the subject of little controversy and served merely as a way for people to identify me and get my attention without shouting "Hey, Wheelie McMuffin!" or "What up, gimp?" In fact, the only point of contention surrounding my actual name was how it was spelled. People tend to treat the name Zach like it's the word "Chanukah," like you can just start with a Z, put a vowel in the middle and some consonants at the end, and you'll wind up with something acceptable. That's not true. My name is Zach. Z-a-c-h. Four letters. That's all you need to remember.

It was important to my mother that I learn how to spell my own name, especially since my dad often misspelled it. I am an "H" Zach. I was not a "K" Zack. I did not go surfing and put lemon juice in my hair to make it unnaturally blond. Driving this point home to my teachers probably got my mother the reputation as one of *those* moms. But as a six-year-old who could neither enunciate nor project, or even hold his head up very well, people automatically assumed that a physical disability was indicative of a mental one. There's no better way to unintentionally reinforce this misconception than answering the question "How do you spell your name?" by shrugging and saying, "I dunno, whatever." So while it might have seemed overzealous at the time to place such importance on a single letter, my mom fought for that "H," and in the end, it was that letter that made all the difference. In the years between when my name became important to me and when it started mattering to anyone else, I paid little attention to it and focused instead on my dreams of stardom.

When we were growing up, my dad constantly filmed my brother and me with his enormous Panasonic video camera, which recorded direct to VHS tapes via a cable attached to a separate tape deck the size of a Ghostbusters pack. Whether he was shooting us licking the cream fillings of Oreos and sticking them to the wall behind the couch or blasting cap guns and covering ourselves in fake blood, my dad encouraged a flair for showmanship and a passion for filmmaking in both his sons.

I love making videos almost as much as I love making people laugh. In high school, I would show up with a handicam, drifting from table to table in the lunchroom and filming pre–YouTube-style vlogs, which I called *The Zach Show*. My intrusive and incessant filming of my peers ensured that instead of being known as just "that kid in the wheelchair," I was rebranded as "that obnoxious guy with the camera." Later, after transferring to film school at the University of Texas at Austin, I starred in a sketch comedy show called *That's Awesome!* where I gained the reputation of being the hilariously offensive guy who could get away with saying anything. But being crass just for shock value quickly lost its appeal, and as I matured, I shifted my efforts toward projects that meant something, that I could be proud to attach my name to. I worked very hard over a period of several years turning Zach Anner, the insult comic, into Zach Anner, the optimist adventurer and all-around positive wheelchair-bound lady magnet.

In the summer of 2010, when I was twenty-five and living in Texas, I became associated with one of the most recognizable names in all the known universe—Oprah Winfrey. At the time she was launching the Oprah Winfrey Network and had a promotional competition where anyone could pitch their "OWN" show. Basically, you'd pick a show category—cooking, health and well-being, fashion, finance, pop culture—and post a short video audition. The public would vote and the top ten hopefuls would then face off on a reality competition called *Your OWN Show: Oprah's Search for the Next TV Star,* where one contestant would ultimately win a season of their TV show. Over fifteen thousand people made submissions, so my mom figured that I had a pretty good shot and eventually convinced me to enter.

My video entry began with a simple introduction, "Hi, my name is Zach Anner, and I have something called cerebral palsy—which I believe is the *sexiest* of the palsies . . ." I then explained why I would be a horrible TV host for each of the proposed categories, showing myself burning toast on a stove while wearing a chef's hat, modeling a sparkly dress and my grandmother's wig as the least convincing drag queen since Wesley Snipes in that *To Wong Foo* movie, and tumbling through improvised yoga poses in a revealing paisley Speedo.

After a minute of pointing out everything I sucked at, I spent the last two describing my concept for a show I'd actually be perfect for: a travelogue for people who never thought they could travel; a show that would inspire the audience to go out and see the world. I wanted to urge everyone to embrace the spontaneous and unexpected nature of globe-trotting through a sense of humor. I closed the video with a rousing promise that my show would prove that "no mountain is too high, no volcano is too hot, and no Atlantis is too underwater or fictional!" In the end, I thought I did a pretty good job selling myself as a television personality for someone with a seven-dollar haircut and an oversize shirt, but just because I put the video up didn't mean that anyone would see it or care.

After a week online, my entry had received high praise from my mom and my childhood occupational therapist, but only a few hundred votes on the Oprah competition Web site, and there were other submissions that had already amassed millions. In a last-ditch effort to get my name out there, some friends, my brother, and I took a spontaneous trip to Dallas to audition for Oprah recruiters in person. When we arrived in the parking lot of a Kohl's department store at dawn, there were already hundreds in line to try out. I was exhausted from driving all night, was generally unkempt, and probably could have used some deodorant.

When it was my turn, I was ushered to a round folding table with twelve other hopefuls and given one minute to sell myself and my show to a casting director. Running on pure adrenaline and no sleep, I gave the most energetic pitch of my life. For someone who had barely remembered to put shoes on, I had surprising command of an audience. But to be honest, it's all a blur now. I can only recall that at the end of my sixty seconds, the round table of other would-be Oprah protégés and exceedingly peppy recruiters cheered. Afterward, my exhausted motley crew and I slugged our way through the rides at the nearby Six Flags adventure theme park to pass the time while waiting to see if my impassioned speech had earned a callback. It hadn't.

As we drove from the amusement park to our crash pad at my friend Marshall's grandma's place, I got word from my college friend Chris Demarais that my audition video was doing well on a site called Reddit. He sent me a picture someone had posted of something that in all my wildest dreams I never thought I would see—my name scrawled out in permanent marker across a pair of naked breasts. Not only that, but it was spelled correctly! I had no idea what Reddit was, but I liked it. At that point, I thought my name had reached its peak, but the world had bigger plans than ZACH ANNER on boobs.

On the evening of June 13, 2010, two weeks after the original posting, my video had picked up steam and garnered about twelve thousand votes, which made me very happy. There was no way I would ever catch up to the leading videos in the contest, but it was nice to see that I might have found a niche audience. Chris and I had tried to get my travel show off the ground for years, writing a treatment and applying for grants, but nobody seemed interested. Now people I'd never met were getting behind not only my idea but behind me as a person. It was a nice feeling for a guy who wasn't sure if he'd ever be able to hack it in the entertainment industry. The sting of the casting directors' rejection faded and I went to bed satisfied with my new smattering of topless fans.

I was woken in the middle of the night and carried out of my friend Marshall's grandmother's house, and then down the street to Marshall's parents' house, because they had Internet. Nobody would tell me what was going on. But my brother and friends sat me down in a chair and I could tell from the huge video camera in my face that either something extraordinary had happened or I was about to get a surprise kick in the nuts. My brother turned on the computer and pulled up the audition video I'd already voted for twenty times earlier that day. I was still three-quarters asleep as my childhood friend Andrew stood behind me biting his nails, waiting for me to realize what they already knew. Then I heard Marshall say from behind the camera, "Why don't you just read how many votes you have there." I looked at the screen in front of me and was overtaken by an excitement I hadn't felt since I was a kid racing downstairs on Christmas morning.

"What the BALLS is this?!" I sputtered in disbelief as it hit me that twelve thousand votes had miraculously skyrocketed into more than two million over the course of just a few hours. It was the most flabbergasting of all flabbergasts. And the only reason this happened was because of the name Zach Anner and the misplaced dedication of thousands of other people whose names I'll never know.

While I'd been peacefully dreaming about riding a humpback whale in a middle school gymnasium, my audition video had circulated through Reddit to the online community 4chan. I didn't know what it was at the time, but I later came to understand that 4chan is an online forum that is frequented by, among millions of other users, a controversial group of cyber activists called Anonymous who use their enormous Internet presence to turn the tides of the Web, depending on the whims of the masses lurking in the shadows behind their keyboards. To this day, I've never made a post on or even visited 4chan. But they thought my video was genuinely hilarious, and, as it turns out, a few posters saw another reason to get behind my irreverent pitch. A case of mistaken identity had made me an unwitting warrior in a battle against the Queen of Television that had begun years earlier.

I suppose the absurdity of a guy in a wheelchair making jokes while wearing wigs and a dress might seem like the perfect prank to pull on Oprah, a personality some 4channers had decried as preachy and disingenuous. But it was my name coupled with my irreverence that started the perfect storm of online conspiracy theories. And it all came down to that H.

It took me years to piece together the story of what happened with 4chan during the competition, and I'm still not sure I have all the facts straight. I don't know when or why 4chan's feud with Oprah began, but they had trolled their way onto *The Oprah Winfrey Show* before by making mayhem and outrageous claims. On those occasions, they'd communicated with the show's producers by using the screen name Opr4h, substituting the vowel *a* with the number 4. Once my video was posted on the 4chan forums, it didn't take long for them to start connecting imaginary dots that unearthed the biggest online cover-up to have never existed.

It was at this moment that the potential in my name, which had been dormant for twenty-five years, awoke and started working its peculiar magic. Imagine you're Tom Hanks in an underwhelming, sloppily scripted thriller we'll just call *The Da Gimpi Code*. If Oprah becomes Opr4h, and you apply that same logic to my name, Zach becomes Z4ch, and all you need to do is be a little liberal with the spacing and use that serendipitously placed H . . . and Zach Anner becomes Z4channer . . . Z - 4chan - ner! And just like that, for better or worse, I had been adopted by the most controversial presence on the Web. Without even realizing it, I had become their star. The idea of me going head-to-head with the most powerful woman in show business on her own turf inspired thousands of deliberately anonymous people to vote thousands of times for the fake person, Z4chAnner. The real Zach Anner was, of course, oblivious to this.

In the days that followed, the attention from 4chan and Reddit caused my video to go viral, eventually tallying nine million votes and earning me a spot on Oprah's reality competition. But no matter how it happened, my audition was seen by *a lot* of people. For the first time the world knew my name, and they knew Zach Anner as the positive funny guy who wanted adventure. I was championed by everyone from John Mayer to David Hasselhoff and was suddenly featured in *Time* magazine, *USA Today*, and the *New York Times*, and on a bunch of TV shows: I was profiled by Sanjay Gupta on CNN, featured on *ABC News* with Diane Sawyer (but without Diane Sawyer), and brought my complete lack of balance over to the fair and balanced folks at *FOX News*. I received thousands of messages from complete strangers about how my video had moved them and changed their perception of people with disabilities. My name actually started to mean something bigger than myself; it meant hope and possibility to a population that had largely been ignored. And then things got ugly.

Despite a general goodwill toward me that people rarely see on the Internet, there inevitably came rumblings of cheating on both sides. Ridiculous rumors circulated that Oprah was trying to rig the competition in favor of another contestant, and for a whole day the number one search on Google was "Oprah Hates the Handicapped." And there were still people out there who thought I was just a big ruse. To them I was some con artist who, instead of posing as a billionaire prince from some obscure country, had opted instead for the much more glamorous persona of a guy in a wheelchair with a lazy eye who sometimes peed his pants if he laughed too hard.

But amid the whispers of "cheat" and "phony," I stayed true to myself. Whenever some shock-jock radio host or a gossip site tried to get me to say something bad about Oprah, I wouldn't engage in the negativity. I refused to speculate about why six million of my nine million votes were abruptly and mysteriously deducted from my video midway through the competition. I just shrugged and said, "The Internet's a crazy place and I'm extremely grateful to everyone who supported me. And I'm a huge fan of Oprah." Weathering that time period and toeing the line between gratitude toward Oprah and toward my fervent but unpredictable Internet saviors helped me realize why "Old Rough and Ready" might be the right nickname for me after all.

When I was born, those who didn't know me would have called my circumstances a tragedy. But my parents knew better. When they looked at me, what they saw was just a kid who was destined to take a different path than that of anyone else they'd known. They gave me the tools to explore and let me find my own identity. It took me years to figure it out, but nowadays when people come up to me on the street and excitedly ask, "Are you Zach Anner?!" I'm able to confidently say, "Yes!" because I finally know who that guy is. I'm a guy who's been able to recognize that sometimes the only difference between mistakes and miracles is what you choose to call them. And the most interesting lives are the ones that have an equal mix of both.

CHAPTER 2

How to Win
a Television Show

"Four thirty in the morning, perfect time to get up!" said no one ever. Day Two of filming *Your OWN Show: Oprah's Search for the Next TV Star* began in the dark, or at least it did for me. Technically, we had a 7:30 a.m. call time for arriving at the studio, but I needed a full three hours to get ready for the day. My morning routine would be repeated and perfected at my new home in the Sheraton Universal Hotel in Los Angeles over the next several weeks. First, my best friend Andrew and I would exchange groggy morning salutations through the wall of our adjoining rooms and then, five minutes later, he'd walk in like a bear fighting tranquilizers, fussing with his glasses and absentmindedly playing with his ample chest hair while he waited for me to pick the perfect outfit for him to iron. My wardrobe for my audition video had consisted of a

Speedo, a dress, and a chef's hat. Somehow that silly video had made me a reality show star, and now I had to dress the part.

Filming this TV competition was potentially a monthlong gig, depending on when you were eliminated, so I'd packed optimistically according to what I thought my prospects were: about five days' worth of clothes. Upon realizing I'd only brought four pairs of underwear (and you need at *least* five), Andrew had made an emergency excursion to Target the day before, to make sure I wasn't competing commando.

"What color you wanna wear, Broseph?" Andrew asked as he ripped the plastic off the Fruit of the Loom five-pack. Today was important because it was the first elimination day and, not trusting in my actual ability, I put all my faith in my boxer briefs.

"Let's go with the purple ones. Those will be my new lucky underwear," I declared.

Like I always say, the best friends provide moral support AND ball support.

Breakfast arrived at 5:00 a.m. with a knock on the door. Andrew answered it in a state of déshabille, greeting our formally dressed bellman, who I came to think of as a less enthusiastic, Indian version of Lumière, the candlestick from *Beauty and the Beast*. He wheeled in our morning banquet, asking eloquently, "How is morning?" before lifting silver covers from each item and announcing them as though the dishes were foreign dignitaries at a ball: "Orange juice ... coffee ... pastry ... bacon ..." and something he ingeniously mislabeled a "fruit melody." I appreciated the pageantry for something that moments later I would be eating on the floor, still half-naked. Breakfast deserved reverence because it was the only meal I would allow myself to eat all day.

My stomach had been a beast since high school. I couldn't

tame or reason with it, and it would unmercifully wreak havoc without warning. No matter how kind and careful I tried to be to my digestive tract, its mood swings were violently erratic. I was living with my own private Grendel in Tummy Town, where fruits, vegetables, enchiladas, and ice cream could happily coexist, until one misplaced bread crumb or Skittle would summon The Beast and the whole town descended into chaos. With no children to sacrifice and no Beowulf, the most I could do to appease The Beast was feed it and sedate it with Imodium. Since we're all friends here, I have no problem dropping eighth-century Old English literature analogies to tell you that I need a good twenty minutes in the bathroom every morning . . . and by twenty minutes I mean forty minutes . . . and by forty minutes I mean *at least* an hour . . . just check back later! My self-imposed early wake-up call was to accommodate this very long engagement.

I had a lot to prove on this competition. There was always the question of whether I could withstand the fifteen-hour days and be a serious contender. I knew my mind was up to the task, but like an elephant on a unicycle, it was a delicate balance getting my body to cooperate. After all, how would I be able to make a travel show that embraced the unexpected if I couldn't thrive in a controlled environment in which makeup artists *thanked* me for allowing them the privilege of trimming my nose hair? In order to make the world more accessible, I was going to have to present the most accessible version of myself to the world.

Andrew was there to make sure that no matter *what* transpired in the three hours before I headed out the door, I was 100 percent straightened, combed, pressed, primped, and brushed by call time (in the industry, they call it "wheels up," just in case you want to feel cool). I was the only contestant out of the ten finalists allowed to have a friend/"medically necessary assistant" in his room at the Sheraton. Then again, I was also the only one with cerebral palsy.

The compromise we'd struck with the production team was this: Andrew could take care of me before and after hours, but I couldn't tell him anything about what was happening on the show. Since Andrew was a trained EMT, I presented him as a medical professional and neglected to mention that he had also been my best friend since third grade. Every morning he'd bid me farewell by saying, "Chew bubble gum," a phrase co-opted from our favorite childhood video game hero, Duke Nukem, who, just before opening fire on his alien foes, boldly declares, "It's time to kick ass and chew bubble gum—and I'm all out of gum." With these three simple words, my best friend had found a way to subvert the OWN competition's strict No Encouragement policy and *chew bubble gum* became our mantra. After we parted, Andrew could go off and have adventures in Los Angeles during the day, and an aide named Hershall would look after me on set, presumably to make sure I didn't break or steal shit.

Because of my filmmaking background, the prospect of reality television terrified me. Reality shows are based on drama and character, and I knew from my own experience working in the TV studio at the University of Texas that both were extremely malleable in the editing bay. My character was in the hands of producers I had only known for a day, and my fear was that I'd be presented as the helpless little boy in the wheelchair. By Day Two, I'd given them plenty of footage to support that depiction.

The format of the show had ten finalists broken into two

teams who competed by producing different types of mock-television segments with a new celebrity mentor each week—makeover segments, cooking segments, late-night talk show segments—basically, any form of TV that requires hosting. Then, the OWN competition's judges, *Queer Eye for the Straight Guy*'s Carson Kressley and *Entertainment Tonight*'s Nancy O'Dell, would judge the segments and someone from the losing team would be sent home.

For the first challenge, we were supposed to do "Man on the Street" interviews with the guidance of Dr. Phil. Both teams were instructed to choose a topic for him to comment on, and I had come up with "How Technology Affects Relationships." I was charged with the task of stopping people outside the Universal Studios Theme Park and talking to them about psychology. I'd done this type of thing a hundred times before when I was a show host for my student television station at the University of Texas, but how can one guy in a wheelchair surrounded by gigantic cameras compete with the magic of Harry Potter and genetically enhanced turkey legs? He can't! They were setting us up to fail! It was an experience so disheartening that when I returned to the Sheraton at the end of Day One, I told Andrew to pack our bags. Given my volume of clothes, this took two seconds.

In my mind, the only thing that could save me from the previous day's disaster was a completely superstitious one—the newly anointed pair of lucky purple underwear I'd put on that morning. I didn't think my magical boxer briefs could save me from elimination, but maybe, just maybe, they could spare me from a brutal public shaming by Dr. Phil, America's Number One Disapproving Military Father.

Dr. Phil is a large man with a looming presence. Immediately upon meeting my team, he had turned our joy and excitement about being on the show into mortal fear of being unqualified. Trying to be cool, I'd asked him casually, "What kind of dynamic do you like to have with folks onstage? What do I need to do to make you feel comfortable?" To which he'd humorlessly replied, "Don't worry about what *I* need, worry about what *YOU* need to do. You are all incredibly unprepared." I knew what I needed to do—crawl into a corner and suck my thumb for a bit! Usually it took people getting to know me before they were so disappointed. This was not a good start. In Dr. Phil's mind, we had no business in television and should all be out digging ditches somewhere, and the last ditch we dig should be our own grave—'cause that's just how useless we were. Or at least that's how it felt.

Today, we had to answer for the losers I was sure Dr. Phil had already reduced us to. When we got to the set, I had just enough time to go up the ramp and find my place onstage, after banging into all the chairs. But when Dr. Phil arrived, he wasn't the imposing figure in a three-piece suit from the day before but rather Dr. Phil Casual, in black dress pants and a polo, accessorized with a completely new demeanor. The rehearsal went smoothly, and he gave my teammates and me the much needed and liberating advice to tone down the hammy shtick we'd pre-scripted and just keep it natural.

When my team got in front of the cameras to film our mock TV segment, the stern and unimpressed Dr. Phil we'd met yesterday magically transformed into a warm and humorous Dr. Phil. He laughed at our jokes, even though he'd already heard them at rehearsal, and made the best out of whatever we gave him. When my teammate Ryan asked how much I knew about sexting, I quipped, "Nothing, but I would like to receive some!" And Dr. Phil added, "Well, that's a whole other show." It had gone well and I hadn't been completely useless. This could only mean one thing—the lucky purple underwear had worked!

But there was still the wild card of the other team's segment. I had no idea what *their* underwear was like. For all I knew, they could be wearing panties made from Pegasus feathers! I hoped my Fruit of the Loom would hold up against whatever under-armor they'd brought to this battle. But in the end, not even wardrobe could have saved them, because they'd chosen to focus their segment on the thought-provoking and socially responsible query: "Does wearing condoms cause depression, and consider-ing this, should you use them?" Turns out the answer was, yes, you should use condoms, because, apparently, getting AIDS is *slightly* more depressing than wearing a condom. Glad somebody finally made the definitive call on that one!

At two thirty in the afternoon, we broke for lunch. We headed outside to the craft services table and the cast entered what is called "lockdown." That means that since the cameras weren't rolling, all cast members had to do their best to pretend the others didn't exist. We couldn't speak to each other, because if something even remotely interesting were to happen that, God forbid, wasn't being filmed, what would be the point? So these lunches became all about the food. Even whispers about the weather were immediately shut down for fear that saying, "It's a lot hotter than I expected it to be," might be a strategic code designed to rig the whole competition. While the rest of my team sought comfort in trays of lasagna, salad, and cob-bler, I maintained my steady post-breakfast diet of air, which is more substantial in LA because of the smog.

All day, as he had the day before, my assistant Hershall tried to get me to eat. Did I want pretzels? Crackers? Cheese cubes? Water? Are you sure no pretzels? Not being privy to my morning ritual, he couldn't understand my rigid fast. I *wanted* to eat all of those things but I couldn't risk waking The Beast! For that reason, it was best not to eat while I was with other people, or in any situation where getting to a bathroom with six seconds' notice was not an option. My stomach was on lockdown too.

Some people fear death or public speaking, but my most consuming fear was crapping myself in public. I would gladly die onstage while giving the State of the Union address before I let that happen. But my steadfast refusal to eat posed a problem for Hershall, who had been hired for the sole purpose of helping me with the parts of the competition that were physically prohibitive, which so far had been absolutely nothing. Hershall had become a man who was being paid to be told he wasn't needed. That didn't stop him from trying.

When he asked me for the forty-seventh time, maybe it was his youthful puppy-dog face, or that forty-seventh-time's-a-charm rule, but I finally relented. "Okay," I said. "I guess I could try to eat some fruit." Hershall sprinted off and in seconds returned with a fantastic fruit medley that put my breakfast to shame: diced-up honeydew, cantaloupe, pineapple, grapes, strawberries, the works. I let him down easy, like a father telling his son he won't be home for Christmas this year. "Hershall, I promise you I will eat this as soon as I get home. This looks great." He put on a brave face, stuffing the fruit into a big ziplock bag and tucking it into the back pocket of my wheelchair.

After lunch, we headed into the red lacquered gallows of Stage Two to face the judgment of Dr. Phil. I didn't know if we'd be meeting the friendly one from earlier, the frigid one from the day before, or a completely new one, with a sombrero, perhaps. Sadly, it was the hat-less, calculated Dr. Phil from yesterday. But it became abundantly clear pretty quickly that my team had won the challenge, simply by virtue of not advocating unprotected sex. We were so close to the end of the day. *So close.* The lucky underwear was living up to its name. We had been sent back to the quiet comfort of the carefully arranged prop furniture in the green room, while leaders from the other team stayed behind to plead for reprieve from Dr. Phil. All we had to do was wait out their fate and film a few more minutes of us clinking champagne glasses in a victory celebration.

I had just begun to relax, anticipating the big dinner I'd eat back at the hotel with Andrew, when I felt a familiar twinge in my stomach; The Beast was stirring. It was hungry and I hadn't fed it all day, which made it very, very irritable. I could hear The Beast's moaning—like a baby whale that's lost its mother, but angrier. If I could just keep it contained, I might be able to chalk up my wincing and nervous sweating to sadness for which-ever contestant was on the chopping block. Can the camera tell the difference between compassion and diarrhea?

There were two hundred people in the crew. All of us had been at work for eleven hours. I knew that if I went to the bath-room, I was going to hold up the whole production. Couldn't The Beast be held at bay for just a little bit longer?

Meanwhile, on Stage Two, the deliberation was taking a few more minutes than expected, and while others feigned con-cern for their fellow competitors, I remained stoic and quiet, trying to fend off internal chaos while my mind kept repeating over and over, *what the fuck is going on in there?* Then The Beast moved lower, causing a spasm in my sphincter so alarming that I knew disaster was imminent. The monster was storming the gates and the defenses would not hold. I needed to find a bathroom immediately!

I pulled Dino, the task producer, aside and confessed that I wasn't feeling well and needed to go to the bathroom. At this point, I was really pushing it, doing gymnastics inside my stomach to keep things from heading where they wanted to go. The other contestants had been denied their requests to take a 10-1 (as they call it in the business), but Dino recognized the horror on my face and just said, "Okay."

Thus began my frenzied dash to the crew bathroom, as Hershall, now essential to the war effort, followed close behind. I couldn't afford a single delay. If I was going to make it, it would be the mother of all close calls. We shuffled past the camera-ready polish of the OWN studio set, into the back warehouse filled with shelf upon shelf of props and equipment. I could see the bathroom door. I was almost there. My stomach was tense and churning, a volcano ready to erupt and engulf everything in its path. But at least I'd made it, and then . . . the door was locked! I have never felt such despair. Who was in there? I had convinced my stomach and my mind that I would be on a toilet in thirty seconds or less, and just like that I had to renegotiate the peace treaty between Grendel and Tummy Town. In the heat of my exasperation, I thought, *How could ANYONE have to go to the bathroom except me? This is bullshit!*

When the bathroom's occupant finally emerged, Hershall trailed in after me as I bolted for the toilet. "You need anything? You need anything?" he asked, with all the earnestness of a squire boy. "NO!" I shouted, and Hershall ran out, closing the door behind him. Finally, the pressure was off. I brought my trembling hands up to unfasten my pants, and, taking a deep breath, looked down and realized that my clip-on mic was still live. This meant that everyone on the crew could potentially overhear the firestorm that was about to take place. With Dr. Phil still in the building, I couldn't risk him accidentally tuning to my channel and concluding: *That doesn't sound like a man who can host his own television show. That sounds like a man who needs medical attention.*

It was this foolish attempt to save my last shred of dignity that sealed my fate. As I fumbled to get the microphone's battery pack off my belt loop, it happened—The Beast came to the surface breathing fire on my lucky purple underwear. They would never be worn again. I had crapped my pants and I was only a bathroom door away from doing it on national television. As I frantically found my way to the toilet, I knew that there was no going back. The guy with cerebral palsy, who'd hoped to erase the stigma of helplessness associated with disability, had shit himself on Day Two.

I spent the next forty-five minutes surveying the damage and my options. Could I just live the rest of my life in this bathroom stall? Meet a special girl (probably someone from the cleaning staff), start a family? Or would it be acceptable to come out when the competition was over? Could it be perceived as charming if I went out there with no pants on? How could I possibly recover from this? As I was sitting there on the toilet, I had a lot of time to reflect.

I remembered how I'd been a slave to my stomach since high school, how I'd missed out on family vacations, friendships, and a normal life because I was afraid of what it would do. And now, at what was the most important and pivotal moment in my twenty-six years, my stomach had done exactly what I had always feared. Just as I was about to have a total meltdown, I remembered a simple, three-word directive: *Chew bubble gum.*

Sitting there on the cold porcelain with my defiled underwear around my ankles, I thought about how I'd tell the story to Andrew, how I'd turn this horrible situation into jokes to make my best friend laugh. It occurred to me that this was, all in all, the most hilariously embarrassing thing that could possibly transpire, and, to my shock, *I* started laughing, right there on the toilet. Even if I had to go out there and explain to Dr. Phil that I'd just crapped myself, I was going to do it because it would make for a funnier story.

I switched into survival mode and took inventory of the tools I had to clean up this mess. I was more prepared for this moment than any young man should possibly be. I had flushable Cottonelle wipes, hand sanitizer, a bottle of water, and a bathroom floor; as far as I was concerned, that was all I needed. If I could emerge from this stall triumphant, I knew that whatever challenges lay ahead would pale in comparison. This probably sounds strange, but once you've crapped your pants, you really feel like you can accomplish anything!

I clutched the grab bars and lowered myself to the ground and, with my newfound confidence, began erasing any evidence that this disaster had taken place. I removed my pants. *Thank God.* None of the offending matter had reached any visible outer layers. I then proceeded to get naked on a concrete bathroom floor that I'm almost certain had never been cleaned. I first removed my socks and then, very delicately, the new pants I'd been given from Kohl's (our sponsor), and the fallen hero of the day—my lucky purple underwear.

Outside the door, there was much conjecture about what exactly was going on. I learned later that my delay had at first been angrily attributed to another contestant. When they realized that it was actually caused by me, the producers just shrugged and said, "Give him all the time he needs." Thank goodness society frowns upon berating the disabled for taking too long in the bathroom.

Because of spatial constraints in the stall, my maneuvers while removing my underwear were the closest I've ever come to performing ballet. About halfway through, the ever-attentive Hershall cracked open the door and whispered, "You okay, buddy?" "I'LL BE OUT IN A MINUTE! NO WORRIES!" I shouted back. As I lay naked on the floor, I had to decide what to do with my tainted skivvies. If I threw them away, there was a chance that some perceptive janitor might retrieve them from the trash, and, having heard of my epic bathroom break, put two and two together. I couldn't put them back on (or could I? . . . no, ew!), nor could I risk clogging the toilet. Where could I put this wretched, noble garment? If only I had some sort of airtight receptacle to contain them in. Hmmm . . .

I headed back out to the set, cracking jokes with my costars. None of them had any idea that in the back pocket of my wheelchair, crammed into a ziplock bag, there was a pair of crappy underpants resting upon a lovingly prepared but now very unhygienic fruit medley. It was at once a carefully sealed bag of disgrace and a badge of triumph. I realized that day that I didn't have to prove anything to Dr. Phil or Oprah. Whatever artificial challenges they put us through for the reality show, I had just faced my biggest challenge in *actual* reality, and I had owned it LIKE A BOSS. I didn't need to win this show because I was already the Champion of Confidently Shitting Myself—and how many people can claim that title? The terror that rained down upon Tummy Town had, for this day, been conquered. I was free in the way you can only be after you've faced down your worst fear and lived to tell about it.

That evening, as I recounted the epic saga to Andrew, I presented the bag of fruit and underwear to him as a final flourish. "Wow! That fruit still looks really good!" he said, briefly considering if it could still be eaten. As a trained medical professional, he concluded that it could not.

By the time I'd built up the confidence to finally tell Hershall about the underwear calamity, I'd worn my remaining Fruit of the Loom supply nearly four times over. It was the day before I won the *Your Own Show* competition, and we were headed to the editing suite to work on my pilot presentation for what would become *Rollin' with Zach*. Over the past month, I'd made a lasting impression on all of the cast and crew as a leader, a hard worker, and someone truly capable of hosting his own television show. Nothing could soil that now. As I finished the tall tale, emphasizing how his fruit medley had saved the day, I was surprised to see a heartbroken look on Hershall's face. Then, after a solemn moment, he asked, "You mean . . . you never ate any of the fruit I gave you?"

CHAPTER 3

Drivers Ed in the Mars Rover

"We did it!" Andrew exclaimed triumphantly.
"That was awesome! This is a day we'll always remember," I declared.

April 20, 2011, was the day Andrew and I were rewarded with ten dollars of free frozen yogurt because we'd managed to spend a hundred dollars at Yumilicious in the previous week. It was the most accomplished I'd felt since I'd won my travel show almost six months earlier. Back in October, all the OWN producers and executives assured me that *everything* was about to change. "Things are gonna get crazy!" they warned. "You're gonna be doing tons of press, flying everywhere. . . . You'll be the busiest you've ever been in your life." As it turned out though, my first job as a newly minted Oprah protégé was to keep my mouth shut.

I'd had to wait three months before I was even announced as a contestant on a reality show, and it was February 2011 before the last episode finally aired, revealing to the public that I had won. Up until that moment, the nondisclosure agreement I'd signed required me to keep the greatest personal success I'd ever had from everyone I knew and loved. That period of my life was underscored by a peculiar mix of euphoria and mortal fear that I'd let something slip to my grandpa, and he'd tell all of my thirty-seven hundred cousins in South Carolina, and one of them would put it on Facebook, and then I'd be served with a lawsuit for millions of dollars by OWN Studios and get an angry call from Oprah herself where she would unironically quote *Home Alone*, scolding, "Look whatcha did, ya little jerk!"

When my victory was finally out in the open, I was told that we'd be starting production on *Rollin' with Zach* by April at the latest and cautioned, "Don't go anywhere or do anything, because we're going to need to start shooting soon so that this show can be on the air by the fall." But now, with April coming to a close, I still had no word on when we would begin filming, and there hadn't even been a single production meeting to talk about the timeline. I was stuck on the brink of doing something amazing. So Andrew and I ate our fro-yo and bided our time in Austin. While I was finishing up my bowl of cake batter and taro tart topped with Cap'n Crunch, Andrew proposed a novel idea: "You know, the space shuttle *Endeavour* is having its final launch in two weeks, and if nothing's happening here, I might really wanna go."

Andrew had been a space fanatic ever since he'd seen *Apollo 13*. In grade school, he'd spend his afternoons with his other more scientifically inclined friends shooting off homemade rockets. On three separate occasions he had traveled down to Florida to watch a shuttle launch, only to have them canceled. Now, after thirty years, the US manned space shuttle program was being shut down. After this, any Americans in space would have to carpool with the Russians.

This wasn't just an opportunity to witness one of the greatest examples of American ingenuity in action, but also a chance to help my friend realize a lifelong dream. So over the next few days, we planned an epic twelve-hundred-mile road trip to Cape Canaveral that would serve as a fitting farewell to NASA's shuttle program. Andrew, my brother Brad, and my buddy Aaron loaded up into a minivan with a cooler full of Gatorade and beef jerky and we hit the road.

Our first stop was Johnson Space Center in Houston, where one of Aaron's childhood friends, Mason, worked as a NASA engineer. Aaron was the handsome, athletic type who always wore Chuck Taylors and loved Hunter S. Thompson, so I was surprised he knew people who were, you know, adults, people who had—what's it called? Oh right, careers. I'd never met a rocket scientist before and I expected them to be socially awkward geeks wearing carpal tunnel braces and nipple-high khakis. But when we arrived, a self-assured man in business casual attire came out to greet us. Mason was as chill as they come and almost as chiseled as Aaron. He printed out our official NASA guest badges, which were not just slips of paper with our names on them, but *plastic* and very official-looking. "Look at how legit this is!" Andrew said in hushed, excited tones, pinning his now most prized possession to his shirt.

When we entered NASA, we discovered that they, like me, were in a holding pattern, uncertain of when or how their next project would get off the ground. In addition to the shuttle program ending, plans for the first manned mission to Mars had just been scrapped. That explained why a multimillion-dollar spacecraft was sitting unoccupied on top of what looked like a three-story mound of dirt and rock meant to simulate the unforgiving terrain of Mars.

Normally four dudes giving a day's notice would not be able to just wander up to a Mars Rover and inspect and admire it as though it were a Nissan Leaf in a showroom. But since no one else was going to be using it for the foreseeable future, we just decided to have a poke around. Taking advantage of our VIP access, I asked Mason my most pressing question about space travel.

"Has anyone ever had sex in space?"

"I don't think so," he shrugged, thus adding another item to my already considerable bucket list.

With everything I wanted to know about manned space travel cleared up, all eyes shifted back to the Rover. It looked like a white MechWarrior on top of monster truck wheels, with a helicopter's bubbled cockpit—something straight out of a sci-fi movie, but it was actual science. First, we watched Mason confidently drive the vehicle over a test course meant to simulate the terrain of our neighboring planet. He expertly commanded the two joysticks in the cockpit, navigating over the mountains of dirt and gravel with ease. Then he opened the doors, climbed down, and casually asked, "Do you wanna drive it?" Did we want to drive the multimillion-dollar vehicle that was designed for the maiden voyage to the harsh, unpredictable environment of the red planet? Why yes, yes we did.

I neglected to tell Mason that outside of my wheelchair, the only time I had ever driven anything was a minivan in a parking lot as part of a test to assess whether, given my horrible motor skills and lack of depth perception, I might still be able to drive a car independently one day. It was a special car with hand controls and I sat with an instructor in charge of teaching me how to man the brakes and the gas, check the mirrors, etc., etc. After never getting above ten miles an hour, but still almost hitting the Rite Aid four times, it was deemed that I was not a suitable candidate to drive any car. But sure, I would take the keys to a complex and ridiculously expensive spacecraft that only a handful of rocket scientists had driven before.

The Rover could only be started when two keys were inserted by two astronauts (or, in this case, a NASA engineer and a high school dropout whose highest degree was a Duckorate from the Disney College Program) and turned simultaneously. This is the same failsafe that they use to launch nuclear weapons. As I stared out at the man-made mountainous ground, rife with dips and craters, I thought I had a fifty-fifty shot of leaving Johnson's Space Center with the distinction of being the man who totaled the future of space travel. But with Mason's encouragement, I went full-throttle, bouncing violently up and down like I was Gary Sinese on a rescue mission. With a sudden grating sound of tearing metal, the Rover stopped cold.

"Um, did I break it?" I asked in disbelief.

"Nah, you're good," Mason assured me, completely unfazed. Aaron, Brad, and Andrew were slightly more concerned because while the cocaptain and I had seat belts, they did not. It was the best joyride I've ever had and I only got stuck twice.

When Andrew slid behind the driver's seat for his turn, he looked like he was having the time of his life but treated the experience with a particular sense of reverence and care. By the end we realized that while it may only require two men to drive the Mars Rover, it requires four to get me out of it. My short tenure as captain of that vehicle ensured that I'd be giving Mars a five-star rating on Google Places, citing it as "pretty wheelchair accessible." But boy, let me tell you, after the high of driving the Mars Rover, getting back into a 2005 Dodge Caravan was quite a comedown.

We hit the road again, and since Aaron had brought a Wi-Fi hotspot with him, I was able to put Facebook updates on my fan page and even post a video from the car. With no news to report about my television show, I decided to let my growing fan base know that I was still alive and no one could stop me from traveling. We made a specific Skype account for the trip, ZachInSpace. I told everyone to add me so we could video chat, and as the Louisiana swamplands raced by my window I watched a hundred screen names pop up on my laptop. Aaron drove through the night while I got to know my fans face-to-face for the first time. I talked to parents who got their young children with CP out of bed just to say hello to me, and two teenage girls even shrieked and cried like I was Justin Bieber or something.

A news report on the radio informed us that we had a new reason to rush to Florida besides the launch; several tornadoes were right in our path. Soon enough, it started to rain—not a pleasant April shower, but a harsh pelting that made the windshield look like we were going through a car wash. Brad was driving and the strong winds were making it increasingly difficult for him to stay straight on the road. I quietly suggested that we should pull over. Andrew pulled up a satellite view of the weather on his phone, which revealed that a tornado was only five miles away. Not knowing exactly what the right call was in that scenario, we decided to stop at a Dunkin' Donuts.

"You want anything?" Andrew asked as he opened the door to a wall of rain.

"Yeah, I'll take a Boston Creme," I said, thankful to be the one traveler who got to stay dry. Ten minutes later, Aaron, Andrew, and Brad returned with doughnuts, coffee, and a box of assorted Munchkins. As Aaron switched to the driver's seat, he gave me even more reason to be grateful for doughnuts. "The guy at the counter said, 'Yeah, you guys are lucky you came to this Dunkin' Donuts. Apparently the one in the next town over—it's just gone. It blew away!' Whelp, let's go!" he concluded, putting the key in the ignition and heading to the Sunshine State by way of apocalyptic storm.

We finally got to Florida the day before *Endeavour* was supposed to launch. To the rest of the world, it was the day before the royal wedding of Prince William and Kate Middleton.

Andrew's girlfriend, Christina, had flown all the way from Boston to be in Florida for the launch with us and we picked her up at the airport before checking in at our hotel in Kissimmee.

We spent the day before the launch the way any adults preparing to witness history would—by fighting grade-schoolers for turns on our hotel's water-park slides and going to Cici's Pizza Buffet. Reluctantly, we turned in early, knowing we wouldn't be able to get a full night's sleep if we wanted to have a good viewing spot for the launch. *Endeavour* was supposed to take off at exactly 7:05 in the morning, and to compete with the thousands of other wannabe astronauts, we'd have to get there at 4:00 a.m. Luckily, the duration of time I'd have to be awake to witness this marvel of modern science was, all told, about a minute and a half.

In the wee hours before we headed to Cape Canaveral, Andrew was constantly checking the NASA Web site for updates. He knew better than anyone that even the slightest change in weather or the smallest mechanical malfunction could debunk the whole thing. For as many launches as *Endeavour* had endured, space travel was never something that was taken lightly. When you're sitting on millions of tons of rocket fuel and leaving the planet's atmosphere, any hiccup can be catastrophic. But as we loaded back into the Caravan, all signs pointed to a perfect day for a launch.

We arrived before dawn but were led by a processional of taillights through acres of tall, swampy grass. It didn't seem like a prime viewing area for anything other than a swarm of mosquitoes, but on this day, to be an audience among the bugs cost thirty dollars. We peered out across the water, and through the fog we saw *Endeavour*. "Is that it?" I asked. From our distance,

I could block out the entire thing with my pinkie. It looked like the kind of tiny rocket you used to win at the end of a marginally good game of Tetris.

"Well, can't get any better than this!" Andrew said. Through the stereos of other onlookers who'd tuned to NASA radio, we were able to hear the technicians going over every detail of launch prep. To Andrew, this was fascinating. To me, it was like one of those *Sounds of Nature* CDs where loons or playful dolphins soothe you to sleep. The crowd had young people who had waited their entire lives to see this event, sitting alongside old people who'd been to every shuttle launch since the program started. In the middle of these superfans, there was me, struggling to stay awake and trying in vain not to drool on my shirt. As I saw the sun peeking over the horizon, my eyelids got too heavy and I conked out. When I awoke, the sun had taken the chill out of the air, but something else had taken the excitement out of it. I recognized the familiar sounds of people folding up their lawn chairs and packing up coolers, and out of the corner of my sleepiness I heard Andrew say, "The launch has been scrubbed."

"What?" I said, trying to sound engaged as I worked my way back into consciousness. The first thing I noticed was Aaron's camera in my face as he confirmed that he had some great footage of me drooling with my mouth open. "That sucks," I muttered. I wasn't awake enough to be coherently concerned, but I tried to string together a sentence. "You mean they're not going to try to launch the shuttle at all today?"

"Yep," Andrew said, genuinely disappointed. "No launch till Wednesday at the earliest." Once again, we were in limbo, waiting on forces beyond our control to give us the green light.

"Shit!" I said, finally coming to and jumping into cheerleader mode. "This is what I say we do. First, we go get milk shakes and regroup. Then, we go to a hobby store, buy a model rocket, and launch it ourselves. Show NASA how it's done—a shuttle rebuttal! Twenty Aught 'Leven!" It was settled. We'd head back to the hotel, deal with our grief, and start planning our own trip to space via toy rocket.

Without a clear date scheduled for the relaunch, we decided to wait out the delay at my grandparents' house in Sumter, South Carolina. If NASA couldn't deliver from Cape Canaveral, my grandpa's backyard would have to do. But before we left Florida, we made a stop at the Kennedy Space Center to take a tour. As we made our way up to the observation deck, we could see *Endeavour* sitting on the launchpad. It stood there, facing the sky, towering over everything, but for the moment relegated to doing nothing. I'd never felt such kinship with an inanimate object before. As we passed through hallways filled with plaques commemorating all the astronauts who'd participated in the shuttle missions and stopped at memorials for those who'd lost their lives in the *Challenger* and *Columbia* disasters, I found a new respect for the individuals who had risked everything just to explore.

Andrew was so enamored with it all that he entrusted me with making sure he didn't spend more than two hundred dollars in the gift shop. "Do you think I might be able to fit into this child's astronaut suit?" he asked seriously. "It's only a hundred and twenty dollars and I think I'd wear it a lot."

We made it out of the museum without Andrew spending his life savings on memorabilia and astronaut ice cream, and got to Sumter in time for dinner. After refueling, Andrew and Aaron headed into town to get the parts for our model rocket while I turned to Facebook to ask my fan page to name the craft.

Some of my favorite suggestions were the USS *Annerprise*, the *ZachBuster2000*, and confusingly, *Atlantis*, which happened to be the name of the only other NASA space shuttle not yet retired.

After a week of poolside tanning and my grandma's home-cooked meals, we picked a name that sounded fitting to all of us—the *Low Altitude Rocket Delay Substitute*, or *LARDS* for short. When she was finally finished, *LARDS* was an impressive vessel that had been outfitted with explosive engines normally reserved for rockets twice her size. Andrew prepared to light the fuse as I started the countdown for our live Internet audience who'd be able to witness the spectacle streaming at a whopping two frames per second. The fuse crackled as Andrew ran back to safety and we all tilted our heads toward the sky in anticipation. The engines ignited and *LARDS* was thrust into the air, but she didn't boldly go anywhere. She did, however, burst into flames.

Theoretically, the oversize explosives were large enough to propel this children's rocket out of the atmosphere—but in practice they weighed *LARDS* down, causing her to sputter and twirl like a giant sparkler being thrashed about by a mesmerized kid on the Fourth of July. *LARDS* was no longer in danger of landing on a roof but rather landing on our heads. Ever the hero when sensing imminent danger, Aaron ran backward, tripping over my wheelchair as he tried to save himself.

When the smoke cleared, we found our rocket, which was surprisingly undamaged by the ill-fated flight. Within minutes, we had stuffed her with smaller engines and were ready to give liftoff a second go. Our success rate may have been significantly lower than NASA's, but our efficiency was unparalleled. Shuttle Rebuttal Redux could only be called a success in comparison to the first launch because it didn't threaten to kill us all. In our failure, we had to admit that even if we didn't get to see her launch, NASA should probably take as long as they needed to ensure their rocket was safer than ours.

The day after failing miserably at amateur rocketry, we finally got some positive news from the professionals. *Endeavour's* launch was officially rescheduled for May 16. If we wanted to witness it, we'd have to stall for another eight days in Sumter, but at least there was a timetable. To amp ourselves up, we spent the next week watching the entire series of *From the Earth to the Moon,* a show produced and introduced by Tom Hanks that dramatized the Apollo missions. None of us could resist quoting John F. Kennedy's famous 1962 speech in which he boldly declares, "We choose to go to the moon, in this decade, and do those other things, not because they are easy, but because they are hard." When we recited this historic and important speech, we made a few changes to suit our own missions. Depending on the day it was "We choose to go to the pool, and drink sangria . . ." or "We choose to go to the Sonic, before midnight, and get Route 44 Cherry Limeades, not because they are healthy, but because they are good!" But when we finally took a break from fast food, drinking, and swimming to watch JFK's Rice University speech in its entirety, the sheer audacity of what he was saying hit me. Check this out:

> We shall send to the moon, two hundred and forty thousand miles away from the control station in Houston, a giant rocket more than three hundred feet tall, the length of this football field, made of new metal alloys, some of which have not yet been invented, capable of withstanding heat and stresses several times more than have ever been

experienced, fitted together with a precision better than the finest watch, carrying all the equipment needed for propulsion, guidance, control, communication, food, and survival on an untried mission to an unknown celestial body, and then return it safely to earth, re-entering the atmosphere at speeds of over 25,000 miles per hour, causing heat of about half the temperature of the sun . . . and do all this, and do it right, and do it first, before this decade is out . . .

Listen to how baller this dude was! We promised to go to space within ten years at a time when computers were the size of rooms and less powerful than a graphing calculator. We went to space back when doctors suggested that if you were pregnant, you should keep smoking so as not to stress yourself out. We hadn't even invented the technology we needed to get to space and we gave ourselves a hard deadline and stuck to it. Nowadays, if there's a budget dispute, our Congress will just pack up and go home for a month. What happened? Hearing those words helped me realize that witnessing *Endeavour* would not just be the grand finale of a cool road trip with friends, but would also honor an era in our country's history, a time when we resolved to make the impossible possible and kept that promise despite the improbability of success.

Maybe the universe heard this bellowing call for progress, because just when NASA announced *Endeavour*'s new launch date, things finally started moving forward with *Rollin' with Zach* too. I had my first meeting with my executive producer over the phone and we carved out the format for the show. The new timeline was for me to move out of my apartment in Austin at the end of May and head to LA in early June to start shooting. If everything went according to plan, the timing would work out perfectly. Andrew could still act as my assistant throughout production and we'd wrap just before his first semester of med school would begin if he got accepted. But as I'd learned from my brief exposure to both NASA and network television, just because there was a launch schedule didn't mean things would actually get off the ground.

After almost three weeks in South Carolina, we packed up the van on May 15 and embarked once again for Florida. In an act of sheer commitment and solidarity, Christina had once again flown from Boston to Orlando for a trip that would last exactly nine hours. She hopped in the car and gave Andrew a giddy kiss as we welcomed her back to Florida with the score from *Apollo 13*. We arrived at Cape Canaveral in the dark once again and were led to a far more impressive viewing area suited for an *Endeavour* that now looked like a rocket conjured by a Tetris master rather than a novice. I wish I could tell you that with three hours to kill we watched *Apollo 13* one last time, but the truth is we watched *Smokey and the Bandit II*.

After a quick Burt Reynolds break, we were ready to marvel at space again and decided that our best viewing angle would come from sitting not in, but on top of our Caravan. So, with five minutes to liftoff, Aaron and Andrew hoisted me up like the world's most excited sack of potatoes. All systems were go. The entire crowd fell silent as everyone tuned in to NASA radio. Resting on two thousand tons of rocket fuel, there were six Americans brave enough to trust that this vehicle would not only carry them to space but also bring them home. Thousands of people huddled together waiting to watch *Endeavour* tear through the sky and leave the atmosphere one more time. Andrew took a few final snapshots with his camera and then we locked our gazes on the shuttle.

The countdown began as the mammoth engines roared. We saw *Endeavour* take off before we heard her. A moment later, I learned that in a rocket launch, it's not what you can see and hear that has the greatest impact, but what you feel. There was a seismic rumble that washed over the crowd like a wave, producing a sound so loud that it could easily kill you if you were close enough. It sounded like static or white noise, like the entire Earth was flipping the channels on reality. It was an auditory experience so thunderous that I half expected that whatever signal was producing the environment around us would cut out at any moment and we'd just be surrounded by the stars. Smoke and fire poured down from the rocket boosters as it soared higher and higher, until it was a tiny speck, and then it pierced through the edge of the sky and vanished into a part of the universe only a few of us would ever see.

Slowly, the volume was turned up on the more familiar sounds of a world I understood. We all exclaimed some iteration of the phrase "*That* was awesome!" hoping to find better words to explain how transformed and humbled we were by the experience. But I think "awesome" is the perfect word. It's just that we use it to describe everything now. This wasn't awesome in the way that half-priced margaritas are awesome, or your grandma's WORLD'S MOST BITCHIN' GRANDMA sweatshirt is awesome, or even the way that eating a hundred dollars' worth of fro-yo is awesome. This awesome actually inspired awe and created something that rocked us to the core, caused us to question what we knew, and made us appreciate the wonders of the world we couldn't comprehend.

A rocket on a launchpad isn't worth much. To get it off the ground requires equal parts faith, fortitude, and the collective vision to chase a dream into reality. Later that summer, I'd finally have liftoff on one of my biggest dreams. Thanks to Andrew and a production crew, I was able to make good on my own bullish proclamation to make a travel show. We didn't go to space, but Andrew was the perfect copilot as we boldly went across the country, exploring oceans when I surfed, the skies when I went up in a helicopter, and diabetes when I went to a jelly bean factory.

But the two of us were destined for different orbits. Just before we filmed the last episode of *Rollin' with Zach,* Andrew got the news that he'd been accepted into med school. From the beginning of the reality show competition to the end of production on my travel show, I'd gotten to spend nearly a year with my best friend. That fall, he'd be heading off into the stratosphere, doing what he was born to do. I had no idea where he'd end up; I only knew that Andrew was a rocket.

Later this year, I'll finally get to see him leave the launch-pad and become a doctor, after twelve years of higher education. I'm sure that when the time comes, I'll only have three words to describe the experience—"That. Was. *Awesome!*"

CHAPTER 4

Comics Without Relief

In a darkened high school auditorium, I sit in the spotlight, looking like a kid in his grandfather's suit. Because in actuality, I am a kid in his grandfather's suit. I'm holding a microphone as Gareth McCubbin, the host of the Kenmore West talent show, presides over my marriage to a random audience member. It's the closing bit to my first stand-up act, and I'm getting to know my future bride.

"What's your name?" I say, shoving the mic in her face.

"Meagan," she says, excited to be onstage.

Before she can say anything else, I yank the mic back and say, "Good enough for me! Let's do this!" eliciting scattered laughter from the crowd.

The whole point of this sham wedding was to get to the kiss and then end the performance by having my new wife hop on my lap, so I could carry her backstage with a wink to presumably consummate the marriage. Pretty juvenile, but I was fifteen, what do you want? As with most celebrity marriages, things went south quickly. Right as we were about to recite our vows, one of the other talent show hosts decided the bit was too long and yanked me offstage before I could get to the punch line. It was awkward. Luckily, there was one person in the auditorium who still believed in the sanctity of marriage, as it applied to high school comedy bits anyway. My friend and wingman Dave Phillips, a scrawny guy with a nerdy exterior who nevertheless inhabited a high social stratosphere in our school, saw that my act was about to crash and burn with no conclusion and began chanting, "Bring back Zach! BRING BACK ZACH!" While I was being scolded backstage by the indignant timekeepers, the whole high school joined in the chant. I wasn't allowed to finish my act that night, but thanks to Dave, instead of just leaving the stage, I was able to leave an impression.

Having a high school auditorium clamor for me was a good feeling at a time in my life when I felt the most isolated and out of place. I missed seventy-three days of school my freshman year. During the month leading up to that talent show, the one thing I'd been able to look forward to were those five minutes when I could be a performer on a stage, and not a sick person hovered over a toilet, violently destroying my esophagus.

My first year of high school marked the beginning of a volatile relationship with my digestive tract. Because I couldn't maneuver in the stalls at school, going to the bathroom required the invasive assistance of my middle-aged personal aide, who would then wait outside the stall until I was finished. As a teenager, the threat of public embarrassment coupled with this surrender of dignity and privacy made the prospect of going to school seem like a recipe for social suicide. This anxiety only exacerbated my stomach ailments, which fed into a vicious cycle that often kept me home. At a time when all of my peers were going through some degree of physical transformation, I was devolving from the social butterfly I'd been all through middle school and retreating to a cocoon of self-imposed solitude. I felt like my body was holding me hostage.

Although I was physically sick during this period of my life, escaping the label of "sick person" was something I'd had to do since the day I was born. Comedy was both the tool I used to convince others I was not sick or different and the medicine I took to heal myself whenever life had me lamenting the cards I was dealt.

When I was six years old, my physical therapists had to teach me the simple yet—because it was me—still unachievable skill of taking off a shirt. Several scholars and scientists had been assigned to the project of coming up with a way that I could independently undress myself. It was *Apollo 13* for basic life skills. Eventually, they determined that the best shirting technique was to go over the head and involve the arms as little as possible. When you have cerebral palsy, every limb is an independent variable that could send the entire operation into chaos. But even with this new approach, I'd gotten the shirt stuck over my head. It wasn't going to come off without the help of either my therapist or Ed Harris in Mission Control. Feeling stuck and helpless in my striped Bugle Boy straightjacket, and having just seen *Sister Act* on television, I did the only thing I could think of: I shrugged my shoulders and said, "I'm a nun!"

Over the years, I've learned that a sense of humor is the

only skill that allows you to turn sucking at life into a career. Even the most embarrassing mishap can be spun into comedic gold. Or, more appropriately, every pile of dog shit you roll through can be used as fertilizer for a great story at a party.

Comedy was a universal language in my family. Saturday nights at my mom's were spent dressing up like lumberjacks and singing along to Monty Python records we got at the library. And when Brad and I spent the night at my dad's house on Sundays and Mondays, he'd take us to pick up costumes at the Goodwill and encourage us to make sketches, which he'd immortalize on videotape. Those home movies were how I became comfortable on camera, and by watching myself on-screen, I eventually learned to sit up straight, speak clearly, and project my voice. When my mom first brought home my future stepdad, Greg, it was a joke he made that instantly won over two potentially antagonistic teenage boys: "Life is like a box of tampons—everything comes with a string attached."

Growing up, comedians were the ones that gave context to struggle—not priests or psychologists or philosophers, but Jerry Seinfeld, Gilda Radner, and Steve Martin, the people who had the courage to be silly in a world that seemed to take itself too seriously. The performers I idolized didn't just give me people to mimic, they gave me a means to express sadness and frustration in a way that actually brought people joy and leveled the playing field.

One week during the competition for my OWN show, the judges were criticizing the editing work on a video segment I'd done, not knowing that I had done it. As soon as they realized that I'd been the one who'd made the poor decisions, they started backpedaling. I stopped them and said, "If the video that I made didn't connect with you as the audience, then I sucked balls this week, and that's my fault." I don't think anyone else in the history of reality television had ever won a competition after admitting they sucked metaphorical balls. My statement immediately earned the respect of the judges and the crew alike. Rather than becoming someone who was inept, I was someone who could make a joke, while simultaneously taking accountability for his own failure. Failing with a sense of humor and pizzazz is what I do best! That was never more apparent than during filming for the New York City episode of my travel show, *Rollin' with Zach*, a few months later.

The show crisscrossed the country, with each episode highlighting a different city. Three episodes into filming, it became clear that we weren't making a show about the spontaneous and unpredictable nature of travel. We were making a show about a boy in a wheelchair who was getting the chance to see the world. The only problem was, that wasn't my story. I wanted to make an honest travel show about making the most of whatever life throws at you. But this production wasn't throwing me anything. It was delicately handing me Fabergé eggs and putting me up in five-star hotels, then occasionally showing me struggling to get up a curb and calling that "roughing it." It seems counterintuitive that having the opportunity to ride in helicopters and stay in high-roller suites would be something I'd fight against, but I knew what network executives could never seem to grasp: I was lucky. Every disadvantage I'd ever had had tipped the scales toward a greater advantage.

A pedestal of prejudice is a hard thing to explain without sounding like a dick. But in a weird way, most of the world places such low expectations on me that there's no way I can do anything but amaze. I recently went on a museum tour of famed illustrator N. C. Wyeth's home and studio. During the tour, I did little more than look at paintings and indifferently notice a slightly narrow dining-room table. Sure, there was the occasional doorway I had to roll through without running into the frame, but it certainly wasn't like docking a shuttle to a space station. This isn't to say that the art itself wasn't beautiful and emotionally compelling to me, but it was an afternoon at a museum, and largely museums only ask their patrons to look at things without touching them. That much I can do. At the end of the experience, the jolly security guard who had escorted us through the tour patted me on the shoulder and said, "Bet you haven't had this much fun in a looong time, huh? You did really good!" I didn't have the heart to tell him that I had in fact, just the day before, been a guest in a house where I was also not allowed to touch anything. And the day before that, I'd kayaked for the first time . . . over a *tree*. But still, in this man's mind, my doing nothing successfully was worthy of praise. Perhaps he imagined that I spent my days looking at empty walls, wishing I had a still life oil painting of two lemons and a potato, and that I was bored to tears with my normal-size dining-room table.

Working in television can leave you feeling equally placated and pampered. So I was excited when *Rollin' with Zach* headed to the Big Apple, because that city can't be controlled by even the most anal-retentive of TV producers. On the surface, New York City seems like the perfect place to live large, but no matter how you dress it up, in order to survive there you have to cut the bullshit. Everybody is going somewhere important and if you slow down, you're gonna get knocked over or honked at. I'm pretty sure New Yorkers would have told Helen Keller to hurry it up and learn sign language already.

The show structure was a countdown of my top five things to do in each place we visited. And by My Top Five Things, we meant "whatever five things the producers could line up in time for the episode." The climax of the New York City episode (or My Number One Top Thing) was something I was equally passionate about and terrified by—a seven-minute stand-up set at Carolines comedy club on Broadway. Eric, the black-bearded hipster comedy producer for *Rollin'*, had dreamt up the idea of me performing at the iconic venue on open mic night.

Eric is the most sarcastic, cynical, and just plain negative funny person I've ever met. His assumption in life was that everyone hated everything as much as he did and so he'd pre-empt every hotel stay or meal with, "It's gross, right? You hate it, right?" When we first started working together, Eric clued me in that my optimism about the show may have been misplaced. As a fierce crusader for comedy, he was sure of one thing: no matter how hard we tried, the other producers weren't going to let the show be funny, because they didn't know what funny was. While it wasn't my intention, making a show that capitalized on mishaps would have essentially highlighted producers' mistakes. What I had proposed was basically putting a boy in a wheelchair in precarious situations, stringing the worst bits together, and then sending them off to Oprah for approval. It just wasn't gonna fly.

When I met Oprah, I thought she had a great sense of humor, and she might have appreciated my freewheeling vision for the show if she'd had the chance to see it. But *Rollin' with Zach* was the first series that Pie Town, my production company, had done for OWN and, understandably, everyone was jittery and playing it safe. What was funny to me seemed cruel and inconsiderate to people who'd spent their lives believing that having a disability was the worst misfortune that could befall a living soul. I knew from experience that traveling with a wheelchair never goes according to plan. Things break, get lost, and, more often than should ever be the case, ramps lead directly to steps. Still, the best trips I'd ever taken were the ones where I'd had to wing it. How was I ever going to prove to people that the inevitable discomfort and inconveniences of travel are worth the rewards if we never showed me improvising around any real struggles on camera?

To my delight, when we arrived in New York City, despite all the meticulous planning, it looked as though we might finally capture on video the catastrophic train wreck of a travelogue I'd always hoped for. As we collected our luggage at JFK airport and walked outside, the wheelchair-accessible minivan that had been rented for the weekend pulled up alongside the curb, only this time it wasn't the pristine Chrysler Town and Country with automatic doors, heated steering wheel, and leather-ornamented everything. It was a Dodge Caravan with black smoke billowing out of the exhaust pipe, dropped off by a man in a baseball cap and shades whose frantic energy could only be interpreted as "I can't be seen at the airport and I *may* have stolen this car." Instead of our standard rental agreement, John, our young, bestubbled, and perpetually overworked field producer, just handed this man a wad of cash. He looked down at it perplexed, perhaps disappointed that it wasn't meth. With mutters of, "The AC doesn't work and you're gonna wanna watch that door 'cause it sticks a little bit," he left us with our chariot fit for a dump, and this alone had me brimming with optimism. Real travelers don't have rides with leather seats—they have vans with suspicious stains!

We made it into the city all right, and the next morning I awoke in my twenty-five-hundred-dollar-a-night suite at the Andaz Hotel on Wall Street. While I was happily distracted by both the television in the bathroom mirror and the confirmation from Andrew that there was in fact a naked woman sauntering across her dining room in the high-rise next door, John was facing the crisis of his professional life in the lobby downstairs. Over the course of the eight hours it had spent in the parking garage overnight, the sliding door of our specially procured wheelchair-accessible van had simply fallen off.

This being John's first time out in the field as a producer, he had a lot to prove. His catchphrases throughout the production included "Aw God, I'm really fuckin' up!" and "Hurry it up, guys!" and "I don't know . . ." whenever he was berated with all manner of questions that should have been delegated to more than one person:

"Where can I get this shirt ironed?"

"Where's the wheelchair-access entrance to the Chicago Pedway?"

"Do we have enough money in the budget to take a picture of me as a Vegas showgirl?"

Everything that happened on the road was John's responsibility. So the rest of the crew took that as a sign that we shouldn't collectively be concerned with things like call times and meals and wardrobe . . . and transportation.

When I got downstairs, I was greeted by Eric, more gleeful than I'd ever seen him.

"John's about to have a heart attack. It's great!"

From the lobby, I could see John in a mortified trance, something akin to when you piss yourself in grade school and you know that everyone is going to find out—it's only a matter of time. I should have known how dire the situation was when I saw John heading outside, a roll of duct tape in each hand. With barely half an hour to get to our first location, he was actually going to try to tape the sliding door back onto our minivan. The color of the duct tape matched the shade of gray paint on the van, and the tape's sheen might've actually classed it up a bit. I wasn't in the habit of overstepping my role as a television host, but this was the one time I felt compelled to give directions to the crew. "Make sure you film this!" I said. "This is great stuff!"

To nobody's surprise, duct tape did not fix the van. It was decided that we would have to get a cab, one with all four doors intact. This was an important shoot. Our schedule had us in Brooklyn at 2:00 p.m. sharp for a root beer float tasting at an old-fashioned soda fountain, followed by a speed-dating session back in Manhattan at 6:00 p.m. But there was another problem. As the cab arrived, our director, Malachi, a short, redheaded Irish man in a fedora, noted that due to the episode order, I would actually be in a *different* outfit for the soda fountain segment than I would be for speed dating. I needed to change clothes.

The cab had already pulled up to the curb and there was no time to run back upstairs, so it seemed like the only option was to get undressed in the middle of Wall Street. I went full *Magic Mike* McConaughey, ripping my shirt off* as Andrew started pulling down my pants. I imagined what this feverish disrobing must have looked like to the businessmen and -women walking by with their Bluetooth headsets and briefcases.

---

*The efforts of that Research and Development team when I was six had not gone to waste.

Perhaps they glanced over and thought, *I wonder if that boy in the wheelchair is about to be gang-raped?*, considered it, and then continued on their way to their job at Oldman Sacks, or wherever.

Now, I'm not complaining—I'll take advantage of any opportunity to be naked in public—but as it turned out, on this particular morning, I'd chosen to wear the one pair of novelty underwear in my entire wardrobe. They had been hand-crafted at my request by my cousins—two sweet southern ladies in their sixties—and featured bold, embroidered letters reading WEAPON OF MASS DESTRUCTION, next to an orange cat, which they'd added as an embellishment for reasons I'll never understand.

When I was finally changed into the proper outfit and Andrew had re-poofed and fluffed my hair, we made it over the bridge to the Brooklyn Farmacy without a hitch. I drank something called an egg cream and learned about "jerking" soda, a process that begged for all sorts of innuendos and puns I wouldn't dare make on the Oprah Winfrey Network. The egg cream tasted like a carbonated milk shake and I would have gladly had three of them, but I didn't need any more of those to bring all the girls to the yard because there were seven lucky ladies waiting to date me in a bar across town.

I wish I could tell you more details about this location, but I inherited my sense of direction from Christopher Columbus. All I know is that it was somewhere in the New York City metropolitan area and across from a Starbucks. The only reason I remember this detail is because that's where Andrew and I went to kill the two hours it took them to set up lighting in an intentionally dark bar. Andrew had a peppermint latte; I had a panic attack. Speed dating was a far more terrifying prospect than doing stand-up. This wasn't a mock wedding, this was actual dating, to be mocked later by a television audience. The speed at which I had dated women previously had been a spritely zero to three dates per twenty-six years. I had no suitable explanation for my lack of romantic endeavors, and Andrew had suggested that instead of explaining my lifelong drought, I simply say I was "between girlfriends."

"Technically it's true," he said, sucking his latte through a straw. "You're between zero and one girlfriends!"

Now I was about to date seven girls in a row for eight minutes apiece, with explicit instructions to become romantically interested in at least one of them. It was in the script and I had learned over the past few weeks of filming, the best way to make reality television was to follow the script to the letter. But if I couldn't calm my nerves, I'd be approaching these stilted rendezvous with all the charm of a sweaty serial killer. You know, the kind in those *Dateline* murder shows where they say, "On the surface, Zach seemed like a picture-perfect guy. But *something* was off when he was around women. Could it have been enough for him to . . . *murder*?"

When the lights were finally illuminating that bat cave of a bar, filming took two hours longer than scheduled. Instead of the standard eight minutes, I was given twenty with each prospective soul mate that were later edited to *look* like eight. I was cordial with each of my suitors but clicked with none. We were encouraged to split desserts and share intimate moments with just me, my date, the two camera guys, the sound guy, the director, the comedy producer, the matchmaker, the bar owner, and a very impatient and nervous producer, yelling over at the director, "We gotta hurry it up, guys. This is going on WAY too long." The camera guys grinned—"Yeah, bitch, get me some more of that Oprah money!"—knowing we were now officially in overtime.

Over the course of my dating spree, I met a woman from Cape Town, South Africa, and another who intrigued me merely because she made her own ice cream. The most awkward encounter was with a girl who broke the ice by declaring, "I like dark Asian horror movies." I sheepishly responded, "I like brighter things, like little romantic comedies," which was followed by unimpressed silence. Our conversation was over and we still had to sit there for either six or eighteen minutes, depending on whether we're talking about reality or reality TV. This girl's name, as it turned out, was Caroline. I took this coincidence as an omen that I should expect a similarly cool reception from Carolines, the comedy club.

In the end, I picked a girl named Ella. Our deepest connec-

tion was made when I remarked, "Oh, Ella! Like Ella Fitzgerald?" and she replied, "Yeah." A woman having the same name as a singer I sort of liked seemed as good a reason as any to date someone after a thirteen-hour shoot day. I also liked how Ella seemed to be the person least interested in the television crew: instead of checking her makeup outside and wondering how she was going to look on camera, she went and got a hot dog. As was preordained, I invited Ella to see me perform stand-up the next night, even though, at this point, it was akin to me saying, "Hey, I really like you. Wanna come to my vasectomy tomorrow?"

I was supposed to start writing my comedy routine after speed dating, but it was close to one a.m. by the time I got back to the hotel and we had to shoot interviews in the morning. In all likelihood I'd be performing my entire set for the first time, onstage, with no rehearsal. The next day there was just one break in the schedule, a two-hour window where I could talk through jokes with Eric and draft material. With the pressure bearing down, I sought a muse that had never failed me before: the Olive Garden, this one in the middle of Times Square.

The rest of the crew had abandoned Eric and me at the mere suggestion that we have lunch at the world's best restaurant, and their snobbery had given us the perfect opportunity to focus. We'd been tasked with taking the whirlwind of the previous two days and making something funny but still airable. We came up with a few icebreakers about my wheelchair and built from there. I'd gone on a helicopter ride over Manhattan on the first day, and the pilot had forced everyone to wear life jackets, then took one look at me and said, "Except you. You don't have to." Why this distinction had been made was a mystery to me, and Eric and I wrote some material explaining that I was in fact a cripple and not a merman. We went on like this, bouncing ideas back and forth while I sipped a Shirley Temple and shoved breadsticks down my throat.

The closer for the act was perhaps the most difficult to pull off because it involved me ranting about speed dating and would be a largely improvised routine. I'd ask if anyone in the crowd had speed dated before and then I'd play out a scene with a random audience member, much like the mock wedding I'd staged ten years earlier. I'd ask her what her name was, and before she could even say "Cynthia" or whatever, I'd cut her off and say, "BOOM! We just dated!" Then I'd explain how the rest of our relationship would go:

"Maybe we realize we both like crochet and that we have the same Michael McDonald album. So we decide to just move in together for a while and give it a shot and see if we're compatible. Then in bed I have to confess to you that I have a belly button fetish, but when we're at Thanksgiving at your parents' house, you get a little tipsy and bring it up, which makes your mom feel awkward, and then I'm on the hook with your parents and we get into a huge argument. But we find out later that night that you're pregnant, and we're not really ready to be parents, but what are we supposed to do? Because you're Catholic and we've gotta have this baby! Then we've got to babyproof the house, we have the kid, and one night you're searching through my browser history and discover I'm into all sorts of weird shit and you kick me out of the house, and then we go into a co-custody scenario and decide that while we're good parents, we're just not that good of a match . . ." And then I'd pause and say, "And that's just the first two minutes!"

This ending monologue required rhythm and timing that took an amount of practice there wasn't any room for in the schedule. Everyone just expected me to wing it. It would be another three hours before I'd even get a chance to go through the jokes again because now, after only one Shirley Temple refill, I had to go out into Times Square and start inviting people to a show I was 85 percent sure would be a disaster. I even invited a few of the stewardesses from the Broadway production of *Catch Me If You Can*, knowing that they wouldn't be able to make it. I just needed it to *look* like I wanted people to come for the cameras. The only two people that I was actually comforted to know would be in the audience were my best friend Andrew and my old buddy Dave Phillips, who had moved to New York City specifically to do stand-up.

Dave's story was a cautionary tale. When I asked him how much material he'd developed over the two years he'd spent in the city, he said, "About twelve minutes of really solid stuff." Let's see, twelve minutes from two years of work, and I'm responsible for more than half that after a single lunch? That sounds promising! Even more encouraging, I learned that Dave hadn't performed in almost a year and a half because of a scarring open mic night of his own. The experience was so unsettling to him that he couldn't even think about getting up onstage again. If that happened to me, ALL of America would be watching. Or at least the small portion of America who had the extended basic cable package that included the Oprah Winfrey Network, were able to find the channel, and tuned in at eight o'clock on Monday night, the day after Christmas.*

With forty-five minutes before showtime, I headed into Carolines. I was humbled when I entered the club and saw the illuminated stage with its colorful background that looked

---

*Which turned out to be twelve people. My mom being four of them.

like the kind of argyle sweater a clown might wear. This is the place I'd watched Louis C.K. perform material for his show *Louie,* and the club where Jerry Seinfeld tested out new material for the documentary *Comedian.* It was a stage that had seen thousands of established comics and helped rocket them to stardom. I'm sure thousands more had crashed and burned into a fiery pit, doomed to live out the rest of their days in much safer careers as unfulfilled life insurance salesmen. This is where so many people had finally realized that they were not funny.

As I headed back into the green room, I told myself that if I could get one laugh and not have a nervous breakdown onstage, I'd count the evening as a success. I passed through a hallway lined with black-and-white photographs of the comics I grew up listening to, and hunkered down in the green room with Eric to get one last look at the jokes I'd written earlier that afternoon. He'd printed them out in an absurdly large font in the hopes that if I were to blank or start to cry, I could look down, find my place, and teleprompt my way to being funny. I didn't have the heart to tell Eric that there was no way I'd be reading that text, no matter what point Helvetica he used, because, as it happens, I have not one but two lazy eyes that can dart and drift like pinballs but cannot collaborate well enough to do the simple things like track a line of text across a page or see the world in three dimensions. As I ran through the routine, my leg began to shake uncontrollably and even though I'd gone to the bathroom just twenty minutes earlier, a whole new bucket's worth of piss showed up in my bladder. I could hear the other prospective comedians as they delivered their own muffled sets through the walls. The laughter was sparse and far from encouraging. Then, as I waited in the wings, I heard the worst possible opener for a joke.

"So I was just speed dating recently . . ."

FUCK! Was I about to go and deliver the exact same joke? I didn't hear his whole routine, but I picked out a few key words, enough to glean that, in his scenario, one of his dates had asked what he liked to eat, and his charming reply had been, "Pussy." I could work with this.

Perhaps noticing that there were four huge production-size cameras surrounding him now, the snarky emcee took a kinder and more welcoming tone for my introduction and said, "This is a guy, it's his first time doing stand-up,* and he's got his own show on the Oprah channel. Please welcome to the stage . . . Zach Anner!"

The lights were like high beams. I felt like I was being interrogated by two hundred people for a crime I didn't commit, and in the absence of an airtight alibi, the only way to prove my innocence was to make them laugh. I opened with tried-and-true material—the cripple jokes.

"You may have noticed something different about me and I just wanted to get it out of the way . . . Yes, I do have a lazy eye."

People laughed. This is a joke I'd used before in my previous (now expunged) stage performances.

"A lot of people come up to me and say, 'Zach, we feel bad for you because you're in a wheelchair.' I don't understand why. I don't think these people realize just how comfortable sitting is!" Then, playing to the audience, I said, "You guys know what I'm talking about, right?!"

---

*Not exactly, but close enough for reality television.

These weren't the greatest jokes in the world. They were easy laughs, but they served an important purpose—they gave the audience permission to laugh at a disabled man and let them know that nothing was off-limits, we were in this together. From those first two, cheap jokes, the audience was mine. I moved through the set fluidly, almost as though I'd rehearsed it for more than five minutes. I couldn't see a damn thing, but for some reason I remembered all the key beats. It was a minor miracle, but there was still the issue of how to introduce speed dating, a topic that the last guy onstage had just discussed at length.

"I *also* just went speed dating," I said. " Unfortunately, I didn't eat any pussy with my speed dates. Must have been a different company or something. Gotta get the name of that one!"

The crowd erupted. When the other comic had delivered his punch line, there was little more than mild groans of distaste and scattered chuckles, but when I'd been introduced as "the guy from the Oprah Network" and had still been willing to go there, I earned some major street cred from the crowd. The last hurdle was that final monologue.

Even though I looked confident onstage, adrenaline forced every muscle in my body to tense up, which in turn affected my vocal delivery. When my adrenaline gets pumping, I'm still able to deliver jokes, but in a much shoutier, ShamWow salesman type of way. I don't know if it's an actual physical response, or if my strategy for getting over nerves is to push past them with sheer volume. But after every fifth word or so, I feel as though I need to sit down, take a breather, and have a juice box. When I started in on the closer, talking through the rambling relationship scenario, I could tell that it was falling flat. My energy was already at an eleven, and there was no place to ramp up to. The pace and the randomness required to sell the joke just weren't coming together, but we'd reached the point of no return. By now, I knew how this was going to end—in a sputter.

The crowd would be silent as I delivered the final punch line. They'd still applaud politely, but the enthusiasm would be gone and the experience as a whole would be reduced to "a really good first attempt at stand-up." My body was so stiff that I was pushing as hard as I could into the backrest of my wheelchair, hoping that I could deliver that last sentence with such force that even though it wasn't funny, people would be tricked into laughing, like a golden retriever named Skippy who also responds to "Ethel" if you use the right tone. And just at that moment, when it was all about to fall apart, Fate intervened.

I'd been pushing so hard on the back of my chair that my seat actually *broke*. Under the force of all my strength and impending shame, two bolts had shot out of the sides of the chair, causing it to slump awkwardly and stopping me in mid-sentence. It was an unplanned disaster. *Hallelujah!* I looked around the audience, shrugged my shoulders, and said, "Ummmm . . . that's new!" They laughed. "I really don't have any more material, but it looks like I'm going to be here awhile, so . . . how are you guys doin'?" They went wild. Where the joke falling off its hinges had threatened to ruin my stand-up debut, my seat falling off its hinges had saved it. The right thing had gone wrong at the perfect time.

I rolled offstage prouder than I had ever been of myself, even though my main contribution to the success of the night had been a fear of failure so intense that it caused me to break steel in half, like one of those mothers who is imbued with superhuman strength to save a child pinned under a burning car. The first person I met offstage was Ella, who'd come to the show bearing a gift of flowers made from Legos. I knew that we probably wouldn't go on any future dates that weren't arranged for the purposes of television, but I also genuinely thought that this girl was cool. And a cool girl thought I was funny.

But the main connection I wanted to make that night was not a romantic one. I looked around for Dave. He came up to me and said, "Man, you gotta be happy with that. Couldn't have gone any better! I really gotta get back into doing this." Dave didn't have to start a chant for me that night, but having him there felt like I was finally getting the chance to end the set I'd started ten years earlier. It had been Dave's initial show of support all those years ago that had made the prospect of going onstage again slightly less horrifying. And it made me happy that, in turn, my performance was able to reignite the same spark for him.

In the end, none of the chaos from my three days in New York made it into the actual episode of *Rollin' with Zach*. The footage was manicured into a triumphant trip to a famous comedy club, mixed in with a successful date, an exciting helicopter ride, and "the best root beer float I've ever tasted!"* It bothered me that they didn't show any of the things that went wrong, because my life has taught me that sometimes the things that seem like mistakes are really just setups for the punch lines of jokes we don't understand yet.

---

*I've actually had a better one since then. It's made with Anchor Ginger Root Beer and Coffee Häagen-Dazs ice cream. If anyone wants to send me a case of that, I definitely am not above accepting gifts.

For me, the success of that night at Carolines had started with an encouraging failure ten years earlier on the stage at Kenmore West High School. I dropped out of school later that year due to my mysterious stomach ailment. In the decade between my talent show debut and my debut at Carolines, I also failed to complete my college degree, failed to get a job as anything other than a TV personality, failed to land so much as a drunken hookup at a frat party, failed to open a box of Lemonheads, and failed to zipper up a single coat without assistance. But the one thing I never failed at was having a sense of humor about these things. If my life has taught me one thing, it's that, like humor, turning failure into success is all about good timing. What comedy teaches you is that if you're quick enough on your feet, opportunities and mistakes are the same thing, and you have to seize both. Twice, I've ended up leaving the stage without even delivering the planned punch line, but both times, life gave me a better closer than I ever could have written.

CHAPTER 5

Who Wants to Smell a Billionaire?

"So, what does Oprah smell like?"

People ask me this question all the time, because in the fall of 2010 I got to sit across from Oprah Winfrey for twenty minutes. It was during the second-to-last episode of *Your OWN Show* as part of a press junket challenge where the final three contestants were interviewed by *TV Guide* and *Entertainment Tonight*, and then at the end were surprised by the queen herself for a one-on-one pleasant chat/the most important job interview of our lives. The only difference between me and the other two contestants vying for their own shows was that I was not surprised. When Oprah came up behind me, tapped me on the shoulder, and said warmly, "Hey, fancy meeting you here!" my response was a casual and generally muppet-y, "Hellooo! I was expecting you!" I'd put two and two together that this was how the day was going to end as soon as I saw that producers who normally wore jeans and an eternal five o'clock shadow were now clean-shaven, wearing sport coats, and whispering about somebody with the code name "Big Bird."

Big Bird and I hit it off instantly, probably because I didn't lean in to sniff her wrist as soon as we met. She asked me a question I'd gotten used to answering over the past couple of months since my audition video had gone viral.

"When did you realize that you were different?"

"Well, I knew I was in a wheelchair, obviously," I quipped. "They didn't shield that from me!"

Oprah laughed, but the truth is that I'd lived with CP my entire life and I'd rarely had to articulate my feelings about it—that is, until I was inadvertently thrust into the role of advocate and spokesperson for everyone with a physical disability.

I'd wanted to be famous for as long as I could remember. First, I thought I'd be an actor. Growing up in the early '90s gave me great hope that the advent of CGI would one day allow me to play the action hero Bruce Willis/Harrison Ford–type roles, with a pair of fully functioning running and jumping legs inserted during postproduction.

When I was five years old I auditioned for the role of Tiny Tim in *A Christmas Carol*. Seeing as I was the only applicant who was both tiny and crippled, I thought I was a shoe-in for the part, but I didn't even get a callback. Undeterred, I continued to audition for school plays and musicals with zero success. I chalked up my lackluster career to a lack of mobility until college, when I realized the truth—I'm just a really, really shitty actor. The only two characters I can play convincingly are myself and a dumber and sweeter version of myself. So sometime in early adulthood, I consciously stopped attempting to act. I decided instead to hone my skills as an on-camera personality rather than holding out for computer-generated movie stardom. If I was gonna make it in entertainment, I was going to have to do it on the virtue of my charisma alone. I just had to find my voice and my angle to break in. I knew that cerebral palsy would probably hinder my leading man status, but I'd be lying if I didn't also say I recognized that it set me apart.

When I was filming my audition video, I checked my friend Aaron's opening frame and gave him a direction I would normally avoid: "Go wider. They've gotta see the wheelchair right away." I knew it would be off-putting to just see a guy with a lazy eye flailing his arms around like E.T. fleeing the CIA. But my instincts told me that if I showed the wheelchair and then went straight for the funny, I'd be more relatable than if I tried to hide it, and if I did this right, then by the end of the video my electric wheelchair and erratic movement would just be background noise.

Over the years, I learned that in my career, unlike in life, sometimes my wheelchair is its own automatic door opener. I was able to win the OWN competition by applying one simple principle: be funny, and admit you suck before anyone else can call you out on it. In other words, make the narrative of your failure a comedy.

I knew I hit the mark when John Mayer posted a vlog about me on his blog,* saying that while watching my video, "the chair simply disappears," which means that to the singer of "Your Body Is a Wonderland," my body was not the focus, or, if taken

---

*We live in a ridiculous time.

literally, it means I can levitate. Both things are pretty cool. John Mayer even made good on a promise to write the theme song for *Rollin' with Zach* and posed with me for goofy pictures backstage at a concert in Buffalo. But the storm of media attention surrounding my video brought with it some things that were far less comfortable than having a rock star sit on my lap. I was given a title I wasn't prepared to own: Disabled Celebrity.

I think we can all agree that Peter Dinklage is the best (technically) disabled person there is. When I was a kid, I didn't have any dwarves to look up to, let alone any role models in wheelchairs. When people ask me who my heroes are, I never know how to answer that question because all the people I admired growing up were comedians and filmmakers and none of them had physical challenges. And though as a six-year-old in a tiny red wheelchair I could see virtue in FDR's New Deal, Roosevelt's reported womanizing barred him from idol status in my mind.

Today the landscape has changed. People with Down syndrome star in movies,* pop stars pretending to be in wheelchairs are on sitcoms, and, for the first time, people kinda maybe know what cerebral palsy is. Josh Blue won *Last Comic Standing,* and RJ Mitte became a household name by being the worst character on one of the best shows of all time. People with disabilities are more mainstream than ever. But there's still one big problem that I see. Usually, the disability still comes first.

Even on brilliant shows like *Breaking Bad,* where smaller ancillary characters are given emotional scenes and complex arcs, the guy with CP is used primarily as a device to make

---

*If you're interested, check out my buddy Josh Tate's work on *Love Land* and *Guest Room* to see some pretty stellar actors with cognitive disabilities.

Walter White more sympathetic. Isn't this drug kingpin's life difficult? He has a son with a disability! RJ Mitte *might* be a good actor, but he's given absolutely nothing to do besides whine and eat cereal. They only show his parents reacting to the prejudices he faces and they never give us any story lines about how *he* actually goes through life. Where are the episodes of *Breaking Bad* where Walt Jr. gets drunk at prom, or where he gets caught smoking pot with friends or masturbating into a meth beaker? So many missed opportunities to flesh this kid out! The reason we never see what he does or how he feels about anything is because characters with disabilities on television aren't really portrayed as people. They're just around to make you feel either good or bad by virtue of how other characters in the show respond to them.

In 2008, when a show I was doing at the University of Texas called *The Wingmen* started getting some attention, a Hollywood agent sent me a script that he thought I'd be perfect for. It was a network sitcom about a crappy after-school chorus called *Glee*. To get me the audition, the agent had enthusiastically lied: "You need a guy in a wheelchair who's a great singer? I got 'im!" I may have looked the part, but I can carry a tune about as well as I can carry an unborn baby. I was a horrible actor, but nevertheless, I put myself on tape reading lines and singing a rousingly pitchy rendition of Bruce Springsteen's "Dancing in the Dark." In the script, the character of Arty is locked in a porta potty by cruel football players, only to be rescued by Finn, the quarterback with a heart of gold. Once again, the guy in the wheelchair is the helpless one. In this sitcom universe, the majority of the world is populated by prejudiced, narrow-minded jocks who trap cripples in toilets, and the one person who would not do that is the *best* person who has ever lived. I don't know if that show ever went anywhere, but I didn't get the role. It didn't resonate with me.

When Oprah Winfrey asked me, "What do you think the biggest misconception about people with disabilities is?" my answer was, "That people think they're helpless and that their personalities are defined by their disabilities. . . . Get to know the person; the chair is incidental." Unfortunately, more often than not, the entertainment industry gets it backward.

When my Oprah audition went viral, I was given the chance to finally share my perspective on what it meant to actually live with cerebral palsy. People with disabilities are given a platform so rarely that as soon as I had the chance to speak, it was assumed that I would and could be the voice for everyone with any physical disability—paralysis, muscular dystrophy, whatever it was that the elephant man had, and the anomaly that caused Bill Murray to relive the same twenty-four hours over and over in *Groundhog Day*.

When I spoke about my own life and how humor helped me face down discrimination and other challenges, most people were very receptive to my story. Others were adamant that in order for me to be seen as an individual, I needed to be on message, reciting a rigidly scripted, politically correct mono-logue every time a journalist asked me about my experience with CP. I had apparently gotten my own life wrong.

That week when I became a household name overnight, I was getting about a hundred calls a day because it hadn't occurred to me to take down a promo reel on my YouTube channel that ended with my personal phone number. Most of the calls were from fans—fathers whose children were disabled and were moved to tears by my message of hope, shrieking teenage girls, even other OWN show contestants who called to wish me luck and give me advice.

There was one phone call in particular that made me super-stoked that my phone number was public knowledge.

"Hey, Zach, this is Stephen Colbert. I heard you might be interested in doing a buddy cop movie. The writers and I had this idea to shoot a trailer where you would play a character called Rollin' Thunder." Somehow, Stephen had seen the Reddit AMA where I mentioned that he would be my ideal partner in an action movie.

"That's awesome!" I exclaimed, trying to wrap my head around the fact that I was talking to one of my idols. "We could put a sidecar on my wheelchair that you could ride in." See? Even with Stephen Colbert, I was still angling to be that leading man. We never got to film it, but my friend Kevin Scarborough did the most amazing concept poster. So, Stephen, if you're reading this, I'm still totally onboard.

My phone just kept ringing, which was overwhelming and exhausting, but I was happy to talk with almost everyone. My work was finally making a positive impact. But amid all the well wishes and positivity, there were also bizarre calls that were tinged with resentment and slightly creepy vibes I couldn't place.

"Are you the guy I spoke with a year ago about my idea for a travel show for people

with disabilities? I think we've had this conversation before . . . ,"
a woman from Maryland accused. Her tone was very menac-
ing. She kept me on the phone for an hour, grilling me, as
though she were recording the call and trying to get a confes-
sion out of me. It was unsettling, to say the least.

There were also chats that started off friendly and then
quickly revealed another agenda.

"I absolutely love your work, and you're very inspiring, but
I was e-mailing with a friend of mine, and let me just read you
what she wrote: *He's got a great attitude, but the stereotypes he's
perpetuating are undermining everything real advocates have
worked for. Maybe he could get us in touch with Oprah and we
could all work together on this show?*"

And then there were the people who were downright furious that I had chosen to describe myself as a "wheelchair-
bound lady-magnet." "You're not bound to your wheelchair!"
they'd yell into the receiver, with all the misplaced anger of a
drunk dad at a Little League game. "Your wheelchair is not
part of you!" a stranger would insist.

Now, I'll tell you what, when I travel with my wheelchair
on a plane, they don't stuff us both in cargo. I get to ride sepa-
rately in economy. But on several occasions, airlines have lost
my wheelchair in transit, and those unfortunate separations
have taught me something.

For instance, when I was heading back to Los Angeles after
meeting with New York publishers to secure the deal that
would eventually become this book, my electric wheelchair
made a connection in Phoenix that I missed.* The next flight

---

*This delay involved me crapping my pants again. Sadly, that theme has already
been thoroughly covered in this book.

to LA wasn't until the following morning, so an airport employee brought me one of those gigantic airport wheelchairs with a pole sticking out of the top of it, pushed me to what would eventually be my gate, and left me there with my bags to spend the night. At my size (a robust youth medium), I'm unable to propel myself in a manual chair that seems specially fitted for The Mountain in *Game of Thrones*. So I spent the night on the floor at my gate, counting ants, unable to leave my bags to crawl to the bathroom. In that moment, I was forced to recognize that while I may not be physically bound to my chair, my autonomy most certainly is. My wheelchair is like the Canada to my Quebec—I wanna be free of it, I have my own identity, but if we split up, all I'm left to do is think of weird things I could put gravy and cheese curds on. Of course, the terminology traps didn't end at "wheelchair-bound."

Other callers were distraught that I had chosen to describe myself as "a disabled person," rather than their preferred "differently abled" or "a person with a disability." I fully understand the intention behind person-first language. I agree full-heartedly with the goals of this movement. But here's the thing: first of all, saying it my way is a full four syllables faster than "a person with a disability" and a whole lot less clunky. These are things that matter when you're struggling to get yourself across in a fifteen-second sound bite on TV or trying to stand out to a casting agent who's read ten thousand descriptions of ten thousand people in two weeks.

And as for the whole "differently abled" thing, do we ever talk about anybody being "differently abled" when they are extraordinary at something, or does it always imply a disadvantage? We don't say Tiger Woods is a differently abled golfer because he's better than anybody else in the world. I've never seen a poster that says *Differently Abled Cellist Yo-Yo Ma, Live at Carnegie Hall!* It just never rang true for me.

But my main problem is that with all of the emphasis placed on phrasing, I've found that people outside the disability community are wary of even starting a conversation with me because they're afraid that if they use the wrong term, I'll be profoundly offended. I never want to discourage anyone who's genuinely interested or curious from asking an honest question. I always wanna be approachable.

Now, anyone has the right to disagree with me. You have the right to be angry, even. This is just my personal take on a much larger issue. But before you craft a differently-abled effigy in my likeness and use this book as kindling, remember— whether or not we see eye to eye on the best route, we're all trying to get to the same place.

Learning how to stay true to yourself while some people expect you to speak for everyone has been a tightrope walk— which is very hard to do on four wheels. I never expected to be a disability advocate. I was a comedian first, a storyteller second, and probably a connoisseur of fine bathrooms third. But in that audition video I jokingly stated that "I have cerebral palsy, which I believe is the sexiest of the palsies." The line caught on, and people with CP started adopting the title. As I was reading through YouTube comments, I was surprised to find that that little phrase was starting to change perceptions. Somebody wrote that they were out to lunch with their family and saw someone in a wheelchair who was severely disabled, and their first thought was not one of pity but of recognition, *Oh, sexiest of the palsies!* This guy was able to see a person in vastly different circumstances than his own and feel an instant sense of familiarity, like that person was somebody he could imagine grabbing a beer with.

One of the reasons Oprah is the best interviewer in the world is because she's able to make whoever is sitting across from her feel like they've met a new best friend. When Oprah and I hugged good-bye, I left knowing that I'd made an impression, but I thought it was along the lines of *Someday I'd like to have this young man over to my house and we'll split a quesadilla!* I'd felt we'd shared a moment of mutual understanding, but when I watched the episode months later, I was surprised to see that after our brief encounter, when they cut back to Oprah for commentary on our exchange, she was in tears. "Zach makes you want to be a better person, with his humor and his heart, and everything he's had to deal with from the time he was born. I've never met anyone like him, and I've met a lot of people."

On the one hand, that's one of the nicest things that anybody has ever said about me, especially from a person who has interviewed so many of the world's most extraordinary people. On the other, I couldn't help but feel that this emotional response was at least in part due to an assumption that I had it a lot tougher than I actually did. Here was an African American woman born in 1950s Mississippi who had elevated herself to become one of the most influential and powerful voices in the world. I, on the other hand, have all the privileges afforded to every white, middle-class American male. On top of that, I have a loving family who has supported me in almost every endeavor I've undertaken. My single disadvantage is that I was born with cerebral palsy.

I couldn't help that. Instead of fighting against it, I worked with everything I had in my personal arsenal: humor, intelligence, empathy, curiosity, creativity, and hotness. Funneled through all those positive traits, my wheelchair and my diagnosis became tools rather than obstacles. I apply them when they can make my work better and try to check them at the door otherwise. They get in my way sometimes, but they also pave it. So when I'm sitting across from Oprah, or anyone else, my goal is to be seen not as someone who is forced to sit down, but rather as someone who chose to stand up. To me, that's putting the person first.

Oh, and for the record, Oprah smells lovely.

CHAPTER 6

How to Lose
a Television Show

When I met Kristina Kuzmic we couldn't say a word to each other. If we had talked, there was the risk that either one of us could be sued for five million dollars. That's the kind of contract you enter into when you agree to be on a reality show. So the bubbly, curly-haired, fresh-faced girl could only be referred to as her initials because we were forbidden to officially meet until the cameras were rolling. Every detail of K.K. and Z.A.'s lives were a mystery to each other. The first thing I noticed about her was that at the mere mention of chocolate she would have what could only be described as an orgasmic response. I had a pretty good inkling that we'd be friends, because I also climax when presented with M&M's. The second thing I noticed was her perfect, beaming smile, which immediately made me regret that I'd not thought to use white strips before making my debut on national television.

On each episode of the competition, K.K., Z.A., and the eight other monogrammed contestants faced off on various challenges, and basically whoever screwed up the most would be sent packing. Their final thoughts and regrets would then be played over a walk of shame as they exited OWN studios with their luggage, got into a 2011 Chevy Equinox, and drove away.

This disgraced exit was what we all had the pleasure of filming first, before the competition even started. The ten of us sat in the back lot of the studio and took turns putting on the black trench coats wardrobe had provided so that we all looked uniformly grim when we wheeled out our empty prop luggage to the fuel-efficient and unexpectedly luxurious disgracemobile. It was a stark reminder that though we were all hopeful, nine of us would be going home as losers. When it was my turn to face the bright lights and head down the ramp while contemplating a future where my dreams had been dashed and I might never get another chance to have a show on television, Corky the stage manager had some advice for me.

"When you go past the camera, try not to look so chipper about just being eliminated. Okay, reset the crane!" he called out to the crew.

I went, as we call it in the business, back to one, filming my sad departure three times.

"That's a little bit better, but it still looks goofy," Corky critiqued. "I know your wheelchair can't actually fit into the Chevy Equinox, so when you get to the car, just duck down behind it and we'll cheat the shot."

I was a terrible loser. It was the least convincing failure in the history of television, and luckily no one would ever have to see the footage of my defeat.

Over the weeks of filming, my interactions with K.K. were few and far between. We'd sneak in little bits of contraband conversation, but if we mentioned anything personal our handler would scold us, and an absolute silence policy would be enforced.

I almost instantly became a fan of Kristina Kuzmic. She was vying for a cooking show and had the same "anyone can do it" mentality about the kitchen that I had about travel. The premise of her show was to teach the world's worst cooks that even they could make a great meal for their friends and loved ones. She was funny and relatable, and I admired that she wasn't trying to be the version of herself that she thought Oprah would like.

Kristina grew up in Croatia but had to flee the country with her family when civil war broke out. She emigrated to the United States at fourteen and learned English by watching *The Sound of Music* a thousand times. Her passion for cooking was passed down from her grandmother, who taught her that food brings family together and to go with her gut on any recipe. She was a tough and relentlessly optimistic survivor who had raised two kids while waiting tables. Despite a difficult divorce, she found the courage to give love a second chance and had recently married a wonderful man named Philip. I didn't know these details of her story until much later, but in her, I immediately recognized a kindred spirit, someone else who'd been through a lot of shit and had still come out smiling.

The two of us refrained from the tantrums, catfights, and tears of reality TV with an unspoken understanding that at the end of the day, this was just a contest, and while we both wanted very badly to realize our dreams, there were more important things in life than winning. We were on opposing teams, but I hoped that no matter how the competition ended, Kristina and I might end up being friends.

On my team, I emerged as the funny guy everybody liked who also inexplicably seemed to be the only contestant with previous production experience. Knowing that everything I said could and would be used against me in a court of basic cable, I was always humble and never had a bad word to say about another person on camera. I didn't graduate from the University of Texas Film School, but all those long nights shooting sketches and editing in my dorm room had adequately prepared me for producing a Kohl's commercial in five hours, and that proved more useful than any degree. The biggest revelation of competing on *Your OWN Show* was that I might actually know what I was doing.

Kristina had no production experience but knew exactly what she wanted. While other contestants were preoccupied with coming off well on camera, Kristina was focused on doing good work. She wasn't afraid to be the voice of dissension (and often reason), even at the risk of being unpopular, and she fought for what she believed in. This impressed me, and as it turned out, it impressed the judges and Oprah too.

After five weeks of competing, I had charmed my way, while Kristina had fought her way, to the final two. On our last day off before shooting the pilots we would present to Oprah, Kristina and I pleaded with producers for permission to have breakfast together at the Sheraton Universal buffet. After weeks of only being able to wave at each other discreetly, we were delighted at the chance to dine together without chaperones. Kristina learned that the mysterious bearded man in glasses with the Boston Red Sox cap was actually my best friend, Andrew, and I was able to learn Kristina's kids' names for the first time. It's hard to describe the kinetic excitement of a breakfast table where two out of the three people sitting there might have their biggest dreams realized in less than three days, and the third person 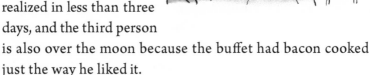 is also over the moon because the buffet had bacon cooked just the way he liked it.

Somehow Kristina and I didn't see each other as adversaries but as underdogs on the same team. We were both people who society had often counted out. Now, through hard work and some serious luck, we were on the brink of becoming celebrities. But life had taught us both not to have expectations for success when things were outside of our control. We couldn't allow ourselves to get our hopes up for more than a passing moment because when one of us lost, we'd have to be okay with going back to life as it had been. After all, one of our journeys would still end with that somber walk to the Chevy Equinox. As we headed back up to our rooms, we wished each other luck, and we meant it.

Within six hours of the most optimistic breakfast I've ever had, I was laid up in bed with a hundred-and-two-degree fever, aching all over, coughing my brains out, and too sick to do anything but desperately drink a gallon of orange juice in a twenty-four-hour period. At the precise moment when I needed it most, my immune system abandoned me. But the next day I loaded up with over-the-counter meds, determined to make the funniest five-minute travel show pitch by a deathly ill cripple that Oprah and superproducer Mark Burnett had ever seen.

Even though the premise of my travel show was how to have a good time when things go wrong, I knew that my zombie-like pallor would cause people to question whether or not I had the stamina to host a half-hour show where I jet-set around the country, filming twelve hours at a pop. In reality, I just had the same bug that had laid out half of the crew, but in reality TV, that bug was drama.

The producers had to take whatever drama they could get because Kristina and I weren't giving them any during our interviews. The last episode of a reality show is supposed to be rife with tension and fierce rivalry, but the last standing members of the show's opposing teams had nothing but nice things to say about each other.

Prodding, producers would ask, "Zach, don't you *want* to beat Kristina?"

"No," I'd say, "I don't want to beat Kristina. I think she deserves this."

"Can you just say the sentence, 'I want to win this show'?" they'd plead.

"I don't know if I'd say that I want to win it. I want to *earn* it."

Exasperated, they'd beg, "Just say, 'I want to win my own show.' Just those exact words."

"I want to win my own show . . . ," I said as producers held their breath, "buuuuuutt I also want Kristina to win!" and everyone behind the camera looked at one another and silently agreed that they could cut out the second half.

On the last day, as Oprah sat onstage with Mark Burnett

watching our pilots, she seemed to genuinely enjoy both of them, but she had more doubts about me than about Kristina. When my pilot was shown, there was a concern that I, one, told too many jokes, and two, as I'd anticipated, may not possess the physical stamina for the grueling production schedule of a travel show.

When Kristina and I returned to the green room, we once again expressed how happy we were that we were in the finals together.

"I think you got this," I said, smiling through the unbearable tension of waiting.

"No, I think you totally won," she reassured me.

We were playing a very gracious game of hot potato with our pending success. But I was sure that my last appearance on television would be that footage of me awkwardly ducking behind the Chevy Equinox and pretending to drive away. The judges deliberated for over an hour.

When we returned to Stage One to hear our fates, Oprah had a surprise for us that I can only describe as Oprah-esque. "Whether you win or lose," she said, "moments like these are important to share with people who are important to you," and then she brought out my mom and Kristina's husband. My first thought was, *Great, Oprah's gonna make me lose a show in front of my mom.* But after talking at length about how much she'd enjoyed our presentations and how she thought we both deserved our own show, she said, "I'm going to make that happen . . ." (dramatic pause) "for BOTH of you."

Holy Mother of Dragons!

No matter what you've heard, Oprah IS magic. In a split second, I had gone from being an unemployed college dropout to being a television personality, and Kristina had gone from being a hostess to the host of her own show. The dream had been realized for two people who, going into it, hadn't allowed themselves to believe for more than a fleeting moment that something like this could happen to them. Oprah and I hugged. "I promise I'll make you a good show. I'm so happy you're my boss!" I told her. Kristina and I exchanged phone numbers with everybody on the crew, and Carson Kressley even told me to call him anytime if I needed advice.

It was like a dream—everything that was happening around me didn't seem to make any sense. I'd grown up with one reality, gone on a reality TV show, and returned to a world where everything looked the same but felt vastly different. TV was no longer a thing I watched; now it was something I was *part* of. Oprah was not a larger-than-life public figure who interviewed world leaders and movie stars, but an affable woman standing right over there, eating a Pink's chili dog in a parking lot, just like the rest of us—just like me. Normally my world is all logistics and limitations, but that day was all possibilities. I didn't have to worry about anything or even hope that one day things would be different because in that moment my actual life had leapfrogged my imagination.

The most magical part of the whole thing was being able to go back to the Sheraton at the end of the day and celebrate with my mom and Andrew. They'd both believed that this could happen for me long before I ever could. As the three of us were sprawled out on the carpet eating a post-victory bounty of In-N-Out Burger, there was a knock at the door. It was Kristina. She ran in, hopped on the bed, and started gleefully shouting, "I can't believe we both have shows!" and then, spotting a Trader Joe's carton on my dresser, "Are those chocolate almonds?!" with nearly equal enthusiasm. We were now officially off the clock, and so could finally officially begin our friendship. October 14, 2010, was the day that Kristina Kuzmic and I both made it.

January 3, 2012, was also an important day. A week earlier, the last two episodes of *Rollin' with Zach*'s first season had aired back-to-back on the Oprah Winfrey Network. I was still in Buffalo for the holidays, but with New Year's over, winter transformed my hometown from a place to frolic in the wonder of Christmas snow to a place to grumpily trudge through January slush and hibernate for five months until either spring or death came to greet you. That's what winter in western New York feels like. To get ourselves out of the postholiday funk, my family and I were planning to go to our favorite Indian restaurant for dinner. It was 4:00 p.m., so naturally I was just about ready to consider putting on pants when the phone rang. It was Maitee Cueva, the executive at OWN in charge of overseeing my show. I knew as soon as I heard her tone what this call was going to be.

"Hey," she said, "it's Maitee. How were your holidays?"

"Fantastic!" I said.

"Good," she continued. "Well, I'm calling because unfortunately I have some bad news. As you know, the network as a whole has been struggling to find its legs and many of our shows are not doing well. We had really high hopes for yours and we're very proud and happy with how it came out, but the ratings were not good. We're all very sad about it, but we won't be moving forward with a second season of your show."

Unsure of how to respond, I just said, "I'm sorry I couldn't do better for you."

"No, no, it's nothing to do with you," Maitee reassured me. "We're all still trying to figure things out. I just got off the phone with Kristina and broke the news to her as well. We loved working with you both and you'll always be part of the OWN family. Please don't hesitate to call us if you ever need anything. We really do wish you the best of luck. I'm sure you'll go on to do great things in the future."

We exchanged good-byes and that was that.

Both Kristina and I had spent the past year and a half chasing down this dream and in two consecutive three-minute phone calls, those dreams were over.

Immediately after I got off the phone with Maitee, I called Kristina.

"He-ey," she greeted knowingly. "Did you get the call?"

"Yep!" I said. "First of all, let me just say that I think that they're idiots for dropping you. Secondly, I was thinking that we could pitch them another show starring both of us, called *Oprah's First Failures*. What do you think?"

"I think that's a great idea! Hold on, let me call Maitee back," she joked.

We consoled each other on the phone for half an hour, and then I went out for Indian food with my family for the first time as an unemployed TV host. It wasn't the most fun dinner I've had, but naan bread does make the death of a dream settle a little easier.

Over the coming months Kristina and I were faced with readjusting to life without a camera crew, wardrobe person, producer, or makeup artist. I had no one to comb the knots out of my hair or halt production for ten minutes while my collar was futzed with. It was like being the star quidditch player at Hogwarts and then going back to being a muggle. The first paycheck I ever got was for a hundred thousand dollars when I won the OWN reality competition. A little over a year later, I wasn't sure if I'd ever have a paycheck of any amount again. But losing *Rollin' with Zach* felt like I was losing a lot more than financial security and a team of stylists to gently explain to me why a neck beard is a bad idea.

When my show was canceled, I felt like I had broken a promise to people—not just those with disabilities, but everyone who'd entrusted me with carrying a torch for the disenfranchised and the underestimated. I'd become a symbol of hope for a lot of people who didn't know how they fit into society. They saw themselves in me and I imagined that in my failure, I had let them down. Months after my show went off the air, people on online forums would ask, "What happened to this guy? I wonder if the show was too much for him."

I was used to being pitied, just not by quite so many people all at once. I had battled uphill my entire life—I knew how to do that. What I didn't know was how to stop from sliding downhill. I was worried that at the age of twenty-seven, I might have already peaked. I hadn't accomplished enough to just join the twenty-seven club, so there was pretty much no other option but to grit my teeth, keep working, and keep dreaming.

The most awkward thing about that post-Oprah limbo was that people still recognized me on the street and never failed to ask, "What's going on with that Oprah show?" I held off saying it was canceled as long as I possibly could because, inevitably, the follow-up question would be, "What are you doing now?" If I answered this honestly, I'd have said, "Oh, just wandering aimlessly through the produce aisle, projecting myself onto a beat-up grapefruit that's been picked up, thought better of, and cast off in the cucumber bin." But the only respectable response I could come up with was, "Um . . . You know, I'm working on some things," hoping they didn't press for details. Kristina, meanwhile, had hooked up with a high-powered manager who sent her to meeting after meeting with network executives who fell in love with her story and her personality and agreed that she had to be on television. All evidence suggested she was well on her way to her next big thing.

I took a different career approach. I couldn't just simply put my entire livelihood and image in the hands of some Hollywood big shot who looked at me primarily as a chance to cash in on that lucrative celebrity cripple market. Plus, no agents approached me. I had to figure something out so I wouldn't have to pawn the super-fancy, electronic bidet toilet seat that I'd splurged on back when I still had high hopes for my earning potential. I just wanted to pursue projects I was passionate about and not have to go back to my previous career as an unemployed person.

Thanks in large part to Reddit cofounder Alexis Ohanian, Google's YouTube Creator Innovation Program, and my online fan base, within two months of losing *Rollin' with Zach*, I was given the opportunity to hit the road again. With the Web series *Riding Shotgun*, I got to make the travel show I'd always intended, this time on the Internet. Basically, my brother and two of my friends from college traveled with me around North America in the wheelchair-retrofitted Chevy Suburban I'd won from Oprah, meeting up with Redditors in person, and embracing every wrong turn and stumble along the way. We did whatever the Internet told us to do, even if it meant my having to be carried on an army stretcher through the woods or confronting my worst fear—hairless cats. Brad, Aaron, Josh, and I were the cast, crew, editors, and producers. Sure it wasn't as prestigious, and I made less for an entire year of work than I did for one episode of *Rollin' with Zach*, but I was still doing what I loved. I was humanizing disability in a way that traditional media wouldn't allow and making good on the promise and the premise of my initial Oprah audition video.

While on the road for *Riding Shotgun*, I'd often call Kristina to see how her post-Oprah life was going. In the time since her show, *The Ambush Cook*, had been canceled by OWN, she had been in talks about projects on the Food Network, NBC, and Oxygen. She'd had book deals, formal offers, and even a pitch for her story becoming a Lifetime movie where she would play herself! Her most promising opportunity was a show on Nick-Mom. There were contracts signed, a production company on board, and excited network executives. Both of us were getting a second chance neither of us had been sure would ever come. And just as we had been on *Your OWN Show*, we were each other's biggest cheerleaders. I was thrilled for Kristina and sure that she'd be the breakout star of NickMom (a network I'd shockingly never watched), and Kristina was confident that all the episodes of *Riding Shotgun* would go viral and my legions of online fans would make me the Rick Steves of YouTube.

Our expectations for success had been raised. I mean, winning a show from Oprah is definitely starting from the top, but I think both of us would have gladly accepted shows from Ellen, Barbara Walters, or, if it came to it, Ryan Seacrest. It would be fair to say that we had a slightly unrealistic perspective about how easy it was to get a show on television. After all, our first television shows only required us to put a homemade video online, spend a month in a hotel not talking to anyone (except the celebrities we had the pleasure of interviewing), and being better at this than the eight other people we were in competition with. As it turns out though, there's no such thing as a sure thing in the entertainment industry.

The NickMom deal fell through at the last minute because the production company and the network couldn't agree on budgets. It was devastating for Kristina. Despite the enthusiasm and commitment of her agent, she hadn't had any paid work in over a year. This was the most recent, and by far the biggest, of a series of near misses for her.

"I honestly think I might have to go back to waiting tables at my old restaurant if I don't get something soon," she confided to me over the phone. "The thing is, I would be *fine* with waiting tables. It would just be hard to wait on the same people who celebrated with me when I won and expected me to do more with my life. Do you know what I mean?" And I did. I knew exactly how she felt. We'd experienced such an extraordinary high together that there was no such thing as going back to normal. We were expected to do big things. We'd grown up with much less than we had now and were still by all accounts very fortunate, but everyone assumed we were set for life. People think that once you're on TV, you've made it. What they don't understand is that there is no such thing as making it. The only thing you can do is seize the opportunities you have, keep working, and be grateful for everything but feel entitled to nothing.

By the time *Riding Shotgun* made it to the Web, I was grappling with my own disappointments. When we wrapped, we had over three hundred hours of raw footage to slog through. The original plan was to release the fifty proposed episodes on a Monday-Wednesday-Friday schedule with the season finale around Christmas 2012. But it was June 2013 by the time we uploaded the last episode. At the height of my media exposure, I was used to my videos getting upward of a hundred thousand views apiece on YouTube, so it was disheartening to watch each segment of *Riding Shotgun* crawl its way to its first thousand views. The lackluster response and the strain of the workload made the unending postproduction schedule feel very lonely. The show turned out exactly how I wanted it to and I was proud of the journey and the work, but almost no one was there to watch it. We'd taken so long that the Internet had moved on. Feeling stuck in Austin, I needed to move too, but I had nowhere to go.

Kristina had one pretty strong suggestion on this front. Every time we talked, she'd prod me, asking, "When are you moving to LA?" I always told her that I'd only relocate to her town if I had a reason to be out there that provided a means to pay the absurdly high rent without selling my body, my wheelchair, or my soul.

Luckily, it turns out you don't have to sell your soul to make pancakes out of it.

Rainn Wilson's inspirational media company SoulPancake had been interested in doing a show with me since they saw my Oprah audition. The chance to make *Have a Little Faith* came to me not through divine intervention but, like most important connections in my life these days, via Twitter.

@soulpancake: *We want to get in touch with you about a potential collaboration! Pls DM us your email so we can get you more info.*

It's a pretty unassuming, unofficial way for a spiritual journey to begin. But over a period of months I developed the concept for a new show and with it my reason to become a

Californian. *Have a Little Faith* is a Web series that explores different world religions from my perspective as a self-proclaimed religious idiot. In each episode, I interview one person about what their faith means to them. The goal was to take the judgment and politics out of interfaith discourse and make a human connection to people with different beliefs. With a six-episode commitment, my brother and I headed to the West Coast, and my mom came along to help us find and move into an apartment.

The City of Angels gave the Anner family the first impression of being an unlivable shithole where *Keeping Up with the Kardashians* is filmed. It's hot, needlessly spread out, and every lunch you have begins with the waiter telling you about the audition they're going to after their shift because they're up for a part in the pilot of a podcast. It's a place where delusions and hope are the same thing. Everybody wants to be there so nobody really cares about making you feel at home. Nobody, that is, except Kristina.

At the time, Kristina, her husband, Philip, and their two kids lived in a modest two-bedroom apartment. Despite the shortage of space, they welcomed us with open arms and said we could stay until we found a place of our own. Her kids were visiting their grandparents in Croatia for a month, so we got free rein of the bunk beds and Legos. We thought we'd be there for three days before we'd find and move into a new apartment with palm trees, an umbrella drink vending machine, and an ocean surf wave pool.

As it turned out, we'd grossly overestimated the number of safe, affordable, handicap-accessible living spaces in the city. On more than one occasion, after what we thought was a promising lead, we drove up to the address, admired the graffiti, noticed the bars on the windows and the broken glass behind them, and decided to cancel our showing. Day after day, we'd go back to Kristina's and she'd do her best to convince my mother that her sons would be safe and find their way.

Ever since our destinies had aligned on Stage Two of OWN Studios, Kristina and I had helped each other keep perspective as we navigated through things that would have been much too foreign and scary to go through alone. To their credit, OWN made good on their promise to keep me in the family and were always quick to help by providing any materials or references I needed. After *Rollin'* was cancelled, they even let me out of my contract early so that I'd be free to move forward with my career and participate in other projects. Brad and I did eventually find a one-bedroom in Sherman Oaks, and I was grateful to sleep on a foldout IKEA sofa in the living room with a roof over my head and reinforced walls to protect me from earthquakes.

In July 2013, I began a year in the Golden State that was filled with personal milestones, and Kristina was there to see all of them: *Have a Little Faith* became my first show ever to be renewed for a second season, and an episode from my personal fitness series, *Workout Wednesday*, became my first video on YouTube to surpass a million views post-Oprah.

What I learned during my time in Los Angeles is that it's full of people who want to get together and make things happen, but everyone is so busy chasing a dream that life almost feels like an afterthought. When I was there, I had a full calendar occupied by meetings and potential collaborations and lunch and dinner dates, yet somehow with all of this I was still free 90 percent of the time. I can't count how many industry people came up and said, "Man, I love your work! We gotta do something someday!" But to the best of my knowledge, you can't call up your dentist's office and say, "I need a root canal. Mark me down for a nine a.m. on Someday." Hollywood is the flightiest place on Earth. But when Kristina and I made plans, we always stuck to them.

Even though we had started off as competitors, we grew to be like family. I spent my twenty-ninth birthday with her and as proof that she knows me better than just about anyone else, she got me the perfect presents—six pairs of pajama pants and a mountain of Skittles. That Christmas, we released our first collaboration together in a segment called "Cooking with Zach," in which I do absolutely no culinary labor and require Kristina to make a completely fictional family recipe for something called Apple Scrumples.

Kristina, like me, has found a new audience on YouTube and recently had a video about breast-feeding go viral that has, as of writing this, accrued over three million views. She freelances for various other DIY cooking sites, writes for parenting blogs, and added a new member to her family with the birth of her third child. Even though Kristina had been very receptive to my suggestions of names for her cooking shows, she refused to accept the brilliance in my proposal of "Han Solo" for the name of her newborn son.* We made a video together the week before he was born called "Talkin' Pregnant," and Brad and I went to see her in the hospital two days after "Han" arrived.

When we stood under the bright lights of OWN Studios waiting to hear our fates, Kristina and I had no idea of the journey that we were about to start together. At the time, I

---

* You guys can call that kid whatever you want, but he'll always be Han to me!

didn't really understand what Oprah meant when she said that no matter the outcome, having someone to share the experience with would make it better. Neither of us lost on that day, but my friendship with Kristina, which was bound together at our highest moment, ended up being the thing that got both of us through the lowest ones.

When you win, good friends make the experience even sweeter, and when you lose, they're the ones who help you appreciate what you have. We won shows together, we lost shows together, and we were able to navigate all of the things in between because we had each other. I don't know if Kristina or I will ever end up with shows on network television again, but I do know that whatever successes we have in our lives and careers, we'll always be rooting for each other. Oprah gave me many things. I lost the show, spent the money, and sold the car. But of all the gifts that Oprah gave me, a sister in California was by far the best. I'm grateful she's the one I've been able to keep.

II

Friends in Search of Benefits

CHAPTER 7

Destiny in a Red One-Piece Bathing Suit

"Check it out. I got your manual wheelchair," Dave whispers, crashing into the side of the tent and dropping his flashlight.

"But I already have my electric," I tell him.

"I know. It's for me."

"What?"

"I'm not walking all the way to the bus station!" he scoffs. "You're not the only one who gets to be lazy."

"Don't yell. You'll wake up my mom," I say, checking to make sure her light is still off. "We should leave in an hour. Are we forgetting anything?"

Dave shrugs. "We got a pillow and a blanket."

"What about the sandwiches?"

"Well, we don't want to make those or the chocolate milk

until right before we leave or they'll go bad. And if that's not enough food, we'll grab some Arby's," he assures me.

"Five for five?"

"Hell yeah."

Unable to contain my enthusiasm, I blurt out, "What're you gonna say when we meet Cindy?"

Dave presses his hand to his chin, deep in contemplation. "I don't know," he says, "but I'll have to stand behind your chair because I'll have a *huge* boner."

So, with everything set into motion, we prepared to venture into the great unknown, bringing a Tiny Toons thermos filled with chocolate milk, six peanut butter sandwiches, two wheelchairs, two hundred dollars of stolen bar mitzvah money, and our suits with matching clip-on ties. To two ten-year-olds with a dream, this list comprised everything we would need to make the four-hundred-plus-mile journey from Buffalo to New York City for one reason, and one reason alone: to track down, meet, and marry Cindy Crawford.

✧

I can't tell you exactly where my love of women began, but I'm pretty sure it had something to do with physical therapy. Some of my earliest experiences with the fairer sex were at the therapeutic preschool at the United Cerebral Palsy medical center in Buffalo at the impressionable age of two. To my parents, learning basic motor skills and being stretched daily was an important phase of my physical development. To me, it was an excuse to get to play games with the program's exclusively female staff.

With my blond curls, baby blue eyes, and sly smile, I was an undeniably adorable toddler. As the cutest cripple of the bunch, I was often used as a study subject for college students learning about CP. One time when I was four years old, I turned to my therapist during a session that was attended by a large group of eager and unsuspecting grad students and politely inquired, "Excuse me, may I kiss your breast?" As I matured, I realized I might have been setting my sights too high, so I focused my affections on someone more attainable.

I was introduced to the transcendent beauty of Cindy Crawford on a used VHS tape from Blockbuster Video. Most people at least pretended to watch the Cindy Crawford workout tape as a way to stay fit, but I unapologetically watched it while drinking root beer floats and eating Doritos, because such angelic purity deserved undivided attention and snacks. She'd instruct me to change positions, and I would respond by eating more popcorn. It didn't seem to make a difference; she'd praise me just the same.

At ten years old, I had found Destiny in a red one-piece bathing suit. My life *finally* made sense—I was born to woo and wed this woman. The early '90s were a wonderfully oblivious time before the Internet age, when supermodels and sex symbols could remain on their pedestals without drunken panty-less photos making the rounds on a thousand gossip blogs. Cindy Crawford was free to become whatever my ten-year-old mind imagined her to be. She collected comic books and baseball cards. She loved Saturday morning cartoons as much as I did. If we ever did get the chance to meet, my down-to-earth, innocent charm would be a welcome break from her supermodel lifestyle and we would form a relationship based on trust, common interests, and occasional boob-grabbing. So, over the next several months, her legend and my infatuation continued to grow.

The adults in my life didn't seem to take the unbreakable

bond that Cindy and I shared seriously. But neither the twenty-year age difference nor the fact that she was a supermodel, whereas I was a small boy in a wheelchair whose mom still had to button all of his shirts, deterred me.

I met my counterpart in prepubescent perversion, a.k.a. Dave Phillips, a seventy-five-year-old Jewish man in a ten-year-old's body, in 1994. While other fourth graders were collecting pogs and Power Rangers, Dave would come over to my house, watch *Blazing Saddles*, and explain the innuendos in his George Burns joke book. Thus, sex education began.

We were beyond excited when our lunch monitor, Mrs. Frazer, who was always up on the latest tabloid gossip, informed us that Cindy was more attainable than ever.

"Heard your girlfriend just got divorced! I seen it in the paper."

We theorized that Richard Gere's dime-a-dozen handsomeness and movie stardom had bored Cindy and, being several years older than her and a Buddhist, he had not been able to match her energy level. But we, as two vivacious bachelors, were anything but Zen at the news that Cindy was single and ready to mingle.

"We could be her rebound!" Dave exclaimed.

"Yeah!" I agreed, wondering what a rebound was.

This was it: our one chance to prove that instead of rushing back into the arms of some forty-year-old millionaire actor, she should spend the rest of her life with two ten-year-olds. It was a convincing argument, to say the least. But in order to believe it, she would need to meet us.

The only thing that was keeping Cindy apart from Dave and me was distance. We knew that our parents, who understood nothing of true love, would dismiss our resolve to find her as "foolish" and "crazy" if we confided in them. After all, we lived in Buffalo and she lived in—where did she live?

"I think they film *House of Style* in New York City," Dave guessed.

"New. York. City. She lives in New York City!" I declared.

The next several sleepovers at my house were spent covertly plotting the perfect plan to escape under the cover of night, leaving our lives as fourth graders behind and making our way to the Big Apple.

At the time, the top speed of my electric wheelchair was four miles per hour and it could travel eight hours before it needed a ten-hour charge. At this rate, after factoring in such variables as time to stop and eat and potential inclement weather, we calculated that the trip to Manhattan would take us, give or take seven minutes, an extremely long time.

"It seems like a pretty easy walk," I assumed.

I was optimistic that at the end of each travel day we were bound to happen upon a lovely family who would take us in, feed us a hot meal of meat loaf followed by cherries jubilee or homemade cream puffs, and invite us to stay the night. This family would be warm and welcoming, but would have a complete lack of interest as to why a couple of transient children would have shown up at their door in suits needing a place to charge a wheelchair for the night. Why, that's the American way.

When Dave brought up the very valid point that one of those families might be psychopathic murderers, the idea of couch surfing seemed slightly less appealing. In our minds, America was comprised of those who would sit down and eat with us and those who would sit down and eat *us*. Luckily, before giving up on our hopes and dreams, we saw a commercial for Greyhound advertising bus tickets to anywhere in the United States for only sixty-eight dollars, and it just so happened that New York City was part of anywhere. Our golden chariot had arrived.

With our Greyhound godsend, the travel itinerary was airtight and we knew exactly where we'd get the cash. Recently, Dave's family had ceremoniously entrusted him with a full Fisher-Price piggy bank, not to be touched until his bar mitzvah, still three years away. Dave's testicles hadn't dropped yet, but he justified using the money for the trip because Cindy Crawford would surely usher him into manhood, even if it wasn't recognized by the Jewish community.

I tried to expedite maturity not from faith, but from knowledge. I knew that Cindy Crawford was an educated woman, and if I was going to impress her I'd need to continue my academic endeavors.

"If I had to go away for a few months, could I get all my homework assignments ahead of time?" I asked my fourth-grade teacher, Mrs. Parsons.

"Under what circumstances would you need to go away?" she inquired.

"A medical thing," I said, pointing to the wheelchair.

"Well, I've only got up to next week's lesson plans but I can give you some stuff."

So, armed with a worksheet on proper verb usage and a blank map of the Middle East, we faced only one final hurdle: my mother. She'd always been a pretty good mom, but she was also capable of crushing any dream with the terrible weapons of Logic and Reason. No amount of explaining would ever convince her of our idea's brilliance, so we had only one option: we'd have to get rid of her. Unfortunately, we knew that if we locked her up in the closet, my chances of getting any video games for Christmas would be considerably lowered.

Luckily, as fate would have it, she was already planning a trip to visit her friend Tammy in Pittsburgh. I invited Dave to come sleep over the night before my mom left so that we could set our escape in motion. In order to make our final preparations, we'd need privacy and it seemed as though the stars were aligning in our favor. We knew this because we could see the celestial phenomenon as we stepped outside the tent erected in my backyard. My mother was preoccupied with her own travel preparations, and thus mom-radar was successfully disabled. As we climbed inside and zipped up the tent flap, we knew every base had been covered. Cindy Crawford was within our reach.

"So once we get to New York, how do we find Cindy?"

The look of panic on Dave's face made me realize that we'd neglected the important fact that New York City was actually, when you thought about it, quite a large place. Maybe instead of slopping gel into my hair, I should have been thinking about how to track down and contact one woman in a city of millions. Never rattled for long, Dave regained his composure and attempted to quell my fears.

"I think I know where the MTV studios are," he reassured me. "She's probably hanging out there somewhere. And if she's not, we could just go and knock on doors and stuff. Everyone knows who she is."

I felt entirely relieved. With our confidence restored, we were able to return to the much more important task of trying to look nice.

We enlisted my brother Brad's help in retrieving our suits from the closet because we thought that the less time we spent in the house, the less chance we had to incriminate ourselves. As Brad had no illusions that this plan was actually going to

work, he had happily made our sandwiches and delivered our clothes to the tent, thinking that these items would only make our inevitable failure more hilarious.

"So do you think she'll let us stay at her house?" I wondered aloud, starting to regret that my last night before becoming a nomad would be spent over hard ground.

"Yeah, probably, as long as we're not weird about it," Dave reassured me.

"I bet she has a hot tub,"* I envisioned. "You know what's really cool? I don't think any other fourth grader has ever done anything like this. No matter how much trouble we get into, after this, at least we'll know we did it."

"Well that's good, 'cause we're going to get into a crap-load of trouble," Dave yawned.

Sensing that the moment might be slipping away from us, I rallied.

"You can't fall asleep! We'll have plenty of time to rest on the bus. We should leave. *Now.*"

"All right, all right! Don't get your panties in a twist," Dave said.

We unzipped the tent flap, prepared to face anything the

---

*Not once did I consider whether Cindy Crawford would have a ramp or an elevator, but I spent a great deal of time imagining her hot tub.

world had in store, but as soon as we were outside something felt off.

"Wow," I said. "It's really dark."

"Yup," Dave added.

"How far away is the bus station, again?"

"I don't know where the bus station is."

"That's cool," I said, calculating the odds that someone would come up and kill a kid in a wheelchair in the middle of the night. "You got your Swiss Army knife, right?"

"No. The Swiss Army knife is my brother's. We have a butter knife."

And then, in an instant, every ounce of excitement that had propelled us to that moment without any regard for consequence was replaced by an overwhelming sense of fear. Sucker punched by the darkness, we had our senselessness knocked out of us and the only one left standing was our most loyal friend, Cowardice.

In five seconds we'd gone from two love-struck adventurers, excited at the prospect of heading blindly to New York City in the middle of the night, to two thumb-sucking sissies, not even brave enough to make the trek from their backyard tent to the familiar comfort of a bedroom fifty yards away. We sat in silence. Like a game of pride chicken, we each hoped the other's last shred of dignity would swerve first.

And then Dave murmured, "I'm just throwing it out there, but what if we left tomorrow morning?"

"WHAT?!" I yelled, feigning outrage. "You're really going to pussy out? No way we're leaving tomorrow morning!"

The following morning, well rested and with our fears subsided, we prepared to leave.

A daylight departure meant that we would have to face the

minefield of maternal awareness head-on. Ingeniously, we made sure that my brother created an intricate web of deception to distract her. "They're running away to New York City," he ratted. "They're just being stupid. They won't actually get anywhere." It was the perfect cover. She wouldn't suspect a thing.

But she did suspect a thing. In fact, she suspected quite a few things and seemed far past the point of suspicion when she confronted us.

"I know exactly what you guys are doing," she told us flatly, "and I'm not in the mood."

"We're not doing anything," I insisted as Dave pushed my manual wheelchair, stacked with blankets and sandwiches, past the kitchen on our escape route to the driveway.

"If you guys don't stop this right now, I'm going to be really angry."

"Stop what?" I mumbled.

This denial was met by that look only mothers can conjure, a scowl that, if translated literally, would mean, "I'm a volcano right now and if you say one more word I will erupt and burn you alive with my smoldering hot lava of rage."

I knew in that moment that if I said anything other than "You're right, Mom. I'm sorry. Here are some flowers and a card I made you to apologize," I would do irreparable damage to my childhood. But the love of my life was on the line and I wasn't about to budge.

Just before this kamikaze confrontation came to a head, the phone rang. It was Tammy, my mom's friend from Pittsburgh. "Sorry, I'm running a little late," my mom said, stepping out of the room. "There's kind of a situation here."

This was our one shot.

As I edged toward the door, I noticed that my mother

had laid all the money for her trip on the kitchen counter, unguarded: a king's ransom of $180 cash. I was past the point of no return. I *had* to make it to New York City now because after what I was about to do, I would never be allowed back in my own house.

I took three twenties and put them in my pocket. "Let's go," I said to Dave. I guess my thought process was that if you dig a hole deep enough, eventually you'll get to China or, preferably, Cindy Crawford.

Under the cover of broad daylight, we headed down my street.

"Whatchya doin'?" asked my neighbor, watering his lawn.

Dave grinned. "Going to New York City to meet—"

"Nothing!" I interjected. As the old saying goes: when in denial, deny everything.

The confused looks from my neighbors might have fazed other explorers, but we happily headed down the block, thinking we were home free.

"I can't believe we actually did it!" I exclaimed. "We're on an adventure that we'll remember for the rest of our lives!"

"We'll probably need to hide in the bushes at some point!" Dave eagerly anticipated.

And for four blocks, Dave and I talked about anything and everything Cindy Crawford. It felt like an eternity of contentment. We'd spent a lifetime looking for meaning and finally, at the ripe age of ten, we were done searching. It didn't matter how far we had to walk because we could see the finish line. Sure, there were miles to travel by foot in some undisclosed direction, and probably a urine-soaked bus ride and an aimless search through a city of millions of people ahead of us, but after that there would be a beautiful encounter with a beautiful woman (who may or may not actually reside in that city). Nothing could stop us.

And then I saw it: the maroon minivan of motherly justice roaring around the corner to collect us and sweep up the fragments of our broken dreams. I looked at Dave, both of us knowing in our hearts that we didn't have much of a chance. Then I suggested that Dave do something we were both unaccustomed to.

"RUN!" I shouted.

I pushed my wheelchair into full throttle, miming a running motion with my one free arm, hoping it would make a difference. It didn't. I knew that the 1988 Dodge Caravan was a far superior vehicle to my electric wheelchair, but I turned my speedometer all the way up to the little cartoon rabbit anyway. Dave frantically chased after me, recklessly pushing my manual chair in front of him. With my mother fast approaching, he shouted, "You gotta turn your chair to Rabbit!"

"It is to Rabbit!"

"Shit!" Dave screamed.

Then, our fatal mistake: the pillow atop Dave's chair flew off and crashed to the ground, a casualty of the chaos.

"Leave it!" I called.

"BUT I WANNA BE COMFORTABLE," Dave pleaded, returning to pick it up and then running as fast as he could. But the damage had already been done.

My mom sputtered up beside us, rolling down her window. "Get. In. The. Car," she demanded, pulling over.

"Never," Dave taunted, but his audacity faded quickly in the face of my mother's fury. Though Dave's heritage had allowed him to see the humor in everything, we knew that resisting arrest at this point would only make things worse.

Ignoring a few defiant kicks and cries to let me go, she stuffed me into the backseat.

The three-minute car ride home felt like the start of a life sentence with the weight of my mother's fuming silence bearing down on our already heavy hearts. Dave and I barely said a word to each other except when I whispered to him, "Do you think we'd get really hurt if we rolled out of the van?"

As we both contemplated our punishments, we realized that our future for the next several decades looked pretty bleak. We knew with every ounce of our ten-year-old bodies that love was not a crime. Stealing sixty dollars from your mother was, however, and unfortunately, I had done that as well. I was grounded for two weeks and was not allowed to socialize with Dave for a month. Lucky for me, we were poor and my mother had nothing, apart from hope, that she could take away from me. Dave's punishment was far worse: three weeks with absolutely no Super Nintendo.*

At school, I tried to approach Dave about a second attempt at busting out of fourth grade, but the lack of Donkey Kong had shaken him to the core. This was a broken man who realized that, when it came down to it, video games were more important than women.

To me though, Cindy Crawford was more than a woman. The flame I held for her had less to do with the countless erections she inspired, and more to do with the promise of freedom. Once I realized that Dave had fully abandoned the cause, I started looking for other ten-year-olds who'd be willing to join me on a pilgrimage for true love. In my most desperate

---

*First you take away a man's love and then you take away his only replacement for it? The cruelty was breathtaking.

hour, I showed up to my classmate Charlie Bennett's house with a plastic bag full of Kix cereal from the bulk food aisle of the grocery store. I didn't have much incentive for him, so I just cut to the chase.

"Wanna go to New York City?" I asked.

"When?" he said.

"Now."

He stayed on his front step, pretending to think about it. "I don't, uh, think I'm gonna be able to do that. I have cello practice at five."

I hung my head and clung to my sack of cereal as I rolled back down the sidewalk to my house. Of course Charlie Bennett couldn't go. He was already a child prodigy and had a bright future that he couldn't just throw away chasing after supermodels. And Dave had had a lot to lose too. He had more friends than I did and a lively Little League career. I just had Cindy.

At ten years old, the only thing I could do independently was dream. I couldn't get dressed or go to the bathroom without the assistance of an adult. I had aides at school and parents at home to help me cope with, but also to remind me of, my limitations. Running away to meet Cindy Crawford was my chance to do something extraordinary at a time in my life when most of the things that set me apart from my peers were subordinary; I was only special for the things I lacked in comparison to other kids.

They say that if you shoot for the moon and fail, you'll still land among the stars. But at the time, it sure seemed to me that if you asked any of the adults around me, their outlook on my future was too hazy to see any stars at all. I had told my physical therapist that I wanted to walk someday and she said that that *probably* wouldn't be possible, why don't we focus on buttons for now? I said that I wanted to live on my own, and they said, "Maybe, someday . . . but there's also this thing called a group home that might work better for you." Running away to New York City was my chance to prove to myself that I was going somewhere.

For many years after Dave and I had run away, I imagined what life would have been like if we'd actually made it to Cindy Crawford's doorstep. I pictured us rolling up to a thick iron gate adorned with the gold-plated initials "C.C." We'd ring the buzzer and after explaining the situation to a butler over an intercom, the gates would fling open. Our hearts pounding, we'd head up the long driveway and make our way past the trees, barely stopping to notice the moat or the pink flamingos, and finally, we'd see it—Cindy Crawford's mansion, nestled deep in the forests of Manhattan.

Then, from around the side of the house, a beautiful woman in a familiar red one-piece bathing suit would emerge. She'd just gone for a dip in the pool and before she could notify the authorities, or worse, our mothers, she'd say, "You two must be exhausted. You wanna come in and have some lunch?"

Dave, having held it in since we left Buffalo, would ask where the bathroom was and leave Cindy and me alone at the dining-room table. We'd sit there, locking gazes, and she'd put her hand on mine knowingly and whisper, "I know what this is about. You can touch my boobs for ten seconds. Just don't tell Dave." And as I blew bubbles in my chocolate milk to charm the woman I loved, I'd feel the type of satisfaction you only get from realizing a dream that everyone else told you was too big.

CHAPTER 8

I'll Have a Virgin Zachary

"I think that's something you should put in your bio: 'My penis works! I'm not a vegetable and my penis is great!'" Brad called out from the backseat of our ride, a white Chevy Suburban we'd affectionately dubbed "Betty" after our favorite Golden Girl.

"That should be your two-minute speed-dating pitch," Josh added from behind the wheel. We were a few weeks into our road trip of a lifetime, but to my friends Josh and Aaron and my brother Brad, *Riding Shotgun* was more than just an Internet-fueled travel show—it was an opportunity to finally get me laid. All attempts to find me a lady on the trip so far had failed, and Josh and Aaron, never having had trouble with women themselves, struggled to understand why. Getting dating advice from them was like living in a village without running water and receiving a cheerfully delivered chocolate fountain. They wanted to help but didn't know how. Josh and Aaron grappled with the idea that for some people, the casual hookup was as elusive as an open bar at a Mormon wedding.

"I imagine that if there was someone in a wheelchair, there would be a sort of desexualization of that person," Josh theorized.

Aaron jumped in, recounting an unsettling experience. "When we were filming in New Orleans and I was riding around in your chair at that parade, I came up to these two or three girls, and they looked at me and were like, 'Hey, how's it goin'?' and I was like, 'Heeey, how's it goin'?' and they were like, 'Awwwww!' and then they walked off and I was like, 'Wait, what the . . . ?'"

The "Hey, how's it going?" method had been foolproof for Aaron in the past, so it troubled him that the same words that had led to so many romantic encounters before could be rendered powerless simply because he was on wheels. He was the same person, with the same chiseled features, the same confidence, and the same pectoral muscles bursting out of his shirt. The only real difference was that he had stolen his friend's wheelchair for a few minutes and now girls saw him not as a Lothario but as a cripple.

"It really did put things into perspective, though, to sit in that chair. I was surprised how tough it is to be taken . . . not seriously, but to be taken . . . equally," he reflected. I thought that this kind of infantilizing dismissal, more than anything, was the reason that I was still a virgin at the age of twenty-seven.

No matter how old I get, there never seems to be a shortage of strangers who invite themselves to pat me on the head and have no qualms telling me to sit up straight in my wheel-chair and buckle the seat belt. It's like they think I'm just a tall, foulmouthed eight-year-old with a beard. The idea of me being an adult, let alone a sexual being, never occurs to them. In nearly every interaction with someone new, my first job is to undo all the misconceptions they have about people with disabilities. Making people see not just a person but an individual—instead of a wheelchair with a boy in it—is a tall order. I'd not been able to make the leap from pity to passion with women in the real world thus far, despite having received several marriage proposals online.

While my lack of sexual experience weighed on me heavily, it wasn't the great white whale my friends had made it out to be. I knew that casual sex was not something that would be easy for me because my body barely fit into my own life and it was going to take a supreme amount of understanding and patience for another person to navigate through my endless list of physical quirks. The random spasms, flailing limbs, and limited mobility were not things that could be easily incorporated into the heat of passion during a one-night stand. I was a guy who, while disrobing, would have to launch into a litany of caveats longer than the list of side effects for an erectile dysfunction drug. Even making out would have to start with a debriefing.

"Is there a way that I could get closer to you? Or if you could, just scootch up beside my wheelchair—and try not to hit the joystick because I'm planning on making a spontaneous move to kiss you," I imagined myself saying.

This is not an easy conversation to have drunkenly while "Gangnam Style" is blaring in the background. Who would possibly pick me when there were other hookup options that wouldn't potentially lead to driving a wheelchair into a wall with your ass? The way I saw it, my sexual awakening was only gonna happen if love was part of the package.

The problem I'd found with being a hopeless romantic is that in holding out for romance, I'd only been left with hopelessness. So as we continued across the highways of North America and no suitable soul mates emerged, my friends shifted their focus from the search for true love to the search for any womanish person who would have sex with me.

Josh and Aaron were optimistic that I possessed *something* that could overcome a culture of sexual dismissal toward the disabled.

"... If women *knew* of you, you could sort of parlay your fame ..."

Josh's suggestion might have seemed shallow on the surface, but it *was* more likely that I would be able to become romantically involved with somebody who knew my work, and through that had gotten to know me as a person and not just a stereotype. I'd gone through most of my life armed with only a sense of humor, a thoughtful personality, and a parking placard. Now I also had an adoring fan base of people who, when shown carefully edited clips of me, might be able to see me as datable. After years of fumbling through an empty romantic Rolodex, I finally had options. I just didn't know it.

Baltimore, despite being called the "Charm City," has the distinction of being Edgar Allan Poe's hometown, the setting of the HBO show *The Wire*, and home to a rat problem only surpassed by its heroin problem. When Betty rolled across the city limits that summer, we were greeted by a fanfare of police sirens. Our hotel in the center of town was conveniently located across from a condemned Burger King. We were too drained from our traffic-plagued drive to Maryland to even care that our rooms' ACs were on the fritz. Sweating and exhausted, we hit our pillows and promptly fell asleep, all of us grateful that tomorrow would be a day off.

The next morning, I was startled by a sound that is only alarming when you hear it through a bathroom door while sitting on the toilet. A young woman's voice drifted through the walls, and I listened to Josh laugh and converse in a voice pitched half an octave higher than his normal register. I didn't need to make out a single word to know that whoever he was talking to was as hot as a summer's day and as refreshing as a dish of sherbet. Josh's type was so specific that his flirt voice acted like sonar, so I knew the person on the other side of the door must have dark hair and very large breasts. When I emerged from my morning constitutional, I demanded to know who this mysterious beauty had been. It was the front-desk clerk who'd come to switch us into rooms that weren't a thousand degrees. All I knew of this woman was what I could gather through a closed door while pooping, but I was nevertheless enchanted and emphatically called dibs.

"Do you have a plan as to how you're gonna woo this girl?" Josh asked.

I had only thought it through as far as asking my friends to stop pursuing her so I wouldn't have any competition. Despite my good intentions, I had no idea how to transition from crushing on a girl to actually going on a date with her. Realizing I was entirely out of my depth, Josh spit-balled some ideas. "Why don't you set up a romantic dinner on the rooftop and

Brad and Aaron and I could come out dressed as fancy wait-ers?" All ridiculous scenarios aside, I knew I'd never have the courage to ask this girl out for coffee, much less dinner. My best-case scenario, if I actually did work up the nerve, was to be let down easy. So I shifted my objective to something less ambitious: proposing marriage.

If my romantic gesture was so grand that it could be per-ceived as a joke, then being turned down would be a joke too. Her rejection wouldn't be that quiet "no" that tenses your chest and closes your throat. By choreographing a hyperbolized romantic stunt for the cameras, I could avoid admitting that I had no idea what I was doing with women and was too terri-fied to even attempt a first move. I was warming up for a "bit," rather than dreading a cold shoulder. There were chains around my heart even thicker than the ones that kept the squatters out of the Burger King across the street.

It was on this day off, while weighing the comedic value of getting the front-desk lady flowers against the cost of a bouquet, that I got a call from a twenty-three-year-old reporter, who we'll just call Stephanie. She worked for a college paper I'd never seen or heard of, but to us, any press was good press.

I was used to doing these interviews by now. None of the questions ever surprised me, and they usually ranged from "What made you want to make a travel show with the Inter-net?" to "Whatever happened with that Oprah show?" Stepha-nie, however, did surprise me. When she called, she seemed giddy to talk to me and spoke with an excitement I thought was reserved for fans of much more attractive people. Five minutes into the interview, she asked, "What time would be good to do the interview?"

Confused, I said, "Well, I'm free all day . . ."

"Okay, great!" she said. "I'm in DC now, so if I take the train, I can be there a little after six. Would that work?"

"Sure," I said, moderately bummed out that I'd have to put on pants that day. "But I don't want you to have to drive across the country!" I continued, because, with my complete lack of geographical knowledge, I had no idea that Baltimore and Washington, DC, were relatively close. "We could just do it by phone," I offered.

"No, no, it's fine. It'll be a lot better for details anyway if we're in person," she assured me. "I'll just hop on the train now," and she hung up before I had a chance to explain that this would really disrupt the evening I'd already planned to watch *What About Bob* with Josh, Brad, and Aaron over Thai food.

What an inconvenience it is that a woman wants to talk to me! I thought, which is a perspective that might explain my dearth of romantic encounters as much as anything else. It was my responsibility to pick the meeting place, but the only things we'd seen in Baltimore were the super touristy national aquarium area and The Block, which was home to both the Grace and Hope Mission and about a dozen strip clubs. Instead of splitting a footlong with Stephanie at the Subway next to the Hustler Club, I opted for the slightly classier Cheesecake Factory located next to the aquarium and the plastic dragon boat rental place.

I got there around seven o'clock and was greeted by a girl with long brown hair, slightly frizzed from the humidity, in a floaty tank top and white shorts. We got situated at a table outside and ordered dessert. I hadn't eaten dinner and was really hungry, but as a rule, I don't generally eat big meals when I'm out with people for the first time. There's no better way to play into a stereotype of helplessness than to have to ask someone, "Can you cut up this chicken?" immediately after introducing yourself. But Stephanie and I didn't have any of those awkward interactions and there was a certain ease of conversation that was almost completely foreign to me.

I didn't have to use any of the canned responses to standard interview questions that I'd perfected over the past two years of being in the spotlight. I thought I'd only be there for half an hour before I could hop back in bed and fall asleep to Bill Murray, my toes gently grazing Josh's leg hair. But before I knew it, the short interview had progressed into a three-hour-long stream of consciousness. I was asking as many questions as I was being asked. I learned that Stephanie was a nanny, that she was moving to Australia, and that she had been engaged but had recently broken off her engagement. Normally, the only information I got from reporters was formal, like, "Hi, I'm Dan from *Time* magazine. Let's get started," or "My name is Natasha. I'm from a podcast called *Lick It, Bite It, or Both*. You've been nominated as someone we'd like to lick and bite. Would you be interested in being interviewed?"* But this was not that same staunchly professional dynamic I'd grown accustomed to.

Normally when you're doing press, there's some element of performance. But with Stephanie, I felt comfortable dropping all the formality because of something I'd later come to recognize as chemistry. But since I had limited exposure to girls enjoying my company, I was unable to imagine this evening progressing into anything beyond our pleasant conversation. Besides, I had other things on my mind—it was nearing ten o'clock and the *Riding Shotgun* crew had a very important morning ahead

---

*This really happened, by the way.

of them. We had to be up at seven to go to the Hidden Peak Cat Club "Strawberry Fields" Cat Show. I would not only have to interview very enthusiastic and serious cat owners in the morning, but also train cats to run through an obstacle course, if not run through one myself. I was first and foremost a host on a job. My mind hadn't been conditioned to think of the action I could be getting, and it hadn't occurred to me that there could be something more beneficial than eight hours of sleep. But Stephanie seemed to at least vaguely know of something that I might rather be doing.

"I just bought all this stuff for an eighties prom party I've got next week," she said, pointing to a shopping bag. "What time is it?"

"Quarter to ten."

"Damn," she said.

"What's the matter?" I asked, signing the check and backing away from the table.

"I don't think I'm going to be able to catch a train back to DC tonight, and my phone's dead."

"Huh," I said. "What kind of phone is it? I've got a charger back at the hotel you could use," a casual offer that for me held the subtext of *I've got a cell phone charger back at my hotel room that you can use to charge your phone.*

"That'd be SO helpful!" she said, and we started walking back to the Best Western Plus together.

When we got to the hotel, I was relieved to see that my future wife's shift was over. I didn't want her to think I was cheating on her when I brought another girl back with me. Stephanie stopped at the front desk and said, "You know what, it's really late. I should probably just stay here." Had I not been an idiot, I would have taken this glaring, flashing neon sign as a cue that I should offer up my room as a place to stay, but, obviously dedicated to remaining a virgin forever, I said, "Oh, I'll get you a room!"

"No, I got it," she said, taking out her wallet.

Newly minted key card in hand, she asked, "What room are you staying in? I'll show you the dress I got for the party! You can tell me if it's too tight. It's a leopard print thing."

Naturally, at the prospect of a pretty girl trying on tight animal print dresses in my hotel room, my train of thought was *How long is this fashion show gonna take? There is no way I'm gonna be ready for the cat show if this girl is trying on outfits all night!*

So, before Stephanie even checked out the private room I'd chivalrously let her book, we went up to my floor. Josh had already been asleep for an hour and had he not been groggy, I'm sure, like any good friend, he would have assessed the situation, taken me into the bathroom, and finally clued me in to what an oak tree could have gathered was a surefire chance to lose my virginity. Well, maybe it was a stretch to think that a woman who'd only split a slice of cheesecake with me would usher me all the way into manhood that night, but regardless of what base I got to, this was certainly the best opportunity I'd ever had to get in the game.

But it was Stephanie who ended up in the bathroom and when she emerged she was in a form-fitting leopard print tube dress with her hair done up in an eighties scrunchie. In retrospect, I painfully recognize that this look was totally hot. I enthusiastically told her she looked great, but I have to admit that in the moment the dress mostly just made me wonder if there would be any leopard print cats at the Hidden Peak Cat Club "Strawberry Fields" Cat Show in the morning.

Gosh, I thought, *if I get any less than six hours of sleep, I'm gonna be completely shot for tomorrow!* So in lieu of acting like a real human being and proposing that we go to her room so she could try on the rest of the outfits she'd brought, I yawned and said, "Well, I've got a really big day tomorrow so I should be getting to bed! Do you want me to come by your room in the morning so we can check out the breakfast buffet?" Reinvigorated for all the wrong reasons, I said, "They've got one of those automatic waffle makers; it should be awesome!"

"Yeeaah, so just, I'll see you in the morning, then?" she shrugged, realizing it was hopeless.

"Definitely!" I said, reassuring her that, and I quote, "I never miss a chance for waffles!"

And with that, Stephanie went down the long hallway to her room. As I went to bed, I thought to myself, *Well, that was nice!*

I awoke the next morning to waffles, still oblivious to the fact that I'd missed out on anything more the previous night than a full forty winks. So as Stephanie left the breakfast

bar to catch a train to DC, I recounted the evening's events to Aaron, who instantaneously was able to translate my night with Stephanie at the Best Western into what it actually was—the best-missed opportunity in the Western Hemisphere.

"You let her get her

OWN ROOM?!" he shouted in disbelief. Then, turning on Josh, "How could you let this happen?! This was *our chance*!!!"

Not yet ready to confront my own shame, I joined in: "Yeah! How could you let this happen?!"

It made me feel slightly better to pretend that this all might somehow be Josh's fault. I was only twenty-seven! I didn't know any better! Josh was a full two months older than me. He'd clearly been the responsible adult in this situation.

"I'm sorry," he lamented, burying his head in a bagel. "I should have done something!" he exclaimed, with all the sincerity of a firefighter who couldn't save your kitten.

"I'd expect this from Brad, but not from you," Aaron continued. Brad just shrugged his shoulders in agreement and ate his scrambled eggs.

With the burden of guilt now squarely resting upon Josh's shoulders, we resolved that if a situation like this were to ever arise again, Team Get Zach Laid would not fail.

With Stephanie now out of state and probably disinterested, I reverted to the only form of courtship I was comfortable with—one that was solely for the cameras. On a piece of hotel stationery, I had Josh transcribe a marriage proposal to the beautiful front-desk clerk. I made sure to highlight all of my redeeming qualities:

You have put the Plus in my Best Western Plus experience.

Now about me. John Mayer wrote a song about me, I've met Oprah twice, and I have an awesome toilet seat! Marriage?

—Zach

P.S. What is your name?

Brad filmed me as I handed her the note, but before she had a chance to open it, I bolted out the door, too afraid to even wait for a reaction, and hopped into Betty White, the only woman I understood.

As we waved good-bye to the abandoned Burger King, my phone buzzed. It was Stephanie, thanking me for the great time she'd had. While in her presence, I'd missed every signal she'd sent my way. But in reading her text it finally clicked that this was a girl who hadn't given up on me. As crass as this sounds, she saw me as "doable," whereas I saw myself as the forever-alone type.

I hadn't just kept my virginity that night with Stephanie, I had earned it, not by trying and failing, but by failing to try. I'd been so used to being looked up to or down upon that I'd failed to see the pretty girl looking right at me. And for all the subtext I had missed, the most important was something I'd longed to hear from any woman—"I see you."

CHAPTER 9

Something to Offend Everyone

I was introduced to Austin, Texas, in a darkened movie theater during the 2002 South by Southwest Film Festival when I was seventeen. I saw forty-two films over the course of that week and spent the majority of my time at the Alamo Drafthouse. It was unlike any place I'd ever been and quickly became my favorite movie theater in the world. You could order food off a menu that was filled with items named for Quentin Tarantino and Robert Rodriguez flicks, and before each show they had a pre-roll featuring everything from long-forgotten B movie trailers to clips from '80s exercise tapes. It didn't matter if it was a documentary at 11:00 a.m. or a midnight slasher screening, the passion from the crowds for both good and bad cinema alike was infectious. By the end of that festival, the Drafthouse felt like a second home to me.

I'd always dreamed of making movies, but SXSW was the first time that the film industry seemed accessible to me. Filmmakers and film fanatics were everywhere. I fell in love with Austin's creative energy and the city itself. I'd just dropped out of high school and had no idea how I was going to move forward with my life. SXSW gave me my answer.

When I told my mom about my idea to go to the University of Texas at Austin's film school, she didn't scoff or try to dissuade me but just said, "If you take the initiative to apply and get in, we'll figure out a way to make it work." In the three years between when I first visited Austin and when I finally moved there as a bright-eyed twenty-year-old, I got my GED, took some courses at the University of Buffalo to make sure I was ready for college-level classes, and worked at Disney World to test-drive an away-from-home experience that wasn't as high stakes. Then, having proven to myself and my family that I could do it, I was officially accepted as a radio, television, and film major at UT Austin in January 2005.

Instead of arriving in the fall with the other freshmen, I had the disadvantage of transferring to UT for the spring semester. During my first month of classes, I didn't make any friends. Where did the Texans who didn't drink or know a single football player's name hang out? I felt lost and adrift in a sea of burnt orange T-shirts and Longhorn pride. Even my RA would sometimes call me Simon, which was the name of the other kid in a wheelchair from my dorm, who should have been easy to distinguish from me because he wore glasses and had a helper dog. College wasn't turning out to be quite the social awakening I'd anticipated.

When I left Buffalo, I'd hoped that Texas would be an opportunity to be seen as something different inside and out.

I was two thousand miles away from home at one of the largest universities in the country. I didn't know who I was or who I wanted to be, but after my awful high school experience I felt like being anyone would be better than being a Sick Person. I moved across the country to get some independence and life experience, rich with parties and beer pong, boobs, and all the college pastimes I'd seen so much of in *National Lampoon* movies. But the way things were going, it seemed like all Texas was turning out to be was a new place to disappear.

I thought Austin of all places had the potential to embrace the quirks and individuality that I'd be dismissed for anywhere else. It was a mini entertainment mecca that celebrated weirdness. UT had a history of producing cultural leaders and trendsetting independent artists, everyone from Walter Cronkite to Wes Anderson and Matthew McConaughey. And though I never thought I could look as good shirtless as any of those guys, I dreamed that one day I would do something notable enough to earn a place for my name among theirs on the plaques and busts that lined the walls of the campus communications building.

I almost missed my chance to shine because it involved getting out of bed. Inexplicably, one of my most important classes, the required Intro to Film, started at eight o'clock in the morning, an hour that was rumored to exist but had faded into the realm of myth for most college freshmen. I took the fact that it was held in a large lecture hall as a sign that I wouldn't be missed if I slept in. Over the course of the semester, I probably made it to that class four times. During one of those four, however, a volunteer from the student-run television station called KVR TV announced that they were going to have their general meeting and welcomed anyone to come work on existing shows or even pitch their own.

As a film major who wouldn't be able to take any actual production courses until junior year, the prospect of getting hands-on experience was enticing. I knew that if I was gonna do anything besides nap through lectures about breaking up the Bell Atlantic monopoly and mise-en-scène (which basically means "the-stuff-in-a-scene"), I'd have to get involved in some extracurricular activities. I couldn't help operate film equipment, but I hoped that if I just showed up and everyone saw how useless I was in that capacity, they'd decide to put me in front of the camera.

Not wanting to wait until the general meeting, I went to the communications building that same afternoon. What I found was not a pristine TV studio with broadcast-quality cameras and high-def monitors but, instead, an unshaven dude in tattered jeans napping on an old couch while he waited for his frozen burrito to thaw out in the microwave. He looked too old to be in college, like one of those thirty-year-old models they cast as high schoolers for network TV shows.

"Hey," I said, "is this the television station?"

"Yeah," he yawned. "Sorry, I'm just hanging out here between classes 'cause I don't have an apartment right now. But what do you need?"

"I was just looking for a volunteer form and wanted to see about getting involved."

"Sure," he said. "I'm Mark, by the way. What's your favorite movie?"

"I think it's a toss-up between *Almost Famous* and *To Kill a Mockingbird*."

"Oh yeah?" he said. "Mine's *Terminator 2*. Do you make movies?"

I'd certainly filmed a lot of things, but I didn't know if you'd call that story of Andrew as a mail-order Russian bride a *movie*. So I decided to dodge the question.

"Yeah," I said, "but mostly sex tapes."

Mark started laughing.

"Hey, Blake, get in here!" he shouted down the hall.

A guy with glasses and a lazy beard poked his head in the door.

"Tell Blake what you just told me about your movies."

And just like that, I'd made my first friend in Texas and found my niche. I was the guy who could say inappropriate things without getting into trouble. It wasn't long before Mark and Blake hatched an idea for a show with me as the star. Its name would be derived from the most common response Mark and Blake got whenever they described it to people.

"We're gonna do a show that features this kid in a wheelchair who's really fuckin' funny, and we're gonna do music videos and celebrity interviews . . ."

"That's awesome!" people would say, and Mark would respond, "Exactly. That's what it's called. *That's Awesome!*" Given my unique ability to elicit laughter from jokes that would normally get people slapped, excommunicated, or kicked in the balls, the content would be informed by the show's slogan, "Something to offend everyone."

In one of the first outings for our new show, we took two cameras down to the bars on Sixth Street on a Saturday night with the premise of "Let's just have Zach interview drunk people." I gave wheelchair rides to anyone that wanted them and made more sexual innuendos about my joystick than is appropriate for print. I even played a game called "Rub the Cripple" with one particularly cute and apparently not picky bar hopper. I told her she'd get three wishes if she rubbed my tummy. She only asked for one.

"I whirsh fooor a fine-ass white boy in a wheelchair to come along and do me doggy style!"

Believe it or not, that trip downtown was one of the more highbrow segments we did on *That's Awesome!* Once we realized that my wheelchair could help us get away with anything, we exploited this get-out-of-jail-free card far beyond the boundaries of good taste.

My goal at the University of Texas was to build a reputation so that one wouldn't be built for me as the Kid in a Wheelchair Who DOESN'T Have a Dog. I wanted to escape the stereotype of all people with disabilities being innocent and helpless, and so I chose to be loud, vulgar, and undeniable. And it worked.

Within a couple days of our Sixth Street shoot, Mark had cut together some highlights and was screening them for other KVR volunteers. I originally thought the segment would be no more than five minutes long, but Mark assured me, "There's so much good stuff, I think we could make a whole half-hour episode out of this!" The only bit that didn't involve me was a lip-synched Fall Out Boy music video where Mark and two other friends wore wigs and dresses. It didn't make any sense, but that was kind of the point. "Also, dude," Mark said excitedly, "instead of putting a beep when you swear, I decided to just use this rubber chicken sound effect to differentiate us from all the other shows." I always kinda hated that rubber chicken sound, but I was happy to be part of something, and in Mark I found my first superfan.

It wasn't long before we landed our official time slot, Fridays at nine, which I loved, because it was when *The X-Files* used to air when I was growing up. Over the next few months, we produced four half-hour episodes of *That's Awesome!* comprised of segments like "Cheap Dates" (a knockoff of *The Dating Game*, where each of the prospective suitors describes what their perfect date would be on a budget of five dollars), celebrity interviews, and several more music videos with Mark in drag. Astoundingly, it wasn't long before *That's Awesome!* was being talked about as the best TV show on campus. Before meeting Mark, I never would have guessed that a freestyle rap about my penis could have widespread appeal, but it did.

For the first time in my life, people noticed me not for my disability but for my crude and relentless humor. All of a sudden, I was a recognizable figure on a campus of fifty thousand students. I'd see people I'd never met wearing shirts with my face printed on them in the dining halls. The arrangement worked out for both Mark and me. He never had trouble with women before, but being the man who shepherded the funny kid with CP to campus stardom made Mark even more attractive and sympathetic.

We were an unlikely pair. Mark had a formidable brow and rugged good looks—so rugged, in fact, that no matter how hot the day, he would never wear shorts, only jeans ("My calves are too big, dude. I don't want girls seeing that"), whereas I wore shorts all the time and my professors were lucky if I remembered to zip up my fly before class. Mark was popular and simply by telling people I was funny, he made them pay attention to me.

I got to talk about music with Neil Young and discuss sexual techniques with Kevin Smith, and I even tried to get the

Beastie Boys to beatbox for me. With a camera in front of my face, I could hit on any girl with any pickup line without running the risk of rejection (although being the host of my own TV show didn't translate into me getting any action). Even my teachers started to recognize me, which made me wonder whether a college professor had any business watching cable access television at nine o'clock on Friday nights.

"Does that move at all?" Professor Schatz asked, pointing to the huge canoe oar sticking out of the back of my chair with the name and time of my show Sharpied on it.

"Nope," I shrugged. "It's stuck in there pretty good."

I may have been obscuring the view of the overhead projection for the students behind me, but Mark and I had our eyes set on a broader audience than the people on campus who stayed in on weekends. The Alamo Drafthouse would give us that audience.

Along with flagship events like Justin Timberlake sing-a-longs and screenings of the Lord of the Rings trilogy with specific twelve-course meals tailored to the films, the Drafthouse hosted a year-round competition series called Open Screen Night. Open Screen Night was like a gong show for video clips that people brought in, everything ranging from short documentaries about the Middle East to old men vlogging while giving themselves a coffee enema. I was nervous about showing anything I had done to an audience of two hundred people, especially when they had permission, and were even encouraged, to boo at anything they didn't like.

"Dude, they're not gonna boo you," Mark said. "I bet you anything we win. And if we do, can I use the hundred-dollar prize money to pay off my phone bill? I just realized that my long-distance plan is only free throughout Texas. I spent a hundred and eighty-seven dollars talking to someone in Buffalo, New York."

"That's where I'm from," I said.

"Ooooh! That makes so much sense!"

When we headed into the theater I was more nervous than excited. We settled into our seats and Mark ordered a bucket of six beers. It was only our first public screening, but we'd managed to bring an entire cheer squad with us, comprised mainly of girls Mark found attractive. One of these unofficial cheerleaders had even designed a flag made of pink felt adorned with glitter and kittens with dialogue bubbles that read, "That's Paw-some!"

We sat through two hours of the most random hodgepodge of videos I'd ever seen, and after watching a hidden camera segment about high school students who wear diapers and attempt to covertly crap themselves in a public library, I knew that at least our video wouldn't be booed. Mark thought that our strongest clip was an interview I'd done with Dennis Quaid. It'd been a hit at the TV station, but I had no idea if the Drafthouse audience would like it.

Finally the host introduced our clip. The video began with me confiding in Dennis that as someone in a wheelchair, I don't get a lot of acting opportunities, and then I invite him to improvise a scene with me called "British Middle-Aged Couple in Crisis." Without missing a beat, he puts on a cockney accent and says, "All right, go ahead." We play out a scene where Dennis is my wife and we're on the brink of divorce. The audience was laughing and even if they didn't know what to make of it, they were just buzzed enough by this point to go along with such a bizarre concept. Exasperated that my wife has spent too much money on new furniture, I shout at Dennis in a faux-British accent, "Oh my God, I can't believe I'm married to you! Why don't you just go drown yourself in vodka?" and Dennis, trying not to crack up, replies, "Well, why don't you go fuck yourself then?!" The crowd went wild.

The prize for the winning clip was a hundred dollars and after the uproarious response to ours, the host said, "I have a feeling that if you guys come in every month you'll be twelve hundred dollars richer by this time next year." Open Screen Night was the first time I ever got to be with a live audience watching something I'd made. It was also the night of my twenty-first birthday. I didn't have a single drink because the rush of being recognized and even paid for doing what I loved was greater than any buzz I could get from a Jägerbomb or Flaming Doctor Pepper (plus, I was kind of a lame Goody-Two-shoes when it came to drinking).

I'd never had a fan base before and it felt great. The dream of making a living as an on-camera personality suddenly seemed like it might be a plausible future. At first, it didn't matter that my notoriety was based solely on being an insult comic who held nothing sacred. But after a while, I started to worry that people thought the asshole I played on camera was who I actually was.

Strangers would pitch me ideas for segments they themselves would never have the gall to execute, suggesting things like, "Our former governor, Ann Richards, just died. You should totally do a sketch where you play her at her funeral."

"And how would I make that funny?" I asked.

"I dunno, you're hilarious. You'll figure it out!"

Students would yell out to me, "Say something funny about AIDS!" or "Riff about Kirstie Alley being fat!"

Complete strangers seemed to have a firmer idea about

who I was than I did. I started to wonder if people were finding me funny for all the wrong reasons. In trying to escape being a stereotype, was I unwittingly turning myself into a novelty?

Little nagging concerns began to creep up in the back of my mind, but I largely ignored them. Maybe these red flags were actually shiny red ribbons wrapped around the gift I was giving the world. After all, there were a lot of people around me laughing and telling me how great I was, so who was I to disagree?

As *That's Awesome!* gained traction on and off campus, Mark and I began to get more and more volunteers who were interested in being part of the show. Every time we headed down the long white hallways to the "War Room" for our weekly meeting, we were hoping at least one hot girl would walk through the door. Instead, one Wednesday night, we met Justin Lowrey and his roommate, Chris Demarais. Justin looked like a laid-back, redheaded Keebler elf and I guess Chris was eighteen but puberty certainly hadn't gotten the memo. Chris had spiked hair like a real-life version of Bart Simpson and a boyish charm that made girls want to take him home to meet their mothers. He took off a backpack, unzipped it, and removed twenty cookies, six crumbled pieces of cake, and a plastic gallon jug of orange juice. As more volunteers filtered in, he announced, "I just stole all this stuff from the dining hall, so if anybody wants it, it's over here." I could understand stealing cookies, but the logistics of lifting an entire gallon of juice meant that he had to stand at the fountain for fifteen minutes while it filled up and just hope that nobody noticed. This kid had gumption!

Chris had already managed to make five half-hour episodes of his own sketch comedy show in high school. He'd even made a thirty-minute sci-fi short called *Adventures of PJ*. It was better than anything we'd ever produced on *That's Awesome!* and didn't have any humor in it that would offend millions of people. Chris and Justin had planned to make their own show but, after watching my Sixth Street antics, decided it would be better to just join forces. They weren't the only ones.

Over the course of the next semester, *That's Awesome!* transitioned from being a project that was shot and edited by Mark alone to a weekly collaboration with ten to twenty volunteers. From this new blood I found colleagues like Chris Demarais, Aaron Marquis, and Josh Flanagan, who are, to this day, some of my most consistent collaborators.

Over time, I worked with Mark less and less and spent most of my nights editing with Chris in his dorm room. His entire floor smelled like piss and the building looked like a prison (not a classy one either). But in Room 610 Jester East, I felt a sense of belonging I never had before. I spent more time in Chris's room than in my own dorm. We'd pass countless nights there together, dreaming up sketches, shooting them, and editing until dawn.

While Mark was the first person to believe that I was going to be a star and worked tirelessly to make that happen, my new friends were more in tune with the type of content I actually wanted to create. They were interested in making me part of a team in which I was valued, not for being able to make dick jokes at the drop of a hat, but for my creative input. The show was still crass and vulgar, but for the first time I actually thought some of what we were doing was funny. Mark still ran our weekly meetings, but it started to feel more and more like the rest of us were telling a joke that Mark didn't get.

"Dude, I just don't think Chris or any of those other guys

are as funny as you. I think some of our best stuff is the first stuff we shot with just you and me. You're why people watch the show!" Mark was adamant that I should always be the centerpiece of *That's Awesome!* Month after month we went back to Open Screen Night, winning each time. But even though we packed the house with *That's Awesome!* volunteers to cheer for whatever video we were showing, I could sense that the rest of the audience was growing tired of the same group winning, and I wanted to give other people a chance to shine. Of course, I never really expressed any of my concerns to Mark.

I had to miss one Open Screen Night because my grandpa was in town. When I'd taken him to the Drafthouse earlier that day, he'd deemed it "too dirty" and said he'd prefer to spend the evening shopping for dorm furnishings at Walmart. The clip we were supposed to show that night was relatively straightforward, so I didn't feel I needed to be there.

Mark had filmed me at a book signing for President Bill Clinton's autobiography, *My Life.* The goal had been to get an interview with the president himself, but the publicist for the bookstore was insistent that no questions would be allowed. Quietly, Mark and I both agreed that if I had a chance to say something, I should take it. So as the former POTUS walked out and the flashbulbs of photographers subsided, I disregarded all the rules and shouted, "Well hello, President Clinton!"

Taken aback, he asked, "Are you the first person in line?"

"No, I'm with the student television station and I work on a show called *That's Awesome!* and I was just wondering if I could ask you a question," I said, pouncing on the moment. Perhaps not wanting to deny a disabled person wearing a homemade shirt that said THAT'S AWESOME! on it, he said, "Ask away!"

Rather than inquiring about his legacy or the actual content of his book (which I had not read), I said, "I know Democrats are very concerned with the environment. But how do you intend to save the trees with a book that's this long?" Always quick on his feet, Bill replied, "Yeah, we should have made it out of plastic."

The best part was not the exchange itself, but that going rogue had sent the publicist into a frenzy and my journalistic chutzpah had caught the attention of a local news reporter. I took the opportunity to flirt with her and give her my number, saying we'd go out to dinner later.

Then the whole segment sort of ends. It wasn't uproariously clever and neither Mark nor I was sure we could win Open Screen Night with it. But the next day, while I was sitting at Schlotzsky's eating a sandwich with my grandpa, Mark called to deliver the news that we'd won yet again.

"That's surprising!" I said. "I didn't think the sketch was that funny."

"Yeah, there were some really hilarious videos this time too. There's no way we would have won if I hadn't changed it."

"What do you mean?" I said.

"Well, you know when you're hitting on that girl from the news and you tell her that you're gonna call her later? What I did was, when you say that, I cut to a title card that says LATER THAT NIGHT and then I found a clip of a porno with this girl getting pissed on who looks EXACTLY like her, so it seems like you guys went on a date and it ended with you pissing on her face!"

"Uhmmm . . . I'm not sure how I feel about that," I said, watching my grandpa enjoy his turkey on sourdough.

"Good sandwich!" he said to himself, not noticing the horrified look on my face.

I don't even think the implications of what Mark had just said sank in until I had to explain the whole situation to my seventy-two-year-old grandpa.

"That doesn't seem very nice," he said, chewing on his dill pickle spear.

When Mark showed me the reedited clip a few days later, it dawned on me that I had taken part in something that could potentially ruin a woman's career. Through Mark's encyclopedic knowledge of all pornographic material, he had indeed found someone that looked nearly identical to the perky blond reporter I'd talked to.

"Dude, it's fine! Everyone loved it," Mark reasoned.

"But she's a public figure," I countered. "This could get around."

What made matters worse was that I couldn't really blame Mark. I had set a precedent that I was willing to do anything for the sake of a joke and that absolutely nothing was off-limits. Mark was just following my lead. It didn't even make sense to him that I would have a conscience.

I'd been able to justify crossing the line before by reasoning that confronting people with the most politically incorrect ideas forced them to hold a mirror up to their own bigotry. But what was this? All I was doing was literally pissing on somebody who'd been kind to me, to win a hundred dollars, and far too many people thought I'd be okay with that. This was the first time I allowed myself to admit that my offensive humor was not actually a subversive way to spark important dialogues. I was being loud but saying nothing, which is pretty much the definition of "asshole." Just look at every twenty-four-hour news pundit who spews opinions at the highest volume about religion and race while having absolutely no regard for how it fans and fuels prejudice. I didn't have the courage or the clarity to express my concerns to Mark in a way that landed, so the content of the show remained. It was a formula. Why change it?

The one piece of moral fiber that I clung to during *That's Awesome!*'s entire run was that I didn't want to make fun of those who didn't have a voice to defend themselves. This meant that I wouldn't joke about the cognitively disabled. It wasn't even seeing an innocent person get urinated on that forced me to acknowledge what was wrong with what we were doing.

For all our differences of opinion, Mark had always been my most steadfast supporter, never failing to go above and beyond by helping me with homework assignments or school projects far beyond the scope of his own interests in *That's Awesome!* So when he approached me to be in a short film for his Intro to Digital Narrative class, I knew that I owed him one.

His inspiration for the story came from a nervous tic I had whenever I flubbed a line. Unable to enunciate clearly, I reset by making a motorboat noise, just going, "Bluh-ruh-ruh-blub-buh!" For some reason Mark thought it was hysterical and he had written a part for me that used this singular talent.

In the same way that Quentin Tarantino wrote a *Pulp Fiction* character specifically for John Travolta or how Wes Anderson revamped Bill Murray's career with *Rushmore*, it was a true honor to have somebody create a role based on your ability as an actor. I was excited, until he told me the title.

"It's called *The Retard*," he said, "but it's not what you think. Basically, the premise is, you're chasing my friend Nick around making all these ridiculous noises and he's frightened of you, and the whole time the audience thinks that you're this retard, but it ends up that you're just trying to give him the meal that he accidentally left at Wendy's. So when the credits roll, your character is The Stranger and Nick's character is The Retard."

"I'm not sure that's as strong a social commentary as you think it is," I said.

"C'mon, dude, it'll be really funny!" he pleaded.

I had several issues with the story, the first of which was who really forgets an entire meal at Wendy's when they've just gone to Wendy's to get said meal? Participating in a project that made fun of the intellectually disabled was bad enough, but then tacking on some credits and pretending like the whole thing had been a brave and bold statement made it even worse. Naturally I said, "Absolutely not!" and explained that he had to come up with a new idea, because I had dignity and morals. I said that in my mind anyway, but in real life I just went ahead and reluctantly filmed it, and then complained to all my other friends instead of bringing up my issues to Mark directly. Real spineless-like. On that day, I revealed myself as not only a douche bag but a jellyfish as well.

All this unvoiced dissent came to a head during the meeting before what would become our last Open Screen Night. Mark was insistent that we bring the three clips he'd chosen, but none of the rest of us thought they were particularly funny. When Mark steamrolled our opinions and said he was going to show them anyway, because "funny is funny," one of my other new friends, Jesse, flew off the handle.

"You're not a dictator, Mark! I think what you're doing is exploitative and Zach doesn't want you to show those clips," Jesse fumed.

I sat in silence. I'd been able to perfectly articulate my problems with Mark to everyone but Mark, and now the cat was out of the bag. Hurt, Mark took the segments to Open Screen Night without me. One of the clips that made me uncomfortable was a commercial for a fictional tracking device you could put on your children called "The Third Eye." In the ad, I gave a testimonial saying something like, "It worked out great because we found them. Unfortunately, they were already dead." To Mark's surprise, the segment was booed and stopped at the Drafthouse. He didn't know what the difference was between this and all my other offensive clips, but I did. The testimonial had been shot from the waist up and the framing cropped out my wheelchair. To the audience, I was not a disabled guy being irreverent; I was just a distasteful jerk making light of a horrific scenario. My golden ticket had been revoked.

I planned to quit *That's Awesome!* live on television at the end of a bit we were doing in a send-up of the movie *Dr. Strangelove.* I'd be sitting behind a desk, and as we signed off, I'd let the audience know that this was my last episode. Then I'd use my arm strength to stand up and exclaim, "Oh my God, I can walk!" and we'd cut to archival footage of a nuclear bomb going off. That was supposed to be the end. But when the time came, I got cold feet; it would have been completely unfair to Mark. I knew I had to confront him before someone else spoke on my behalf, but when I called him, it was clear that he already knew something was up.

The setting for our final showdown was not in a desert at sunset or on the top of some picturesque snowy mountain, but at the Pita Pit on Guadalupe Street. It's an unassuming place where students go to grab a bite between classes, an eatery whose mascots are cartoons of animals as well as personified versions of the meat they're cooked into, smiling side by side. There were two freshmen working behind the counter, unwittingly about to become the audience for an impassioned three-hour-long breakup of a bromance.

It started with terse hellos. Neither of us ordered anything besides sodas, and even though Mark looked like he was ready to knock me out, he still put the lid on my drink and got me a straw, knowing that I'd spill it on myself otherwise. When he sat down, he had one question.

"I want you to be honest with me," he said. "Were you planning to quit at the end of last week's episode?"

I wasn't gonna be able to sugarcoat it, so I just replied with a meek and simple "Yes."

"Why do I have to hear that from somebody else?" he demanded.

I didn't have a good answer for him because the honest one was that I was a coward.

"I worked nonstop on this show for a year and a half and always put you first," he went on, "and you can't even tell me to my face that you're quitting? Dude, I only made this show because of you! I wanna be making action movies! And I put that all on the back burner because I think that you have a better shot than anyone I know of getting famous."

"Mark," I said, "I feel like a scapegoat. We're not making

anything *good*. And nobody else's opinion matters but yours, but I'm the one people *see*. I'm responsible for whatever's on TV. You're not the only one who works on this show—there's a LOT of people."

"But none of them work as hard as me. And just because you don't like something doesn't give you the right to stab me in the back!" he shouted.

What followed was an unleashing of every grievance the two of us had ever had over the past year and a half. Now certain that I would burn the bridge of our friendship to the ground, I told him how I felt exploited so that he could look better in front of girls, and that I had a huge problem with his commandeering of Open Screen Night.

"And another thing," I said, impassioned, "I'm ashamed of *The Retard!*"—a sentiment that would have benefited from further explanation for the uncomfortable Pita Pit staff.

"Uh, can I get you guys anything else?" asked a nervous teenager as he tried to take away our tray without making eye contact.

"If me leaving the show means that you keep doing it, I'll leave," Mark said emphatically, ignoring the scrawny server in his monogrammed visor cap. "Whatever you do, don't call it *That's Awesome!* anymore. It's a show that I created and if I have no control over the quality, I don't want my name associated with it."

I told him I wasn't going to change the name because I thought that it would be disrespectful to all the other people who worked on the show.

We both left the Pita Pit as bitter and spiteful individuals. After that conversation, I contemplated how I'd gotten into this whole mess. If I had just been frank with Mark from the beginning, this meeting might have been a friendly chat instead of an all-out verbal brawl. But in an effort to be liked and avoid confrontation, I'd become somebody I didn't even like—a backstabber and a hypocrite.

If for no other reason than to prove a point, we continued making *That's Awesome!* without Mark for one more semester. The production value was higher, the sketches were better, but it was still lacking in any good judgment. After our last episode aired, I confided in Chris that I thought our work on *That's Awesome!* was self-centered and that I knew I could and should be doing something more meaningful. I wasn't sure how yet, but I knew I needed to chart a new course.

Mark and I rarely saw each other for the remainder of our time at UT, and when we did, I couldn't make Mark laugh anymore. In the years between *That's Awesome!* and Oprah, I came to the conclusion that, for me at least, humor without humanity isn't worthwhile. In my *That's Awesome!* days I thought I was using humor to break down barriers, but in reality I was only building walls. It took me years to figure out the difference: laughing at somebody is just another way of dismissing them, but laughing *with* somebody is a bridge to understanding.

Sometimes you can only find your boundaries after you've crossed them. I'm just grateful that my moral compass got calibrated in the age just before YouTube could make my worst gaffs immortal. I often get asked for advice by young YouTubers starting out on their own channels, and I always tell them, "Make sure you know what you want to say before you start, because everything you put online lives forever." My generation was the last one to have the luxury of growing up without social media. I was able to learn from my mistakes rather than become defined by them, and for me, that made all the difference.

When my Oprah audition went viral, Mark was one of the first people I called to thank. We may have had different sensibilities, but I never doubted that he wanted to see me succeed. In the time since *That's Awesome!*, I've transitioned from an insult comic who made dick jokes to an inspirational leader (who still occasionally makes dick jokes). I've become known as much for my positive spirit as I am for my work, but the truth is that being positive is not an inherent trait of mine, but rather a choice. I've grown out of using my voice to be loud and obnoxious and learned to only speak up when I have something meaningful to say. It's easy to get a laugh by making fun of stereotypes, but it's much more rewarding when you can use that same humor to bring people together. So I do a lot less shouting and a lot more listening these days.

Over the course of my time at UT, Austin became home and I went on to produce other shows and shorts that I can still watch today without cringing. My brother Brad moved down a year after I did, excited by the work I was doing there. He never formally enrolled in UT but got a job, moved into an apartment, and starting collaborating on shoots with my classmates and me. Later, a handful of us formed a comedy troupe called Lark the Beard. Among our many projects was a mockumentary series called *The Wingmen*, which you can still watch on YouTube.

The last time I visited the University of Texas, students stopped me on campus, but it wasn't so that I could spout vulgar one-liners—they stopped me to say "Thank you." Winning the Oprah competition had given me the opportunity to divvy up a $100,000 donation to charities of my choice, and after hearing that the TV station at UT was struggling, I gave a large portion of that money to them. My time producing *That's*

Awesome! provided me with a safe place to experiment, define, and refine myself into not just a persona but a person. Giving back to a place that was so important in the development of my voice and values was an opportunity I couldn't pass up.

Roaming the white halls of the comm building, it didn't seem like much had changed. There were still stacks of VHS tapes, corkboards with newspaper clippings about the station, and posters for all the current student-run shows. *That's Awesome!* was still one of them. They'd changed their slogan from "Something to Offend Everyone" to "We're a Comedy Show That's Really Lacking in Comedy, and 98% of Our Fans Are Usually Vomiting." I had no idea what this incarnation of *That's Awesome!* was like, but part of me was glad that Mark and I had started a legacy so that other lost Longhorns could have their own creative experiences to fondly regret down the road. As I made my way down to the end of the hall, there wasn't a plaque or a bust but a laminated sheet of paper taped on the door that read, "The Unofficial Zach Anner Studio." It was fitting because, even though I never officially got a degree, it's fair to say that behind that door is where I completed my most valuable education.

CHAPTER 10

Hope, Salad, and Breadsticks

August 23, 2014, was Andrew's anniversary with his girl-friend of six years and they'd be celebrating with an inti-mate twelve-course meal at a five-star restaurant, followed by a night at a four-star hotel with a rooftop pool in the heart of Boston. This was no ordinary dinner but a six-hour-long journey through a parade of culinary pleasures so extravagant and delicious that it would make the lords of Downton Abbey feel like hot dog vendors at Fenway Park. The meal would begin with an amuse-bouche of cantaloupe foam and rhubarb *macarons*, and progress through a smorgasbord of immacu-lately prepared and artfully displayed delicacies, all illumi-nated by glowing candlelight.

A processional of pampering waitstaff would float to the table with the precision of dancers waltzing at a royal wedding, removing each dirty dish with the same smoothness of the cucumber ice cream they'd return with only moments later. For each course, the sommelier would meticulously detail the origins of the wine pairing, listing its characteristics as though they were milestones of a best friend receiving a lifetime achievement award. The notes of chocolate and robust bouquet of the Madeira would perfectly complement the foie gras with Black Mission fig, smoked almond polvorón, and arugula. To someone with a less refined palate, it could also be described as having a general wine-like flavor with some sugar in it that distracts you from the gross alcohol-iness, but still makes you long for a Sprite.

The only reason I am able to provide the uncultured swine's point of view is because on this particular occasion, that swine was me. I'd called Andrew two weeks earlier to see if he had time during his med school rotation at Harvard to finally introduce me to the legendary French cuisine of L'Espalier. He checked with his girlfriend to see if the weekend I suggested worked for her too, and within a few hours we had made our reservation. But in my haste to organize a romantic bro-down weekend with my best friend over some real hoity-toity grub, I'd inadvertently planned an intimate dinner for two plus one. Andrew hadn't mentioned that I'd be a third wheel on four wheels until I had already arrived in Boston. As we sat down for a light snack the night before all the real estate in our stomachs would be taken up with gourmet food we couldn't pronounce, he clued me in.

"Hey, so you're actually gonna be taking part in something that's pretty special for Christina and me. We kind of have two anniversaries, but this one is almost more important to us than the official day."

"Oh, okay!" I said, thinking that the mere concept of two anniversaries was bullshit. "I didn't mean to infringe upon your special day . . ." *the dinner I planned . . .*

"No, no, it's fine! We love having you here. It's just a very emotional day for us."

Christina was more forthcoming with the details. "Andrew and I weren't exactly dating at the time, and it was a stressful period for both of us. So instead of going to an RA event that we were supposed to attend, we just got pizza. I made the decision to put my head on Andrew's shoulder, and that was the moment I knew I loved him."

"So it's like, your pizzaversary?" I asked.

"Yes," Andrew agreed, "but it's very meaningful."

So I was graciously allowed to tag along for the celebration of a tender and personal milestone I had no business being a part of. By every measure, it was a night I'd remember forever.

I was a fish out of water the entire evening, or, more appropriately, a poached salmon out of heirloom tomato water. While Andrew's drink orders were self-assured and sophisticated, suggesting the particular spirits and dryness of cocktail he preferred, I asked the bartender, "Can I have the girliest cocktail that tastes the most like candy? Just the closest thing you've got to juice." When Andrew and Christina pointed out the rudeness of a guest who had worn his T-shirt to dinner, my only thought was *Gosh, I wish I were rich enough to wear shorts and a Batman T-shirt to this place and not give a shit! I wanna be so classy that having no class at all just shows how important I am!* When the *maître fromager* brought out an extensive cheese platter, I tried to be respectful while knowing that the only types of cheese I can tolerate are on pizza and goldfish crackers. I convinced myself to try everything and resisted the urge to ask if I could substitute the Roquefort Papillon for one of those string cheeses I used to swordfight with in grade school.

By the end of the evening every table but ours had emptied, and when the final chocolate truffles arrived with the bill, the chef came out to thank us. Our stomachs were full and our bank accounts were empty.* Each dish was carefully preserved in an iPhone photo uploaded to a cloud for all eternity. But for all its extravagance, the evening was, at its core, commemorating a humble pizza shared between two people who had taken a leap of faith to be vulnerable with each other. We left the restaurant knowing that though we'd scarcely tasted better food or received finer service, we'd all had meals that had meant more to us than this one. Most of mine were at the Olive Garden.

The fact that you are currently reading a book and not playing Angry Birds means that you are probably judging me right now. But I urge you to stop swishing your snifter of brandy, take the needle off of that *Goldberg Variations* vinyl you've got spinning, and hear me out, Evelyn, or Chauncy, or whoever you are.

Before L'Espalier, Andrew and I treated Olive Garden as though it was the most elegant place to dine with a lady. Whenever Andrew had a date, I always suggested he take her to the Olive Garden to seal the deal. We built up the OG's prestige and wonder so much in our heads that we actually started to believe it.

Now, Olive Garden on the surface may not seem like the most magical restaurant. You won't find organic chicken or

---

*It did cross my mind that I might have been able to feed a small village for a month with the money we'd spent, or at the very least save a kennel full of those abused dogs that Sarah McLachlan gets so sad about.

delicate Rorschach dabs of truffle oil on your plate, and the waitstaff will not tell you a story behind the pretzel bread you are eating, but they will shove a basket of breadsticks in front of your face whenever you shout "More breadsticks!" with a mouthful of breadsticks. They'll even substitute the iceberg lettuce in the salad with mixed greens if you specifically request it. And when the waiter or waitress brings the bill, it's signed with the server's name next to a smiley face, just to let you know that Tiffany also had a good time.

This affection for the Olive Garden has found its way into much of my work. I mention the restaurant whenever possible. I've even written erotic fan fiction about it, which both my literary agent and publisher refused to include in this book. My most important day on social media was not when Sanjay Gupta did a piece on me, or when John Mayer wrote about me on his blog, or even when David Hasselhoff said I would be world famous. Rather, it was the day that the Olive Garden followed me on Twitter. Is there better food in the world? Sure, I guess, if you wanna look at it scientifically. But on several occasions, my outings to the Olive Garden have been less about food and more about nourishment.

The story of how I grew to have such unbridled affection for what most people would dismiss as a typical chain restaurant can be traced back to my time at the University of Texas.

Up until that point, I would describe the OG and me as casual lunch buddies—a real hit-it-and-quit-it-type deal. I wasn't looking for a serious relationship with a restaurant at the time. I had just moved to Austin the year before for college and had been introduced to Tex Mex, barbeque brisket, Thai food, two-pound doughnuts, and an unlimited buffet of unexciting but still edible dining hall fare. Food-wise, I was having fun playing the field.

At the time, I was working on a radio show, a television series, and a documentary. I had a core group of close-knit friends and collaborators in Chris Demarais, Aaron Marquis, and my brother Brad. We turned my apartment into a makeshift editing suite—which was really just a bunch of computers set up on two stolen folding tables from the UT business school—and for a few years during college, we didn't just work together, we practically lived together. In some ways, it was the most creatively rewarding period of my life. But when I returned home one Christmas break I got an unexpected reminder that no matter how full my calendar was, my life was still missing something.

The most exciting part of a month back in Buffalo was getting the chance to tell stories about my new life to my oldest friend. Even in our early twenties, Andrew and I still had sleepovers, our Shirley Temples now replaced with my brother's homemade eggnog. I told Andrew about my adventures in Texas, like the time I screamed at Andy Dick that I would eat his face. In turn, Andrew recounted tales of cadavers and patients in cardiac arrest who voided their bowels all over him.

Before he left our holiday slumber party, Andrew surprised me with a present. There had been no precedent set for us getting each other stuff over the holidays, so my first thought was

Fuck! I didn't get him anything! "It's just a little something," he reassured me. "My mom and I saw this while we were out and thought of you," and then he tossed a twenty-five-dollar Olive Garden gift card onto my desk. "Take a hot date," he said. This directive should have been easy enough to carry out, but Andrew's optimistic suggestion forced me to face a harsh truth: after four semesters of college in Austin, there was still not a single woman I felt comfortable asking to a dinner with even the slightest hint of romantic pretext.

I've racked my brain for a concise reason why I thought of myself as undatable for most of my adult life, but I'm still trying to figure it out. When I flipped through old pictures, I was surprised to find that I actually did attend middle school dances with girls, and from all appearances it looked as though I was on my way to being an active participant in the dating scene. Then in high school, I got sick and something changed in me; being social became scary, and the idea of being intimate was taken off the table altogether.

For almost three years, I was home from school nearly every day. My social circle was no longer made up of my peers but of doctors, specialists, and homeschool teachers. When I finally emerged from my Gollum phase, it was good to see the light of day, but I could never shake the feeling that I'd fallen behind. While I was vomiting over toilets, my friends were going on first dates, practicing awkward first kisses, and spilling water on their pants to disguise just how heavy the petting had been. While they moved forward with their romantic and sexual development, I was stuck, even regressing. I couldn't face being forced to explain this period to a girl I assumed was assuming I was further along. It was too scary. So I built walls, constructs, and characters.

Instead of expressing romantic interest for a woman I pined for, I lapsed into what I would call a cowardly Casanova groove, where I would execute big romantic gestures under the guise of extreme, completely platonic thoughtfulness. I'd give my friends with girlfriends romantic advice, telling them the exact gift that they should get their significant others to melt their hearts. I'd use any excuse to be romantic without the threat of rejection and embarrassment.

The best example of this, I think, was when my friend Holly confided in me that the most romantic thing that had ever happened to her was when her then boyfriend got her roses for their anniversary. I was unimpressed and wanted to prove to her that women deserved to feel special on more than just specifically designated days. The problem was that if I got Holly flowers unprovoked, people would start to talk, make assumptions. My friends Chris and, worst of all, Aaron would have opinions. I never wanted to hear what Aaron had to say about my love life because it would inevitably transition into a story about a blow job that *he'd* gotten. So instead of wearing my heart on my sleeve, I decided to take the upstanding gentleman's route and be an asshole to Holly for an entire day so I could buy her roses as an apology without blowing my cover and revealing myself as a secretly decent person.

So there I was, an emotionally stunted romantic idiot with a twenty-five-dollar Olive Garden gift card weighing heavily in his pocket. More than anything, I desperately wanted to shed the obnoxious character I'd created in my *That's Awesome!* days and make real human connections with people. But I couldn't just call up Holly or one of the other four girls I'd talked to on a campus of fifty thousand because that would be too direct. If I was gonna bare my soul, I was going to do it someplace safe and private. Like Facebook.

So one Saturday in January when Chris had a date night and Aaron was off in San Marcos helping his father contest a parking ticket, I sat down at the computer, opened up a Facebook note, and went full Jerry Maguire. I wish I had the note to reference here for posterity's sake, but in all likelihood it would be less moving and more cringe-worthy than I'd care to remember. The gist was that instead of baring my soul for a person I actually wanted to go on a date with, I opened up to all of my Facebook friends. I spent a full eight hours typing out the note and doing my best to put my heart on the line online.

I recounted the whole story of the Olive Garden gift card and explained how I felt like I'd been social without ever taking the time to get to know anyone. I wanted to make a legitimate effort to just talk to people rather than perform for them. So I invited ALL of Facebook to dinner at the Olive Garden with the sincere hope that they would share a meal and some genuine conversation with me. I posted the note, tagging everyone in it, except for members of my family.

The heart-pounding minutes after my Facebook confessional went live took me back to the nights as a kid when I'd call the radio station with requests. With every ring I got more and more nervous, sweating from the inside out, and wondering every half second if I should just hang up. When the DJ finally answered, my throat was so closed off that I could barely squeak out the words "Hi, could you play 'Gangsta's Paradise' by Coolio?" Though I was never made fun of on air or had my request greeted with that dreaded toilet flush sound effect, the threat of public embarrassment made the wait almost unbearable.

To my relief, the response to my Facebook note, which almost certainly provided fodder for ridicule, was universally positive, even from the people I was sure would call me out for being overly sentimental. Over the coming days, I received long personal notes from Holly and other friends about things that they were going through. A coworker of Andrew's, whom I'd met for all of five minutes a while back, was convinced after reading this note that we were soul mates, and to this day she'll ask me when we're going to Olive Garden. (For the record, if you're reading this, the only reason we haven't gone is because you live in Hawaii.)

The response from my male friends was surprising too. It seemed that many of them were wrestling with some of the same things I was feeling—isolated, unsure of themselves, waiting for permission to be vulnerable. . . . If I'm being completely honest with myself now, when I look back, the Olive Garden gift card was just another device that allowed me to dance around the idea of dating without committing to it. In the moment, though, it was a first step toward cutting the bullshit and taking a stab at the type of man I wanted to become. As a result of this note, I went on a slew of one-on-one dinners with classmates and acquaintances I hoped to know better. But I saved the gift card for Holly. She was the closest person to a hot date that I could think of and, after bringing her to the verge of tears on my douche bag flowers day, I figured she'd earned it.

Two weeks later, while Chris, Aaron, and Brad were burrowed in my production studio of an apartment, I was granted a two-hour leave of absence to go to the Olive Garden with Holly. She came up to my door in a red cardigan, with her blond hair done up in a bun, and exchanged brief hellos with the boys' club while I transferred into my manual chair. As we headed down the hallway, Aaron instructed Holly sternly, "You have him home by ten!"

Holly and I didn't talk much on the drive over to the OG. She seemed preoccupied with finding the right music on her iPod, which made me preoccupied with not dying because she paid more attention to her playlist than she did to the road. As we pulled into the parking lot, instead of following the gentlemanly tradition of hopping around the car and opening the door for a lady, my only option was to stay put and listen to Holly curse my wheelchair as she struggled to get it out of her trunk. Setting a romantic scene is tricky when the first thing your date has to do is reminiscent of hauling a sofa up a flight of stairs, but five minutes later, when she finally came around to the door with my wheels, we let the excitement of the Olive Garden whisk us away.

How can you not be enchanted when "Come Fly with Me" is being piped through an outdoor loudspeaker and the aroma of dried Italian herbs and spices hits you like a love potion as soon as you walk through the door? Perhaps the most exciting thing about our dinner together was that Holly and I shared the same unbridled passion for this fine eatery. "I'm gonna get the Three Cheese Ziti," she exclaimed, " 'cause it's my favorite and I always get it!"

As we waited to be seated, we set out our plan of attack for the meal. Holly was a salad fanatic and I was a breadstick junkie. We were both equally committed to making the most of this dinner and keeping our waiter on his toes. "We need to make sure that we ask for more breadsticks before we're out of breadsticks," I said. "That way there's no gap." Holly added that even if we didn't feel like we wanted another bowl of bottomless salad when our food arrived, we should order it anyway because we could always take it home. I was impressed with her savviness. Even though I was only three miles from my apartment, I felt like we were stealing away on an adventure.

When our "Your Table Is Ready" vibrator thing buzzed in my crotch (bonus), I gave myself permission to admit that this felt like a date. As she pushed me to our table, Holly just smiled and said, "You make me happy." The words escaped like a gentle sigh that couldn't be held back. They meant more to me than Holly could possibly know. It felt like hearing someone say "I forgive you." For years, I'd only been the guy who could make girls laugh or wince. I'd never gotten the impression that I could make a girl happy. Just the smallest acknowledgment that someday I could be the right guy for someone was something I was starving to hear.

That moment passed when we sat down to dinner and Holly told me about her crushes on several of my friends and her complicated relationship with her ex-boyfriend, who she was still sort of seeing at the time. This revelation didn't crush me. In fact, it was probably a relief. I felt like I was off the hook because I wouldn't have to worry about what would happen after dinner, and honestly, dinner alone had taken all my courage.

I just listened intently as the waiter brought basket after basket of breadsticks. I wasn't datable yet. I didn't even know how to flirt. But I was taking the crucial first steps to becoming somebody that a girl could see potential in. It was gonna take a lot more than some fettuccine Alfredo and Michael Bublé for a girl to make that leap, but this dinner was my way of announcing to the world, and admitting to myself, that I wanted to be considered.

For the next hour and a half, Holly and I conversed about nothing in particular, which was everything I'd hoped for. At the other tables there were families with kids in booster seats surrounded by whatever globs of food they'd haphazardly flung to the floor, people on first dates making small talk about what it's like to be a manager at a tanning salon, and elderly couples seeing how many questions they could ask their server before they have to actually order something. Seemingly, one table had very little in common with the next. The only connection among us was that whatever journey had led to this point, we'd all arrived at Olive Garden and were glad to be there.

As a creative person, I often find myself in the mind-set that if something great happened, but I forgot to record it, then I missed my chance to immortalize a moment. But dinners at Olive Garden aren't something you Instagram or rave about on Facebook to make your friends jealous. No journal entry has ever opened with "Dear Diary, you'll never guess what happened to me at the Olive Garden. . . . I met Sir Ian McKellen and he signed my forehead!" You don't go to the Olive Garden to make memories. You go to the Olive Garden to live life. It's also a great place to commemorate one.

In September 2001, my closest aunt, Bethany, passed away after a ten-year battle with cancer. After the memorial service, while my family was milling aimlessly around the church parking lot, unsure what to do next, it was decided that we should all go out for dinner. At a time when all decisions were difficult, the Olive Garden became the easy and obvious choice. With a menu and setting that was predictable and inoffensive, it was the one place everyone could agree on, if not enthusiastically, then with a shrug.

Sitting at one of the long, dimly lit tables, away from the formality of the church, everyone in the Anner family was suddenly free either to reminisce about Bethany or to distract themselves by having the waiter list all the ingredients in Italian Wedding Soup. While the funeral had been beautiful, the task of summing up my aunt's life had fallen to the pastor, a man who had never met her and could only resort to recounting vague stories he'd heard from various family and friends. What was missing from the service was my aunt's personality—her sense of humor, her resilience, and the fact that every time we got together, I'd laugh so hard that I needed a change of pants. I'd regretted not sharing my memories of her at the church but was able to make up for that at the Olive Garden.

While my uncle Steve scolded my aunt Anne for eating the marinara sauce meant for the breadsticks with a spoon, my family and I shared stories of the vibrant and unstoppable woman we all loved. These tiny little nuances of a life told over lasagna were enough to help us focus not just on the tremendous loss, but on the extraordinary gifts that Bethany had given to all of us. Being at the Olive Garden didn't make those memories any sweeter; it just gave us a place to share them. There's not much else I remember about that dinner, only that it felt necessary.

People's opinions of the Olive Garden range from "I kinda like it" to "I don't really mind it." Ninety-nine percent of Middle America thinks that the Olive Garden is just fine. That's as high as it gets, "just fine." In reality, I suspect the Taste of Tuscany means that something is taken out of a freezer in the back, thawed out, and smothered in either marinara or Alfredo sauce, and then they'll grind delicate snowflakes of parmesan cheese onto it, and all you have to do to stop this blizzard is say "When." Yet somehow, to have this little bit of control is comforting. No matter what you order, the check isn't gonna break you, and it comes with mints. You know what you're gonna get—the friendly waitstaff, with their white shirts and black ties, the same sound track of Frank Sinatra songs (or people who sound exactly like him), and food that's tasty and entirely unremarkable. And, if you're me, you'll down a dozen breadsticks and somehow not feel an ounce of shame.

At the Olive Garden, a hot date might actually turn out to be a warm meal and some pleasant conversation. And you may not go home with the girl at the end of the night, but she'll drop you off at your apartment and make sure that your leftovers make it into the fridge. In between the best meals you've ever had and the worst, there are the ones that give you exactly what you need. In life, unlike in restaurants, you rarely get what you order. But sometimes it's not what's on the plate that makes the meal, it's what you bring to the table.

CHAPTER 11

Barking Up the Wrong
Tree House

This may not be popular opinion, but when I was eight years old I came to recognize lifeguards as a plague on society. To the untrained eye there was nothing particularly remarkable about our local public pool in Buffalo, just the standard concoction of thousands of gallons of piss mixed with chlorine and a dash of H_2O for good measure. What set this pool apart was its waterslide. Listening to the muffled laughter and shrieks of delight from the other children, I resolved to make 1993 the summer when I'd finally convince my dad to let me take the plunge. After hearing my impassioned testimony, he carried me up the vertical steps, our laborious ascent interrupting the flow of fifty grumbling kids who could just dash up for their fourth ride like it was no big deal. They didn't understand the enormity of this moment. I remember standing there on the platform, my father holding me up, watching the boy ahead of me prepare to plummet down the tube. As the lifeguard on slide duty saw me approach, the only thing she knew was that there was *something* wrong with me.

I asked her if I could go down backward and on my stomach, thinking it might be more fun to see the next sliders chasing after me, but the lifeguard replied, "No, everyone has to go down the same way. You have to be on your back, keep your legs together, and hold your arms flat against your sides. Can you do that?" "Yeah!" I said enthusiastically, but what I meant was "I'm not sure. I wouldn't count on it!" The lifeguard, who looked like an adult to me at the time, was probably only fourteen, but even then, I think she knew in her heart that I was only masquerading as someone who could keep his limbs together for thirty seconds. I tried crossing them like a dainty woman at a tea party, but they popped open like those spring-loaded cans of novelty peanuts. Still, she took pity on me, and as I stared at the rushing water, turned an inviting brownish hue from the rust, I knew that this was finally my time to experience the unabridged epicness of summer that every kid standing impatiently in line behind me or sliding down carefree in front of me had taken for granted. I just hoped my bathing suit stayed on.

What followed was a singular joy that lived up to everything I'd imagined while looking longingly at that slide so many summers before. Ever since I'd watched Milo and Otis go over that waterfall, I'd wondered what this was like.* For

---

*I live through that dog and cat duo less vicariously now, ever since I read a rumor that suggested that they may have just thrown the critters over that waterfall and had a new pair emerge at the bottom, unscathed. I don't mean to ruin anyone's childhood—but that's exactly what I'm doing.

the thirty seconds I was racing through the turns of the slide, my legs freely flopping about, I was just another kid, encumbered by nothing. But thirty seconds is all it takes for a dream to splash to Earth. After I plunged into the pool, the first thing I saw was the bare ass of a kid frantically searching for his swimsuit, but my mind was cleared of all thoughts save a single word—*Again!*

My dad, not wanting me to have my head smashed in by the next kid barreling down the chute, escorted me to the side of the pool. In between generous gulps of chemically contaminated water, I was able to stave off drowning long enough to tell him, "I want . . . to go . . . again!" But as we approached the steps leading out of the pool, I looked up and saw what I would later come to recognize as a Buzzkill Mustache.

As I've gone through life, I've noticed that, more than any badge or title, a man's mustache alone can signify how much he's going to disappoint you. This one was as thick as a scrub brush and gray with speckles of blond that were still fighting time and the idea that a fifty-year-old man should have no business working at a place where most of his colleagues still had their learner's permits and braces. In the half minute I'd spent on the waterslide, this man had decreed from his tiny chair, high in the sky—like Saruman with a suntan and a beer belly—that I would never again go down the waterslide at the pool. He spoke, not with the bellowing oration of a white wizard, but with a familiar Buffalonian disdain for soft vowels.

"He can't ride da slide. If yous guys go down the slide, he could hurt himself or someone else, and dat's too dangerous, dat's MY ass! I'm just lookin' out for yous AND me."

Whatever he had deduced my condition was—multiple

squirrelosis, muscular disastrophy, Lou Reed's disease, Splendabifida—I was no longer just another kid enjoying the summer. I was a liability. Despite our adamant protests, Summer Saruman would not be moved until all the Earth was scorched and every bathing suit was dry. I left that day vowing never to return and my dad even gave me permission to call the mustached man an asshole on the car ride home. In the summers that followed, whenever we'd pass by the pool, I would curse it with obscenities that only a ten-year-old would find offensive.

"Stupid, fart-breath, penis-face pool!" I'd shout out the window.

To this day, if I see it from the highway, I still have the bitter tinge of chlorine in my mouth. It would be two decades before I was introduced to an online community that had a similar distaste for arbitrary gatekeepers.

Reddit is the self-proclaimed "Front Page of the Internet," filtering out the best of the Web with no bureaucracy but rather a truly democratic voting process. With the mantra that all links are created equal, anyone can submit a video, a meme, a news story, or an animated GIF of a sea otter dancing in the shower, and the Reddit community will upvote the content they like and downvote the stuff they don't. They'd been my bombastic cheerleaders ever since they discovered my audition video for Oprah.

One of the best things to come out of that whole experience was my friendship with Alexis Ohanian, who is the cofounder of Reddit and the sort of guy who could accomplish more on a groggy Sunday morning than I could in four years of college. Alexis has been one the most outspoken advocates for Internet freedom. He successfully lobbied in Congress against many old men and women with mustaches who didn't understand the value of an open Internet and, in trying to regulate it, were in danger of just shitting the pool and closing it down for everyone. His book, *Without Their Permission*, is a rallying cry for Net Neutrality that also features a picture of me naked in full color.

When *Rollin' with Zach* was unceremoniously dismantled and swallowed up in an endless and unforgiving sea of basic cable, I knew that if I got a second chance to make another travel show, I'd have to forgo conventional channels and get back to my Internet roots. When I told Alexis over Skype that my show had been canceled, he immediately asked, "What kind of show do you want to make next?" without skipping a beat. Luckily, I'd thought about this ever since I realized that *Rollin' with Zach* would be far less spontaneous than I'd envisioned. It bothered me that the Internet community that championed me to begin with was completely shut out of the creative process of the show they helped me win. If I was going to be hitting the road again, I'd want Reddit to be not only involved but in control. And on top of that, I actually wanted to meet up with Redditors in person and hang out with them. With that simple concept we were off and running.

Alexis had already been meeting with Google to discuss original online content that the company was looking to fund. They hadn't been sold on his idea for a talk show, so he started pimping *Riding Shotgun* instead. With all his charm and charisma, he was able to convince them that I had the same Internet appeal as a sneezing panda. And just like that, I went from being Oprah's first flop since *Beloved* to being a travel show host again. When we finally hit the road at the end of July 2012, it was clear that the freewheeling "Just roll with it" mantra that had been missing from *Rollin' with Zach* would be on full display this time.

Riding Shotgun promised to be the first travel show "For The Internet, By The Internet"—sixty-five hundred miles, four friends, and a Wi-Fi hotspot. With the power of the Internet to fuel the adventure and thousands of dollars of petrol to fuel our SUV, I jumped into the passenger seat and set out across North America for six weeks with two college buddies and my brother. Acting as both on-camera talent and film crew was Josh, a well-built warrior teddy bear*; Aaron, our token underwear model; and Brad, channeling a '70s domestic beer spokesperson with his long blond sideburns. We asked the Internet where we should go and what we should do, using only Reddit for suggestions and meeting up with actual Redditors in the cities we visited. It was either the perfect recipe for adventure or a sure-fire way to be murdered.

Over the course of a month and a half, the Internet guided us on an unconventional journey from the stage of the grimiest strip club in Montreal, to the VIP room of the nicest restaurant in New Orleans, and everything in between. And while the Reddit community digitally shouldered the burden of creative spark for the show, my friends shouldered the physical weight of the show's host on more than one occasion—which is how I got to piggyback my way to remote waterfalls in the wilderness of Blacksburg, Virginia, and over the peaks of mountains in Denver, Colorado.

The drive between Denver and our final city, Vancouver, was the longest of the whole trip. To break up the monotony of

---

*By the time we wrapped, Josh had also been labeled a "bear" by Reddit's gay community and had his own substantial following.

nights on the road, Josh decided to spend our remaining hotel budget on lodging that boasted indoor water parks. We were willing to get up at seven in the morning in Billings, Montana, to make sure we had time to splash and frolic without eating into the day's drive, because nothing washes away a month of road fatigue like chlorine. At the mere sight of that slide, I slid right back into my childhood, singing improvised verses to "Part of Your World" from *The Little Mermaid*.

"I wanna go on a waterslide / at eight in the morning in Billings, Montana / swimming around in that . . . whatchamacalit? / pool!"

All of the feelings I'd had that first time on a waterslide at the pool rushed back to me like a tidal wave, eroding away any bitterness I still held toward these marvelous, whirling, plastic pleasure chutes. They were like crazy straws for people—who could ever stay mad at these things?! I was in my element and was again lulled into a false sense of security that summer, along with my waterslide privileges, might last forever.

We'd hoped to compare and contrast these wet and wild attractions, but when we arrived in Spokane, Washington, an unsympathetic white sign with cruel black letters greeted us with the news that their water park had closed for the season, just the day before. On the surface, this may seem like a simple instance of bad timing. But it's actually because Spokane, Washington, is the worst place on the planet and you should never, ever go there because it's a city of false promises and filthy liars. That dry, empty waterslide should have been a red flag about what was to come, and I guess it was, except the next flag we encountered was a red and white flag with a maple leaf in the middle of it. We discovered that while Canada gave unfettered access to its oceans and waterways, it was rather protective of its trees.

All I knew about Vancouver prior to our visit was that it often doubles for America in a lot of movies because it's cheaper to film there. I also assumed that all Vancouverites were big fans of hemp because my cousin who lives there had, at one point, owned a hemp store. At Christmastime, when the family got together, she'd often gift us with various hemp products— hemp rope, hemp soap, hemp chocolate, hemp notebooks— that would always elicit the same knowing glare of disapproval from my grandma Ruthie. So, as an American who knows very little about the world outside of Walmart territory, I expected the whole city to be pot-smoking hippies who all owned juicers powered by bikes.

By the time we made it across the border, the end of our journey and our budget was in sight. We couldn't afford some of the things that the Vancouver Redditors wanted us to do, so for the first time in the trip we reached out to a local government tourism board for assistance. The partnership gave us access, but it also meant that we felt obligated to follow both their itinerary and their rules. The oversight wasn't ideal, but it meant we wouldn't have to pay for anything, which also meant we wouldn't have to handle ridiculous, Monopoly-colored money with fuzzy owls on it. I mean, if somebody offered you free Canada, you'd take it, right?

So we found ourselves at the Capilano Suspension Bridge, which is proclaimed by Canadians to be the eighth wonder of the world but is more accurately labeled by the world outside of Canada as . . . a bridge. We met up with a tour guide in a bowler cap and suspenders who went through a rigidly scripted timeline of its construction, which revealed that it was, as I had suspected, originally made of hemp rope. He then took us to the bridge itself, proclaiming, "There it is, the eighth wonder of the world, the Capilano Suspension Bridge, strong enough to hold 203 moose." Apparently our guide was oblivious to the notion that, outside of Canada, wonder is not measured by the number of moose a structure can hold. "Well, I only weigh as much as three moose," I quipped. Our guide ignored me, continuing, "The bridge is so high that if you placed the Statue of Liberty in the river below, the bridge would be roughly at her shoulders." I don't know why but I tried again, shouting, "You would like to do that, wouldn't you! I know about the War of 1812. You tried to burn down our White House!" His reaction taught me the important lesson that if you're attempting to lighten the mood, it's probably best not to insinuate that the person you're talking to and their entire country are terrorists.

Even if our tour hadn't, thus far, produced the most exciting content or the most charismatic guide, there was still the appeal of getting to cross the bridge itself, which was placed precariously over a stunning ravine in the middle of the Canadian Rockies. Though no one had ever fallen off the bridge, it looked bouncy enough and certainly high enough to make the heart jump. For us, the big draw was not the bridge itself but the enchanted treetop town that lay in wait on the other side. I'd always wanted to meet an Ewok and/or reenact scenes from *Robin Hood: Prince of Thieves*, and this seemed like a grand opportunity to realize one, if not both, of those dreams, putting a glorious ending on an otherwise lackluster first day.

But I felt an all too familiar sting of disappointment when both our humorless guide and several large signs informed us that no strollers or wheelchairs were allowed on the bridge under any circumstances. I interpreted this as a challenge to crawl across it, a proposition that was also denied, despite having previously established that I was far under its maximum moose capacity. It was just like the fable of the Billy Goats Gruff, except the trolls were exceedingly pleasant Canadians, and the only goats they wouldn't let pass were goats with pacifiers or parking placards. Naturally, I was devastated, not just because we were told I couldn't do something but because, after six weeks of finding a way to do almost anything, we'd finally come to a bridge we couldn't cross. And it was an actual bridge!

There was some discussion that we should have just crossed that sucker and taken whatever repercussions came as a result in stride. I was sure Canadian prisons were nicer than most American schools, and I imagined guards apologizing to me for not having enough maple syrup for my pancakes. But our liaison at the Vancouver Tourist Board had been so accommodating that we didn't want to break the rules, even when those rules were keeping me sidelined and excluded in a way that felt frustratingly familiar. Not willing to risk another war with

Canada, the four faithful comrades looked across the bridge and decided that unless all of us were able to cross the bridge, none of us would. That steadfast resolve lasted precisely seven seconds before Josh, Brad, and Aaron

sprinted across, unable to resist the allure of the woodland wonderland that beckoned from the other side. It was hard to see the forest for the trees that day as I listened to my friends recount their frolic in the Ewok village, but luckily Canada is rich with treetop treasures and, thanks to Reddit, the most elusive of all of them would be accessible to me. Sort of. If we could find it.

While scouring Vancouver's sizable subreddit page for ideas, Josh, my friend, producer, and excessively hairy person, stumbled upon a gaggle of Redditors who were planning a weekend expedition to find the HemLoft, a legendary tree house hidden deep in the mountains of Whistler. Nobody knew exactly where the HemLoft was, which only added to its mystique: a secret tree house, perched on a dangerous slope amid a hemlock grove, discovered by only the boldest of explorers. These Redditors thought they'd cracked its location, so we decided to piggyback off their weeks of research, while I literally piggybacked on Aaron and Josh through the woods. Using a community to discover something few had ever seen was what Reddit was all about. Even if we didn't find the tree house and simply got lost in the woods and eaten by bears, we all concluded that any outcome of this expedition would make for a glorious ending to the show.

Gone were the guidebooks, bowler hats, suspenders, and scripts. As we drove up the mountain to the meeting point, the skies were gray and threatening rain. Our detailed intelligence on the location of the HemLoft turned out to be little more than a few scribbled notes on a crumpled-up piece of paper, probably hemp paper at that. When we arrived, one of our new Reddit companions had already been decommissioned by a vicious bee attack. That early casualty might have shaken lesser men's confidence, but what was *Riding Shotgun* if not aimlessly wandering until we found something cool? So, for the last time, I resumed the Yoda position and hopped on Aaron's back. We trekked into the woods, leaving my chair along the side of the road, reasoning that even if it was stolen, it was our last day and no one gave a shit at this point.

For the next hour we confidently fumbled through the forest. I lost a shoe early on and my socks didn't shield me from the fear that every leaf my foot touched was poison ivy. "Leaves of green, let it be," I'd always misheard. To make matters worse, there were surprisingly few benches in the forest. Josh and Aaron were understandably exhausted from carrying my useless body, and Brad was characteristically exhausted just from walking and being outside. These types of excursions always left me conflicted because I didn't want to be perceived as a helpless sack of crap that everyone had to lug around, but, for better or worse, *Riding Shotgun* had taught me that sometimes that description is pretty spot-on. My pride aside, we were getting nowhere.

As we became more tired and desperate, we entertained other less plausible methods of finding the damn hut. "We should just burn all the leaves in the forest down so it's easier to see," Josh suggested. I considered it.* Let's be real. We were all very moved by *FernGully* as children, but that's a cartoon. Trees don't actually feel anything. And in all likelihood, Smokey the Bear doesn't care about Canada.

---

*I mean, I'd miss the maple syrup, but we've already got Ryan Gosling and Rachel McAdams, and that's all we need to keep hope alive in America. If our neighbors to the north were left with nothing but scorched earth, that would mean that our side of Niagara Falls would start to get some tourism. This might actually be the best possible option.

Our only rays of hope were the occasional hikers who had arrived in these woods through a genuine love of the outdoors and might know some navigational techniques that were better than holding a smartphone up in the air and cursing Google Street View for not including mountains. Whenever one of these wildlings would pass by, we'd frantically call to them, "Excuse me, do you happen to have any idea where the HemLoft is?" And they'd say, "Um . . . I think it's a-boat five minutes that way," gesturing so vaguely that *that way* could be anywhere. With renewed purpose, I'd cling to whoever's back was less sore at that moment and set off again. Not once, but twice, we ran into a little boy who cheerfully informed us that the HemLoft was actually in the *opposite* direction. We were officially in a Canadian *Twilight Zone* episode. At this point, even MY legs and arms were starting to give out. It was that awkward moment when you realize that the nothing you've been doing is just too much for you.

I suggested that my friends set me against a tree and leave me to die, but although we'd been lost deep in the woods for the past hour and a half, it turned out we were only about a two-minute walk from where we'd abandoned my chair on the side of the road. So instead of leaving me for the white walkers, they just set me back down in my comfy chair. Brad stayed with me to recover from his brief but traumatic exposure to sunlight and physical activity, while Josh and Aaron went back to search for the HemLoft, following the lead of whichever small boy they deemed more trustworthy.

I sat on the side of the road, peering into the forest with anticipation and making idle chitchat with Matt, a mellow Redditor and bassoon craftsman who'd opted out of the search in favor of relaxing with my brother and me. Even though I was tired and it was the last day of filming, I remained the consummate host and asked Matt deep, probing questions like "What does your tattoo say?" and the more philosophical "Nice up here, huh?" while we waited. Finally, echoes of excitement were heard coming from the trees, cries of "It's over here!" and "We found it!" Josh and Aaron emerged from the wilderness, beaming with pride and glistening with sweat, to report that they had, in fact, found the mythical HemLoft.

A feeling came over me that was similar to when you're driving into Orlando and start seeing the signs for Disney World . . . only more Canadian. But getting to the HemLoft wasn't going to be easy. Josh explained, "It's not far, but it is an *interesting* path." "Interesting" meant that in order to get to the HemLoft, we needed to climb up a small but almost vertical cliff side with very few solid footholds, and I couldn't simply be carried up it—I'd need to be handed from person to person.

If this had been an officially sanctioned Canadian tourist spot, there might have been ropes, pulleys, helmets, or, more likely, a simple declaration of "Hell no, you can't do that." I responded to this news of imminent peril with all the concern of a golden retriever on his way to the park. All I heard was ". . . *blah, blah, blah,* tree house, *yadda, yadda* . . ." as I had trained my mind to only recognize words that I liked. So, blissfully unaware, I wrapped my arms around Aaron's neck, pulled up my legs, and went for one last piggyback ride up a mountain.

The gravity of the situation didn't hit me until the actual gravity of the situation hit me. As we ascended farther up the rock face, I could feel my grasp slipping. My whole body clung for dear life. Aaron, now understandably out of breath, stammered, "I'm not going to be able to hold your legs, so you gotta hang on tighter." It dawned on me just how difficult this climb was. The grip of my atrophied swizzle stick legs and the brute strength of Aaron's sculpted Roman statue body were the only things between me and a splattered mess of Zach on the rocks below. I had never been more grateful to be on horizontal ground than when we reached the top of that cliff side. I also felt the familiar mixture of gratitude and embarrassment for nearly strangling and/or crushing my two helpful friends.

It wasn't long after we continued down into the trees that I spotted the HemLoft, where the other Redditors had gathered. It stood like a proud Hobbit hole in the sky, a wooden orb supported by the trunk of a towering old-growth pine tree running through its center. The ordeal we'd just been through to find this place made it feel as though we'd uncovered an ancient relic. I finally knew what it was like to be Indiana Jones, if Indiana Jones was wearing a lavender hoodie and blue track pants, and had to be carried by a man in much better shape than he was. Still, it was an incredible rush.

The HemLoft was on a steep slope, and a bridge of five dainty wooden lily pad steps connected the tree house to higher ground. Aaron got down on his knees with me on his back and started crawling across, carefully using every ounce of strength and balance to avoid slipping and killing us both. The trip was treacherous to begin with but was made even more dangerous when I, ever helpful, started choking.

"Don't cough, you son of a bitch!" he said.

"Your head . . . *cough* . . . is on my . . . windpipe!" I gasped in response.

As I was clinging and hacking for dear life, I suddenly understood why the mustaches and moose enthusiasts of the world would be afraid to let me go down waterslides and crawl across rickety bridges. If I had taken that second ride down the slide at the pool all those summers ago, I might have gotten stuck and snapped both my legs off, or caused a fifteen-kid pileup in the waterslide, creating a dam of children and drowning everyone. And if that bowler-capped killjoy had let me roll over the suspension bridge, I guess there was a chance that the friction of a steel wheelchair could spark a fire that would burn across the ropes to ravage the Ewok village beyond. I could see the headlines: "Crippled Boy Allowed to Have Fun, Fifteen Dead" or "Disabled American Destroys Eighth Wonder of the World, Revenge for War of 1812?"

With one final forward heave, Aaron slung me off his back and sat me up inside the tree house, both of us exhausted but satisfied. After we caught our breath, we saw a ladder bathed in sunlight that led up to a tiny loft and thought, *What's a few more steps?* Reaching the top, we poked our heads out of the hole in the HemLoft's roof and waved to the Redditors below, basking in our triumph.

The journey had been unconventional, unsafe, and profoundly uncomfortable, but in spite of all the hiccups, we'd accomplished what we had set out to do. We'd made a show that embodied the spirit of adventure and the camaraderie of Reddit. We'd gone forth not hindered by fear, but propelled by friendship. As we sat together, with Brad behind the camera capturing the exchange, I thanked Aaron and Josh profusely for carrying me all this way, but for the first time, I allowed myself to admit that, in my own way, I had carried them too.

The show may have been called *Riding Shotgun*, but I had

been a driving force the whole way through—despite doing none of the actual driving. A year earlier, I was wrapping up a different kind of road trip entirely, where I was the star, yet still very much a passenger. That travel show had a bigger crew and a bigger budget but a lot less heart. On *Riding Shotgun* we never asked whether something could or should be done; we only asked how. Where *Rollin'* was about showing me the world, *Riding Shotgun* was about my discovering it for myself.

When the four of us had set out six weeks earlier, we had no idea what we were getting into; we only knew that we would be figuring it out together. There was always the risk of bruises and broken bones, but they weren't worth missing an adventure over! The gatekeepers and network executives and lifeguards of the world might've seen me as a liability, but Josh, Brad, and Aaron saw me as an equal. To them, I wasn't a disaster waiting to happen, I was part of a team who made a journey richer for one another. Sink or swim, climb or fall, we were friends, and friendship is something that is crazier than any slide, more deeply rooted than any old-growth pine tree, and stronger than any amount of hemp rope hundreds of moose can trample.

CHAPTER 12

With Apologies to Gene Shalit

No matter what good fortune falls into my lap, people always tend to view my life as an underdog story. The only times I really agree with that assessment are in regard to my love life. I was the runt of the romantic litter. I was the guy who, at twenty-seven, had never had a girlfriend or even really made a move, and seemed to be well on my way to playing the title character in a real-life reboot of *The Forty-Year-Old Virgin*. But even then, I still held out hope that I would one day emerge as the romantic lead of my own story, that after years of mishaps and missed opportunities, I'd finally seize the moment and get the girl.

On the morning of September 23, 2012, I woke up in my childhood bed at my mom's house in Buffalo, optimistic that I had finally reached the moment of truth in my own personal RomCom. Though no one in my house knew it, it was one of those Today's the Day! kind of days. Sure, I was nervous, but I was ready to take on the world and confident that no matter what happened, everything would turn out well. That was a really nice two minutes. My next thought was *Where the hell are my dress shoes?*

"I don't know," my mom said, "but it doesn't matter what shoes you wear, you're just meeting Alexis there, right?" I couldn't tell my mother the real reason why the geriatric white Velcro sneakers wouldn't be the optimal choice for this particular trip to New York City. Even at twenty-seven, uttering the words "Hey, Mom, I'm going to the Big Apple to lose my virginity" was not something I possessed the maturity to do. Instead, I did what I was most comfortable with—blatantly lying.

"Yeah, but it's a business meeting" (technically true) "and there's gonna be lots of guys from Google there" (hopefully not true). My cover story was that I was going to New York City to meet with Google to go over *Riding Shotgun*, now that we were in postproduction. In reality, the only "business meeting" I had was a guest spot on an Internet talk show called *What's Trending* that was filmed in LA, not New York. I could have just as easily Skyped in from Buffalo, but this trip wasn't about business; it was about pleasure.

In the movies, all it takes to make a romantic connection is a little bit of serendipity, but in this case it took an elaborate web of misdirection, meticulous planning, and a team effort as I'd be joined by expert field agents: my best friend Andrew and newly transplanted New Yorker friend Kevin.

With the exception of my misplaced "business" shoes, I had planned this expedition to a T. A flight at 9:30 that morning would get me into New York by 11:00 a.m., then the trip into the city would take forty-five minutes by shuttle. Taking into account that I'd be the last person off the plane and had to pick up my luggage, I should be at the hotel by 12:15 p.m. This schedule would leave me nearly five hours of prep time—interrupted only by my brief video chat with *What's Trending* at 3:00 p.m.—to converge with Andrew and Kevin at the hotel and do a complete body overhaul, learn how to put on a condom, freak out, shower, get dressed, and, at 5:30 p.m. sharp, saunter downstairs to the lobby of my swanky four-star digs in my George Clooney–est outfit and begin charming the pants off Stephanie, the delightful reporter who had inexplicably given me a second chance after I'd idiotically chosen waffles over a one-night stand with her at the Best Western in Baltimore.

By all accounts, I didn't deserve a second chance with Stephanie. Still, in the months that followed my epic fail in the Charm City, Stephanie and I had kept in touch in a manner that I was now able to discern as flirty. As Josh, Aaron, Brad, and I had continued across the country filming *Riding Shotgun*, Stephanie and I had continued our correspondence across texts and social media. Dissecting that night at the Best Western over and over again worked as a sort of Rosetta stone and allowed me to receive messages and draw conclusions like *Oh! When she talks about her boobs in the shower, that must mean . . . ::* checks Google translate :: *. . . she wants ME to imagine her naked in the shower! By George! I must report this to my colleagues.* "Hey, Josh!" I'd say, looking up from my phone, "she's talking about her boobs!" The sexual tension implied in our winky-faced emojis was palpable.

Over the course of *Riding Shotgun*, the objective of Team Get Zach Laid shifted from finding me any willing woman to facilitating a do-over with the right one. But my second encounter with Stephanie had proven far more difficult to arrange than the first. Our two biggest hurdles were geography and timing. I was staying with my mom in Buffalo but was due back in Austin in a week to start editing *Riding Shotgun,* and a few days after that Stephanie would be moving to Australia for a year. Our window to connect was exactly four days. It seemed next to impossible until Stephanie, ever proactive, offered this: "Sometime during the week before I leave, I'm gonna be going up to New York again to say good-bye to some friends." For once, I recognized an invitation, took the hint, and bent the truth to meet her halfway.

"Actually, I'm supposed to go to New York sometime to talk with Google about how *Riding Shotgun* went. I should know in a couple days when they want me there. Maybe we can time it so we can meet up?"

Relieved that I'd finally picked up a cue, she said, "I'd love to spend a day with you in New York, if we can make it work."

We were both forcing the stars to align in our favor, setting the scene so that two leads could come together in a way that felt plausible and satisfying, though even I'll admit there was some pretty heavy-handed writing going on to make the story work. With the dates set, I booked a four-star hotel on Madison Avenue called The New York Palace—a single room with a king-size bed that felt like a sufficiently grand stage for my long-overdue initiation into the world of the sexually active. I didn't discuss any of this with Stephanie, but I was pretty sure it was implied by one of the emojis I'd sent.

With the details and the sheets ironed out, I shifted my focus to the all-important business of preparing myself mentally and physically for my new role as heartthrob. I'd be playing against type, but if Tom Cruise can be an action movie star at like four foot three and Arnold Schwarzenegger can be a governor, then I was pretty sure I could convincingly play the part of a man who was confident in the bedroom. As Dave Phillips would have put it back in our Cindy Crawford days, I just had to "prepare to be doable." While no one could give me concrete steps or a manual on how to make my presumed deflowering go smoothly, everyone agreed that *something* should be smoother.

"You're gonna have to shave your pubes and your balls. No way around it," insisted Aaron.

To back up a second: there's an unwritten law among my friends that if you've known me for more than two weeks, you've seen me naked. Cerebral palsy forces you to be naked a lot in front of your friends, whether you're changing, getting ready for a shower, or simply propositioning them for a sensuous massage, so letting it all hang out is the only option.* So, depending on your perspective, I was in either the fortunate or the extremely unfortunate position of everyone I know having seen my undercarriage or, as I like to call it, Fangorn Forest.

"You're gonna have to trim it back *at least,*" Josh added.

Even I could suppose that few women would be turned on by a crotch that resembles a mini Gene Shalit. In fact, I think from time to time in this story, I'll refer to that whole situation as "Gene." Even my best friend, Andrew, who always tried to quell my concerns by telling me that different women like different things and that I should just do what's easiest and most comfortable, conceded that a little manscaping would probably be a good idea.

---

*Cerebral palsy: a condition that causes clothing to explode on contact with the skin. See *Playboy*—the cerebral palsy magazine.

The thought of taking a razor to Gene was unnerving. You're talking to a man whose dexterity is so poor that he has spilled almost every cup of coffee he's ever been handed and, when gesticulating, regularly pokes himself in the eye with his own finger.

There were, of course, more professional options. I mean, I could go and get a Brazilian—although that presented its own hairiness.

I once tried to get my eyebrows waxed so that I could look younger and pass as a high schooler for an audition. But each time the very patient Chinese lady pressed the Popsicle stick of hot wax to my face, I involuntarily flinched, spasming backward like Frankenstein's monster recoiling from fire. If it had just been my face that moved, I would have stuck with it, but my arms flung back and my legs tensed up, kicking the barber's chair in front of me. My whole body did not want to get my eyebrows waxed and, after five attempts, I gave up. It was terrifying to consider having wax applied to an even more sensitive and important area of my body. I decided that self-improvement, however risky, might be the lesser of two maimings.

The intimate nature of my mom's house in Buffalo prevented me from having any privacy in which to attempt this massive deforestation project. So, with little to no forethought of what this might mean for my day in Manhattan, I put The Scouring of The Shire off and decided to wait until I was in the hotel. I didn't know it then, but some things are way more important than privacy.

As I slid into my most flattering and form-fitting oxford shirt and my mom loaded up my bags in the car, I went down an exhaustive mental checklist of the tools I needed to become a sexy beast who was a little less beastly.

Sugarfree Orbit gum—*check!*

Q-tips—*check!*

Deodorant (NOT body spray because I was going to a hotel, not a CrossFit gym in New Jersey)—*check!*

Newly acquired basic knowledge of female anatomy—*check!* (Thanks, Google image search!)

Norelco Bodygroom Pro—*check!*

I had everything I needed to make sure this evening went off without a hitch or a stray hair. After today, when my family doctor asked me during my annual exam if I was sexually active, I could finally answer with a knowing wink and a "Yes!" rather than my go-to response of "I wish." It was all smooth sailing from here—baby smooth!

But in remembering all my toiletries and trimmers, I'd forgotten to bring any personal identification to the airport. This mistake cost me two hours while I waited for the next flight to JFK. Still, it was better to get the bumps over with early; I'd padded the schedule in case of a close shave anyway.

During the flight, I was less concerned about the physical preparation of my crotch than preparing myself mentally to embark on virgin territory. As the captain called over the PA system to let us know that we had begun our initial descent into New York City, I felt like I was cramming for an exam in a language I'd neither heard nor spoken. Now, all of a sudden, after sleeping through the entire semester, it was the morning of the final. I had so little knowledge of what was supposed to happen that, in the weeks leading up to this day, my friends had fielded questions as relentless and random as a bumblebee darting back and forth between ice cream cones at a fair.

"If she's on the bed and I'm in the chair, how do I kiss her?"

"What's the best way to give oral sex on a woman?"

"How do you tell which condoms are the smallest?"

"What do I do if she starts laughing?"

"How far open should my mouth be when I kiss this girl and in what quadrant of her mouth should my tongue be? Do I hold my tongue back?"

"How the hell do I explain why this has taken so long?"

Did I even know why this had taken so long? The lie that I always told myself was that things would happen naturally when the time was right. But as I got older, nothing about life in my body felt natural. After a while it wasn't the lack of experience or opportunity that stunted my sexual development, but rather the fear of having to explain my lack of experience to someone. There were not enough *GQ* magazine tips in the world to make me feel comfortable in my own skin.

Out of all my friends' suggestions, Andrew gave me the best advice: that communication and honesty were the most important things.

I thought that was bullshit. "That just means that I'll be honestly communicating what a loser I've been while I'm trying to be sexy in front of this girl. Everyone says, 'Be yourself,' but I've been myself for twenty-seven years and that's how I got into this mess! I think I should try being *anybody* else." Technically, I said this as a joke. But it was a joke I took as gospel.

However this night went down, I knew I had a whole team of people who were eagerly waiting to hear about it and assess how things went. I'd raised the stakes and now people were counting on me to lose my virginity. Aaron and Andrew had had meetings about this that I wasn't even invited to. Whatever happened behind the door of that hotel room, I wouldn't be able to hide it from my friends.

Just as I was about to let my imagination get the better of me, the landing gear hit the runway and the lights came up in the cabin. The captain informed us that it was a sunny seventy-two degrees in New York City. I thought to myself, *It's a beautiful day and you've landed safely, so just take it one step at a time.*

But as it turned out, the next several steps were stumbles. Due to construction, only one lane into the city was open, so what would have been a forty-minute drive turned into an hour-and-a-half-long slog. I got to the hotel just in time for my *What's Trending* appearance, which had thankfully gotten a late start. The interview went off without a hitch but it still ate up a half hour of time I no longer had to spare. Nothing else could go wrong in the next two hours. I still had to shave, shower, and buy condoms.

My phone buzzed and I saw a text from Stephanie: *Hey, are you here yet? We're going to the zoo, if you wanna join!* Feeling the pressure of time bearing down on me, I quickly tapped back, *Got a late start, but maybe in a bit? Have fun!* I tossed the phone aside and then, with great precision and purpose, pulled my Norelco Bodygroom Pro from the outside pocket of my laptop case. I stared at it curiously, thinking to myself, *I know when I packed this, there was an attachment where I could choose the length of the trim, and now there's just a bare blade.* I looked at the other side of the device, thinking that I might be able to just use the electric razor part, only to find that it too was missing. I combed through every pocket of my luggage, finding nothing.

If I used this thing, my tender romantic comedy would be in very real danger of becoming the next movie in the Saw series. My only consolation was that Andrew would be arriving soon. Surely, he would be able to make the trip to the Duane Reade and buy condoms and a new ball shaver for me.

That was well within the boundaries of what anyone would do for a best friend, right? We were on the same team, after all, and this de-virginizing was nothing if not a group effort. Then, another text came in. It was Andrew.

Train's delayed. Won't be in until around 9:00 p.m. Sorry man, call Kevin if you need anything.

This was grim news. Kevin hadn't planned on joining us until later, and he was in Queens, well over an hour away by public transportation. I had to think and move fast. I raced down to the lobby and found the bellman.

"Where's the closest place I can buy an electric razor? One that has the attachments for beard trimming?"

I wonder what crossed through this man's mind as he looked at my daylong stubble that was barely a five o'clock shadow. But maybe it's a bellman's code that you just don't ask questions like that.

"You turn right and head two blocks up and there'll be a Duane Reade across the street. They should have somethin'," he advised.

"Thank you so much!" I said, and then bolted out the door and took a left.

I didn't realize my mistake until I was five minutes down the block, then backtracked, shouting, "EXCUSE ME!" at any pedestrian in my path, snappy even by New Yorker standards. Peeling into the Duane Reade, I headed straight for the cash register, blurting out, "Could you tell me where the electric razors, the condoms, and the Reese's Peanut Butter Cups are?"

She must have heard this combination before because, without skipping a beat, she said, "The razors are along the wall, the condoms are upstairs, and the candy's in aisle four."

"Thanks!" I said, rushing to take inventory of their personal grooming options, and as luck would have it, they did have a razor with every attachment and setting I'd need. Or at least, they had an empty spot on the shelf where it would have been if it were in stock.

"You got any more of these trimmer things in the back?" I called to the cashier.

"If it's not there, we don't have it," she said.

My heart sank when I realized what this meant. Either Gene would be tagging along for the date, which was not an option, or I'd be left to make do with the only part of my Norelco Bodygroom Pro that was still at my disposal—the bare-toothed blade. I couldn't let fear take over. I still had candy and condoms to buy. I took the elevator upstairs and was daunted by the number of prophylactic options. So I took out my phone and had a private conversation with Andrew at full volume in the middle of the aisle.

"How the hell do I know which of these condoms to get? What does ribbed mean? These ones say they add heat AND ice—and are any of these flavored ones any good? I have no clue. Not a single one of these boxes has a sizing chart on it!"

Going into full medical professional mode, Andrew said, "You probably don't want to get anything that's super lubricated or flavored, and I wouldn't go with the ribbed or the lambskin ones. And Lifestyles are the smallest, just so you know."

So I did what any twenty-seven-year-old who had never tried on or even touched a condom before would do. I looked for the box with the largest quantity, because I knew that half would be wasted just trying to figure out how to get them on. As I was reading the back of the jumbo pack of thirty-two Trojans, I heard a voice coming from down the aisle.

"Excuse me, I'm sorry to bother you, but aren't you that boy from the Oprah show?"

I looked up to see an African American woman in her mid-fifties smiling at me. As I'm fairly certain that I'm the only person who looks remotely like me in the public eye, I had no choice but to respond, "Yup, that's me!"

"Whatever happened with that show?"

"It was canceled." I shrugged, still holding the giant box of condoms.

"Oh, that's too bad," she consoled. "What are you doing now?"

Right now? I thought to myself. *Well right now, I'm drowning in embarrassment.* But I replied, "I've got a new travel show!"

"Well, that's wonderful! It was so nice to meet you!"

"You too!" I lied.

Stopping in the candy aisle on the way out, I grabbed the biggest bag of Reese's Peanut Butter Cups I could find, because Stephanie had told me that they were her favorite, and checked out. I zoomed back to The Palace and barricaded myself in my room. It was already 4:30 p.m. I texted Stephanie to let her know that I definitely would not be able to meet her at the zoo.

Aw, that's too bad, she texted back. *I saw a snow leopard!*

Having bought myself some time, I had to prepare for what could very easily turn into self-mutilation. But then, how bad could it possibly be? After all, this device had been designed expressly for the purpose of managing unwanted body hair, so surely they wouldn't equip it with a tool that could castrate a man. I'd gone through ALL the reviews on Amazon and none of them had said, "Stay away, I lost a ball! One star." I wasn't exactly sure if the blade was ever meant to touch exposed skin or if the trimmer attachment was designed to be removable for cleaning purposes only. In retrospect, the latter seemed more likely.

I stripped naked in the bathroom and told myself that I had no other choice. I sprawled out on the floor and tried to position myself over a towel. But who was I kidding? I couldn't have kept that room clean if I had wrapped it wall-to-wall in cellophane. I would just do what needed to be done and worry about the mess later. The key, I theorized, was to be as delicate as possible so that if I did find myself facing unimaginable pain, I could stop before Gene looked like he had alopecia. I didn't even pause to consider that it might be a problem that, from my angle on the floor, I couldn't check the mirror to keep tabs on how the hairdo was coming along.

I grabbed the razor and tilted the blade toward my manhood, hearing the rattle of the motor as it came closer and closer. Then came the first snip. It was a familiar sound that I'd heard a thousand times before while shaving my face, except it was less of a buzz and more of a metallic scraping. But for all the fuss the motor made, it didn't seem to make a dent in Gene's formidable forelock.

Damn it! I thought. *If I'm gonna get anything done, I've gotta commit to this!* So I plunged the Bodygroom deep into the wilderness, and the sharp teeth grazed my sensitive exposed skin with all the delicacy of a forklift moving scrap metal. I wouldn't describe the feeling as pain so much as a piercing anguish that caused every cell in my body to retreat. My survival instincts kicked in, and I yanked the razor out of range. There was no way in hell I would ever let that thing near my pubic hair again. I didn't care what Stephanie thought, and I reasoned that while unkempt hair was probably a turnoff, it wouldn't be as much of a red flag as bleeding, which might prompt her to cry out, "Oh my God, what war was your penis just in? We need to get you to a cockspital!"

I lay there, now sweating, wondering if I could apply little toilet paper pieces to stop the bleeding like you do when you nick your chin shaving. At least I knew I hadn't done irreversible harm and I hoped that my body could heal in time. I surveyed the damage. I had definitely broken the skin. But for all that effort, it didn't look as though I'd actually trimmed anything.

Then I rolled over.

A sizeable clump fell to the floor and I saw the heinous crime I'd committed. Somehow I'd managed to shave down the middle—and *just* the middle. With one ill-advised swoop, I had turned Gene Shalit into Danny DeVito. This looked neither deliberate nor healthy. I flinched instinctively as I heard a buzzing sound and was relieved when I realized it was just Stephanie texting again.

Hey, um, my friends and I are wrapping up at the zoo. Should we head toward your hotel?

It was now 5:30 p.m. Panicked, I texted back, *It'll be a little while. Still doing some interview stuff!* and by "interview stuff" I meant crying, both from physical agony and from feeling overwhelmed. How in God's name was I gonna bounce back from this one? I lay there on the floor feeling defeated—no matter how hard I tried, everything always ended up in disaster. Even the normal things that seemed to come as second nature to everyone else in the world were insurmountable hurdles to me. Maybe I was never destined to be a romantic lead after all.

I heard the vibration of my phone against the cold tile again, and I gingerly rolled over, sure it would be Stephanie saying she'd decided to turn in early and call off dinner. But instead, I saw three familiar words from Andrew:

Chew bubble gum.

Those words were more inspirational than any long-winded speech that Denzel Washington or Al Pacino ever could have delivered at the end of some sappy sports movie. I couldn't give up. I was going to make this date, even if I'd be limping and bleeding all the way through it. The first thing I had to do was finish shaving.

I pressed the button, reengaged the motor on the jaws of death, then held my breath and shut my eyes. I wish I could describe exactly what followed, but I've mostly blocked it from memory. Until I've gone through some extensive therapy I won't be able to cope with it. But over the course of the next excruciating hour, I became as smooth as a gorilla who had shaved himself in the dark. My phone pulsed again.

We've grabbed some coffee but are getting pretty hungry. Can we meet at your hotel?

Yeah, sure, I replied, *head on over!* and I reluctantly let Stephanie know the name of my hotel without giving the room number. It was now quarter to seven.

I took a shower and started trying to clean up the evidence. While I was on all fours naked on the floor with a persistent pain in my groin, I received another text.

Hey, so we're downstairs in your hotel. What room are you in?

It was clear that the universe was not going to be giving me any breaks today. I texted, *I'll be down in ten, still changing!* and then did my best to clean the bathroom floor with a towel before shoving it into the darkest recess under the sink, and began transporting stray pubic hairs into the trash can one by one. In all honesty, even Amelia Bedelia wouldn't have made such a cock-up of the whole thing. But I finished erasing the evidence of my crimes, got dressed, fastened my Velcro shoes, and rode the elevator down to the lobby, ready to pull off the mother of all comebacks.

So what if nobody in human history had ever lost their virginity in shoes that were meant to be worn on a beach in conjunction with a metal detector, a straw hat, and a nose covered in zinc? And so what if I'd just nearly turned myself into a eunuch? Stephanie didn't know that, and I was hopeful that if the night went well enough, I could tell her the whole story and maybe even get an "A for effort."

When I saw Stephanie, she was sitting on a couch in the lobby in a cute tank top with two friends in tow. Everyone was laughing about the day's events at the zoo.

"Hey!" she said warmly as I rolled around the corner. "We're starving. There's this restaurant called The Standard that's not too far from here and it's supposed to be really good."

"Sure!" I said. "I'm game for anything!"—not mentioning that "anything" didn't include fish, cheese, or things that I would have to cut with a knife and fork.

"The lobby of your hotel looks pretty magical, by the way."

"Yeah, that's the vibe I was going for."

"These are my friends, Tim and Sarah. We've been hanging out all day."

"That's cool, my buddies Kevin and Andrew might join us."

"Great!" she said.

As we headed out the door, my attentive bellman interjected, "Hey! Did you find that razor you were looking for?"

"No, they were all out!" I said.

"All out of razors?" He lifted his eyebrows, confused.

"Yeah, well, see ya later!"

As we made our way to the restaurant, Stephanie's friends struck me as a couple who were perfectly at ease with each other. They were finishing each other's sentences and trading laughs back and forth. I wondered how long it would take to feel that comfortable with Stephanie. By my estimation, we had about four hours. While we were both very excited to see each other, there was still that awkward transition between the digital world we'd been flirting in and the real world. As we walked along, making idle chatter about all the friends she was seeing before she left for Australia and how her mother was taking the move, I remembered the bag of Reese's stuffed in the back of my wheelchair.

"Oh!" I exclaimed, presenting them to her. "I got these for you!"

"Thanks!" she said, delighted. "These are my favorite!"

"I know, I remembered." I smiled.

This sentimental exchange prompted an "Awww!" from Sarah. I took this as a sign that I was doing well, because Sarah was probably in place to be the barometer as to whether I was a decent guy or a piece of trash.

For all the tenderness on display, we had barely touched, and so when Stephanie mentioned how she'd been walking around the city all day, I instinctively offered, "Well, you could just ride on my chair if you want."

She gleefully accepted and sat on my lap, tossing her legs over the side of the chair as I started out slow and then kicked into high gear, running over the crosswalk. Stephanie giggled the whole time. I was enjoying myself enough to ignore the discomfort that a person's body weight brought to my still extremely sensitive groin. Despite all my earlier stumbles, I felt like I was doing a pretty good job of being romantic.

As we got settled in at the restaurant, I was feeling more optimistic than I'd ever allowed myself to feel about women. I approached the menu at The Standard the same way I approach any menu: by asking myself, *What can I actually eat here without a) looking like a baby or b) worrying about my stomach?*

"They have a cookie platter!" I said. "I think I'm gonna have to try that!" So I ordered cookies and meatballs. As the night progressed, I got to hear all the stories from the day that I had missed while trying to get into the city, learning about condoms, and brutalizing my balls on a bathroom floor. Stephanie recounted that she'd been so excited to see the animals that she basically pushed little kids out of the way to get in front of them.

"I'm really sorry I missed that," I said, meaning it. The conversation among Stephanie, Tim, and Sarah was full of charming little details and inside jokes I had no frame of reference for. I started to feel out of place at the table. And then the conversation shifted from the day's highlight reel to plans for the immediate future.

"So," Stephanie said, turning to me, "we can't stay out too late because I'm staying with Sarah and she lives in Brooklyn and has to work tomorrow."

We'd only spent a little over an hour together, so inviting her to stay at The Palace with me still felt too forward. My only shot of extending the evening was to transition to drinks somewhere and present a more appealing alternative to a cozy night in Brooklyn.

"How late can you stay out?" I asked.

"Well, Sarah's shift starts at eight, so I don't think we can do much later than eleven."

This was a considerable roadblock. It was already past nine. If I was going to convince Stephanie to stay out later, I'd have to convince her friends that I wanted them to stay out too.

"You should just take the day off tomorrow," I told Sarah. "Where do you work?"

"The 9/11 Memorial," she said.

If there's a tactful way to suggest blowing off one's job at the 9/11 Memorial, I haven't yet discovered it. My last hope was that Andrew and Kevin could come up with a brilliant plan. Maybe if we had fancy cocktails at an enchanting New York bar with a 1920s vibe surrounded by old library books, I could change the tone and sweep Stephanie off her feet with nostalgia or something.

As I was grasping at straws, Andrew texted: *Just got into Penn Station and hooked up with Kevin. Should we still come to meet you?*

In Andrew's ideal version of this night, things were already going so well that I wouldn't need any wingmen. But I texted him back saying that they should definitely come, and they should hurry.

Clinging to a last shred of optimism, I asked, "Do you guys wanna grab a drink?"

"Yeah, but it's gotta be quick," Sarah said.

"Uh, where should we go?" I wondered aloud. "Who has fancy drinks around here?"

"I dunno," said Sarah, and Stephanie took out her phone to Yelp which bars were close. Then came the nail in the coffin.

"Well," she said tentatively, "there's a TGI Friday's right up the street. You wanna just go there?"

There are very few things I am absolutely sure of, but one of them is that no one in the history of recorded time has converted drinks at TGI Friday's into a passionate one-night stand, and if they had, they had to've been more intoxicated than Stephanie and I could ever get from a pitcher of Blue

Moon. It was crystal clear now that even though I had been fully aware of what was happening this time, and had a made heroic effort, I'd still be a virgin in the morning, and probably every morning after that until the morning I woke up dead. It was bleak, but at least I had my future planned out, and how many people can say that at twenty-seven?

As we headed to Friday's, I did my best not to seem somber. But seeing Tim and Sarah's playful chemistry as they walked ahead of us made me wonder if I'd ever have that kind of connection with anyone. If there was someone out there for me, it certainly wasn't Stephanie. She'd be heading to Australia in less than a week, meeting guys with far more charming accents than I had to offer. But still, I tried to make pleasant conversation.

"They're a really cute couple," I said, gesturing toward Tim and Sarah.

"Oh, they're not dating," Stephanie clarified. "They just met today."

"WHAT?!" I said in disbelief.

"I know, crazy, right?"

Then it dawned on me what I'd really missed while I was so preoccupied with my fuzzy balls and obsessing about losing my virginity: I'd missed the opportunity to spend time with a person I genuinely liked, and because I'd failed to establish a rapport on the one day I had with Stephanie, I'd likely never see her again. This stung more than anything else. Romance isn't preparation. It's paying attention. This girl wouldn't have cared that my nether region looked like Art Garfunkel, but she would care that I'd missed out on sharing a day at the zoo with her because I'd been too self-absorbed to focus on anything but Gene Shalit's hairdo. I wouldn't get a third chance.

As we sat down to our red-and-white-checkered tablecloth and met our waiter with his silly vest adorned with a thousand buttons, what should have been a celebration felt more like a funeral.

When Andrew and Kevin arrived, they immediately sensed that they were too late. All our energy deflated as we sipped our pints of domestic beer, which tasted even more bitter than usual. Stephanie still smiled and made eyes at me, but these looks couldn't go anywhere now. When we had finished our drinks, she stood up from the table and came over to hug me. As we embraced, I whispered, "Don't go."

She chuckled. "I have to."

Andrew, Kevin, and I stayed at the table and watched Stephanie, Sarah, and Tim walk out the front door. With them went every dream of finally being intimate with somebody. I'd go back to being the naive guy in my group of friends, completely ignorant of the intricacies of relationships and sex. I was not a leading man but a character actor in my own life, someone to add comic relief while everyone around him got to experience real change and progress. The plan of action would revert back to hypothetical scenarios and I'd continue to wonder whether I was worthy of being wanted. The three of us sat there in silence until I finally spoke up.

"Well," I said, using all the showmanship I could muster, "what the fuck just happened?"

Andrew and Kevin both laughed as I continued. "Do you think it would be rude if I texted her to ask, 'Why aren't we having sex right now?'" That was the only joke I could manage, but at least now the pain in my chest exceeded the pain in my testicles. Even though we were in arguably the most exciting city in the world, it all felt like white noise.

The only thing I had energy left for was watching a movie with my friends back at the hotel. I wanted to stream *Midnight in Paris* on Amazon, so we went to the front desk to plead with the receptionist because this was a luxury hotel and the luxury of Wi-Fi cost eighteen dollars a day. The connection had been so slow during my earlier interview on *What's Trending* that I had called to cancel my Internet for the room, demanding a refund. Not in any emotional place to handle even the simplest transaction, Andrew took the lead, explaining, "The three of us just want to have a quiet evening in. Is there any way that you could cut us a break on the Wi-Fi? We've had a really rough day." Our humble request was declined. And so we went back upstairs and Andrew thumbed through the room service menu.

"Would it make you feel any better if we got a bottle of Grey Goose with ice and a plate of lemon wedges for $1,700?" he asked. "Oh, here's the scotch! It's only eleven hundred!"

And so, what was supposed to be a romantic evening with a special lady concluded with three friends falling asleep together in a king-size bed while watching the only movie that was already on my laptop, *The Incredibles*. In the morning, I divvied up the remainder of my once promising romantic future, giving Andrew and Kevin sixteen condoms each. I'd not even had the time to try one on. We tossed the empty box in the trash can and checked out.

At certain points like these, all evidence suggests that my life is, at best, a comedy of errors or, at worst, a full-blown tragedy. Normally, my role as a storyteller allows me to filter painful experiences into something relatable and valuable to an audience. At the end, no matter my folly, we've learned something and hopefully laughed our way to the conclusion.

In this instance though, no matter how hard I tried to find the silver lining, I couldn't escape the reality that this was just another story of a guy who'd screwed up, again. There was no other way to spin this ill-fated fable. That is, until I thought of the tall tale that the hotel staff might have pieced together given their limited knowledge of the night's events.

The bellman had witnessed a guest return to the hotel with two strange men requesting a quiet night in with Wi-Fi access. And the next morning, when the maid unlocked the door, she found not only a towel covered in hair and blood, but an empty box where thirty-two condoms used to be. I smiled at the thought that someone could imagine I'd had a night so crazy and orgiastic that it became legend among the staff at The Palace hotel. My love life was not a romantic comedy or a tragedy to them, but more of a mystery, and that's fine because it

was still a mystery to me too. Now, that's not the story I wanted to tell, but it's at least one I could live with for the moment. I didn't lose my virginity that night, but I was grateful that all I had lost would grow back, probably stronger and thicker than it was before, so that someday, I could try again, and finally get my happy ending.

III

The Learning Curve of a Late Bloomer

CHAPTER 13

Have a Little Faith

The bar district of any city at two a.m. on a Saturday night looks and feels pretty much the same. The sound track is an atonal cacophony of slurried jibber-jabber atop the booming distorted bass lines of pop hits remixed by DJs in panda suits, or the last shredded notes of a cover band's approximation of "Free Bird." It smells like a mixture of stale beer, cigarettes, and greasy street food. You might see a flood of well-marinated coeds pour out into the streets, stopping traffic as they stumble back home, or a bachelor party so crazy that it's fifty-fifty whether it'll be followed by a wedding or a breakup.

On rare occasions, amid this chaos, you might find me—bored out of my mind and sipping a Shirley Temple while trying to avoid being tripped over. For a sober person, the bar scene is kind of like a zombie movie with nachos and sobbing girls in tiny vests. Whenever my friends insist that I be "social" and drag me downtown into this sloshed mosh pit, I generally only have three types of social interactions.

Number One: The Drunk Do-Gooder High Five, when an inebriated guy sees either one or two of me in my wheelchair and thinks, *I'm gonna make this guy's night!* Which to him means holding up a sticky palm for a high five. When I hesitate, considering where that hand might have been all night, he says, "High five! Come on, man, high five!" as though he was Annie Sullivan trying to teach me how to express joy in the grossest way possible. And when I finally give in, he says, "All riiiiight!" then staggers off, thinking to himself, *I am a wonderful person. I just gave a retard a high five!*

Number Two: The Fuck Yeah! Centipede is a trio of girls holding up the drunkest companion in the middle. I lock gazes with her, as much as a guy with a lazy eye and a girl who can barely keep her eyes open can. I think to myself, *Did we just make a connection? Could this be my future wife? Should I start picking out wallpaper for the nursery?* Completely oblivious to my inner monologue, the future Mrs. Anner thrusts her head back and yells, "Fuck yeah!" before falling back into semiconsciousness and the arms of her friends.

The third type of encounter isn't restricted to bar districts at two a.m., but its presence there is almost more unsettling. A young man or woman with a sense of purpose, seemingly sober and friendly, approaches and makes warm and coherent conversation. IMMEDIATE red flag! "Hi, how are you? What's your name?" they ask. To an onlooker, it might seem like I'm about to have my first pleasant encounter of the night. But inevitably, the tone shifts. It's still friendly, but tentative, like a grandson who finally gets around to asking Grammy May for money to cover his gambling debt.

"Hey man, can I ask you something? Would you mind if I prayed for you? To fix your legs, I mean."

At this time of night, I don't have the heart or energy to tell them that there's actually nothing wrong with my legs; it's just a symptom of the brain damage I have.

This attempted act of God has been offered to me dozens of times over the years and I've never really turned it down. I always try to treat these interactions with as much respect as I possibly can. I mean, I don't wanna be a Negative Nancy and tell them, "You know what? This probably won't work," so I let the holy spectacle play out. They close their eyes, I do the same, and they improvise a prayer.

"Dear Lord, please hear me, Lord. Please help heal my brother . . . Dude, what's your name again?"

"Zach," I say.

"My brother Zach's legs, and help him to walk, Lord. Use your infinite love and healing power to lift him out of that wheelchair . . ."

Unable to shut out the cries of "Jägerbomb!" I briefly open my eyes to catch a glimpse of a guy pissing on a slice of pizza and shut them again just in time for:

". . . in Jesus's name we pray, Amen."

Usually, my self-anointed friend is content to go along their merry way and wish me a good night. But one particular miracle worker outside the Chuggin' Monkey in Austin wanted to see a result right away.

"Do you feel any different? Can you stand up?"

Not knowing how to respond, I removed my footplates, balanced on my feet, and actually tried to stand for a few seconds, only to plummet the six inches back into my seat cushion. My would-be savior looked so disappointed that I couldn't help but reassure him. "Maybe it takes a while to work."

"All right," he said, deflated. "If I give you my number, will you text me in the morning if anything happens?"

The next day I responded with, *Nothing yet :(* to which he replied, *Who is this?*

✧

I don't know why, but my cerebral palsy is interpreted by people who can walk as the one thing God didn't do on purpose. I don't even know if I believe in God, but I thought that was his whole deal: everything happens for a reason, we just don't always know what the reason is. God made possums with a forked penis and they piss and defecate on themselves as a defense mechanism . . . and *I'm* what people are worried about?

There are times I've wished I could take swing dancing lessons or drive a car without the risk of steering off the road into a pile of grandmothers, if, say, a fly landed on my windshield and startled me. But there's never been a time when I've asked a higher power to heal me. I did ask Santa once for the ability to fly, and when I didn't get it I wept, because I thought doing cool shit like that was supposed to be Santa's job.

I always thought that if there was a God, he must be crazy busy and underappreciated. I grappled with the idea that he would let children starve and allow genocide, but would still be pulling the strings of every football game and actually had something to do with Sean Penn winning an Oscar. (That doesn't make sense, that guy's a douche!)

When we were kids, my brother and I attended St. Peter's United Church of Christ where my grandmother was the organist for thirty years. My family was the Easter Sunday type of Christians who went to play dress-up. Church struck me as a sterile and impersonal environment, with the hard pews and the elderly people who only knew who I was because I looked so much like my father had when he was a boy. After church let out, the conversation was always on the grim side— kind of a next-to-go talking about the last-to-go scenario. Even as a young boy, I mostly associated church with my own mortality, which didn't inspire much religious fervor.

When I was ten, I went to a summer camp for physically, emotionally, and mentally disabled kids called Cradle Beach that offered parents on fixed incomes a safe, welcoming place to send their children. It was at once a fun-times, clichéd, '80s-movie summer camp experience, while simultaneously being a disquieting glimpse of what my life might've been like if I'd been dealt different cards. Cradle Beach Camp was the first time I'd ever been surrounded by other people who society indiscriminately lumped together under the "disabled" umbrella. It was also the first time I saw someone wet the bed, intentionally, while standing three feet away from it. The only thing that united us that I could see was that we all had to be dressed in the morning by our counselors, and every single boy in that cabin woke up with an erection that lasted at least four hours. Yep, it was just a bunch of boners every morning. Now, where was I? God!

The reason I brought up my summer camp experience is because it's also the first place that I can recall attempting to pray. Every day after lunch we would have a mandatory siesta, and since many of our counselors loved Jesus as much as we loved toasted marshmallows, we were encouraged to pray during this quiet time. Kids would say their prayers out loud. There was nothing that I wanted apart from Power Rangers toys at the time, and I didn't really feel it was appropriate to ask God to wait outside the Toys-R-Us at five in the morning to get me a Megazord. So I prayed differently. I asked God how he was doing and struck up a conversation. "Oh yeah? That's great!" I'd say, and then I'd relay to my bunkmate that God had told me he's having mac and cheese for dinner.

My casual rapport with the Almighty seemed to rub the more devout campers the wrong way. But it also rubbed me the wrong way that people only talked to God when they needed something. I couldn't really grasp the concept of an omnipotent, all-loving, all-seeing presence. All I thought was *Man, that's gotta be a tough job!* Even then, without faith, I had empathy. As I got older and realized that there were a multitude of religions in the world, I noticed that most people's empathy only extended to those who had similar beliefs. But the most connected I've felt to something bigger has been in moments when compassion trumped belief.

When I had to drop out of high school, one of my few routes to a promising future was through a Catholic Charities' GED program, confusingly named Tomorrow's Youth

Today. (Today's youth—they're adults tomorrow. It doesn't make any sense!) Despite that nonsensical name, they were the sole reason I was able to complete my education. The organization would send someone over twice a week to tutor me, but instead of getting hit on the hands with rulers by a crotchety old nun, I got the "I'll come to your house and we'll drink lemonade on the porch and maybe talk about math a little" variety of Catholic school.

I wasn't Catholic and I knew very little about Catholicism, yet these people were more committed to my education and success than my own school district. While my faith may not have been strong, my view of the faithful was mostly positive. Still, I never told my tutors that I'd only taken communion once, and that's because I thought they were just handing out bread and grape juice. I accidentally ate double Christ that day.

✦

In June 2013, I moved to Los Angeles with my brother Brad. Instead of moving to Hollywood to become actresses like most people, my brother and I set off for the West Coast with a higher purpose—to find God. And by "find God," I mean make a television show, and by "television show," I mean Web series. *Have a Little Faith* is a YouTube show I hosted for Rainn Wilson's company, SoulPancake. In each episode, I interview people from different religions and get to know them, without all the judgment and self-important sanctimonious crap that people normally inject into discussions about anything that's different from exactly what they believe. My take was "You're a person, I'm a person—let's talk about this God thing."

If you can't tell by now, I'm a self-proclaimed religious

idiot, but I felt like my experience with disability gave me a unique perspective to broach a topic that people normally don't want to talk about. I'd grown up as the Other to everyone. I knew what it was like to be categorized and generalized out of my individuality and personhood. While I couldn't endorse any single religion as the one true answer, I could provide a means for people to talk about what was most important to them on their terms, and give them the opportunity to do so without being judged. The concept of the show was simple: What if you didn't have to defend your religion, and what if you didn't have to promote it? What if you just said what it meant to you? For me the show was less about understanding a higher power and more about understanding humanity.

At SoulPancake, I found a way to explore different faiths, as well as a team of collaborators who had faith in me and my vision. I don't think I've ever felt so supported during a project. The CEO, Shabnam Mogharabi, and everyone else I worked with there—Krissy Wall, Jessica Jean Jardine, Georgia Koch, and Bayan Joonam—were all committed to making something special where the focus was on changing perspectives rather than chasing views.

When we started filming the show in Los Angeles, I expected everyone I interviewed to have something to do with "the Industry." That turned out to be only partially true. I did meet a Buddhist who chanted to the Universe to help her sell her spec television script, and at a gathering of people from the Baha'i faith, we definitely thanked the Lord for helping a member book a Target commercial. But in every episode, I found something I hadn't necessarily expected: a person I actually liked and a sense of community. All of a sudden, the guy who had always felt like an outsider was being welcomed in by Quakers, Muslims, Baptists, Jews, Mormons, Atheists, Witches, and Hindus alike. I built lasting friendships with people I might have otherwise written off as stereotypes.

When I approached the Quaker episode, I assumed, like most uninformed people, that Quakers and Amish were interchangeable and that they'd all look like that guy on the oatmeal canister. But I was taken by surprise when I met Joe Franko. When he came to the door, Joe was not in stockings, a wide brim hat, and an ascot—he just wore a red polo with black pants and had a grandfatherly warmth. Joe confessed that he didn't even like oatmeal, to which I replied, "Blasphemy!" He had been a Quaker for forty-five years and over the next couple of hours taught me more about love and loss than any other single human has to date.

His husband of only a few years had succumbed to complications from HIV just two months earlier. When they met, Joe knew that David was HIV positive, but none of that mattered because he also knew they were soul mates. When I asked him how having a finite amount of time with someone he loved so much affected life in the day-to-day, he said, "You learn not to sweat the small stuff." But the truly beautiful thing was that before California had legalized gay marriage, Joe's Quaker Meeting had married the couple in a ceremony where the entire group of Friends had signed a Quaker marriage certificate affirming that, in their eyes, and in the eyes of God, these two people had been married.

When we put the episode up online, I was nervous for Joe when I considered how anonymous YouTube commenters might react. The Internet is a wonderful place that provides an equal voice to everyone, but like most public forums, the loudest voices tend to be the dumbest ones. It's hard to go through the comment section of any video without someone spouting grammatically incorrect hate speech like "Your such a stupid faget." But with Joe's video, something unprecedented happened—there was not a single negative comment in the bunch. Most people wrote about how moved they were by Joe's story, and how sorry they were for his loss. For once, love and humanity had transcended ideology and ignorance.

It came as a shock to everyone when, two weeks after the episode aired, Joe Franko died. Shortly after we filmed, he'd been diagnosed with an aggressive form of bone cancer. I only got to spend a few hours with Joe, but in that time I came to know what the term "unconditional love" really means. It's what religious people say God has, but I saw it in Joe's love for David. Joe told me that he had searched for years to find a church that would accept him as a gay man, and he discovered that Quakers believe that we are all made in God's image, and that God made us all perfect. "God made you perfect, Zach," he said. That's a sentiment that had never been expressed to me before, and it was contrary to the way most people seemed to see me, as someone who needed to be fixed or healed. The most common question I get from strangers on the street is either "Do you need help opening that door?" or some version of "What's wrong with you?" It's nice to know that in at least one person's perspective, the answer to that last question was "Nothing."

CHAPTER 14

The Most Magical Life on Earth

"You guys wanna come with me to drop off Papa?" my mom asked one Wednesday afternoon in October 1997. "I haven't seen the new airport yet," she continued, "but apparently on the floor there's a map of the entire city of Buffalo!"

"Wow!" I exclaimed, completely sold. "Yeah, I'll go!"

My brother just shrugged. He was fourteen and had fully embraced the apathy of adolescence, but I still had a month before all my childish excitement expired on my thirteenth birthday and soured into teenage cynicism.

"You guys haven't seen your grandpa in a while and I'm sure he'd like to spend some time with you."

"Can't we just do that at, you know, NOT an airport?" Brad asked.

"Come on!" I pleaded with him, determined not to miss out on that map.

Begrudgingly, my brother obliged and we piled into the car.

We picked up my grandpa and as soon as we pulled up to the US Airways terminal, I rushed inside the doors of the newly erected Buffalo Niagara International Airport, all the while looking down. I was disappointed to find that the stone floors were merely covered by colored lines with the names of a few streets and not the comprehensive topographical representation of my neighborhood I'd anticipated.

"Where's Parkwood?" I asked my mom, hoping to locate the exact spot where our house would be.

"I don't think Kenmore's on here," she said, "just downtown Buffalo."

"Oh," I said, putting on a brave face, but thinking, *Then why the heck did you drag me all the way down here?*

Just as I was ready to write off the trip as a bust, my grandpa casually asked my mom, "Susie, would you and the boys wanna come with me to DC? You know, just to stay in the hotel room and see some sights?"

Oh my gosh! My grandpa was not only suggesting that we take a completely unplanned, spontaneous vacation, but he was asking us to come with him to *Washington, DC*. Having just learned about it in history class, I couldn't think of any more exciting place to go than the home of the Vietnam Memorial. "Can we go, Mom?!"

Even my despondent brother couldn't hide a glimmer of enthusiasm. "Yeah, can we?"

I was sure my mom would never go for it, but to my shock she said, "If you both promise to do your homework the minute we get back and not complain once, then I don't see why not."

"I can't believe this is happening!" I marveled. "Do you know anyone who died in Vietnam, Mom?"

"Nope."

"That's okay," I said. "It'll still be fun," and we boarded the night flight to DC.

This had to be the best trip to the airport ever. Not only did we get to skip school, but we'd be staying in a hotel that probably had HBO, a pool, and a snack machine. Life couldn't get any better than this.

But when we landed at Dulles International Airport, I was surprised to hear a familiar voice from behind me say, "Hey!"

As I turned around, my eyes didn't believe what they saw. Standing right there in front of me was my uncle Rich, my aunt Terri, and my cousins Corey and Travis. Shocked, I just wondered aloud, "What are you guys doing here?" My aunt was laughing. "Did you read the sign?" she pointed.

"What? What sign?" Then I saw that Corey was holding up a piece of construction paper covered in glitter that read, "Surprise! We're going to Disney World!"

"WHAT?!" I shrieked, my brother stunned to silence.

This masterful plan was inspired by a simple phone call I'd made to my uncle over the summer. My cousins went to Disney World every year, but my mom couldn't afford to take my brother and me on her adjunct professor's salary. Plus, the only thing she likes about theme parks are the benches where you can sit down and rest. But I desperately wanted to go and casually asked my uncle how much I'd need to save up to pay my own way. He didn't give me exact numbers, but I gathered that it was out of my price range.

This early thirteenth birthday present was not just the best surprise I'd experienced to date, but a testament to how committed my family was to creating truly special experiences for one another. You can imagine how a kid who was over the moon at the chance to see the Vietnam Wall would blow a joy gasket when presented with the news that he was going to the Magic Kingdom instead.

For five days I got to be in the most magical place on Earth with my favorite people on Earth. My wheelchair, which was normally the manifestation of all my problems, was, at Disney World, imbued with wondrous properties that allowed us to cut to the front of the lines. I rode Splash Mountain three times in a row with my cousin, and we stayed on the Tower of Terror for back-to-back rides as the other park goers who'd waited in line for hours watched with envy. There were parades, breakfasts with Aladdin and the Genie, and benches as far as the eye could see for my mother to enjoy.

The only problem with Disney World seemed to be that you couldn't live there. I'd have to go back to the real world after this fairy-tale vacation. I'd become a teenager, and if my brother was any indication, being a teenager meant painting your fingernails black and wearing sunglasses regardless of what time of day it was. Twelve is that special age where adulthood no longer feels a lifetime away and your narrow understanding of it allows you to imagine that being a grown-up means you can eat as much ice cream as you want, whenever you want, and ride roller coasters all day, every day. If only there was some way to make Disney World the Real World.

I didn't know that was a legitimate option until January 2004. By then, my concept of adulthood was more realistic but a lot less hopeful. Now nineteen, I wasn't on my way to becoming a professional amusement park guest—instead, I had dropped out of high school, gotten my GED, and was freezing my way through a few classes at the University of Buffalo while keeping my fingers crossed for my transfer application to UT Austin.

As I made my way through the man-made hills of brown snow, enduring gusts of freezing wind, I found a beacon of hope at the student union. I saw two sophomores outfitted with sunnier demeanors than anyone has a right to in February in upstate New York and uniforms I recognized from Disney World. I thought they might be running a raffle for a free trip, so I stopped and struggled to grab a flyer while still wearing my mittens. At the top, it read, "Disney College Program." The words "Disney" and "College" didn't really fit together. They seemed like synonyms for "Vacation Degree" or "Relaxation Doctorate."

"What's the Disney College Program?" I asked one of the students.

"The Disney College Program," she replied, "is a way to earn college credit while you work at Disney World."

At that moment I realized that while God had not healed my legs or brain, he was in fact listening and had answered my prayers in the order that would be the most beneficial for me. After all, if I could walk *before* I worked at Disney World, I wouldn't be able to get to the front of the lines anymore. It was nothing short of a miracle. This opportunity was everything my twelve-year-old self could have possibly wanted and it ticked all the boxes for nineteen-year-old me as well. This was my ticket to get out of Buffalo and away from home for the first time; a four-month retreat fronted by an academic institution requiring absolutely none of the course work and roughly

5 percent of the accountability of your average summer school program. Not only that, but we'd be getting paid *minimum wage* for this! As I was currently making the actual minimum wage of nothing, the prospect of money in any quantity would make me the richest I'd ever been—a king fit for a magic kingdom. There was warm weather and sunny days ahead.

Within a week, I'd set up a meeting with my academic adviser and applied to be a Disney student. I waited for months to hear back and when the large, white envelope finally arrived in the mailbox, my heart jumped in anticipation. This was either an acceptance package or a very lengthy rejection with some party favors thrown in to soften the blow. I read, *We are pleased to inform you that you can now get the hell out of upstate New York, make something of yourself, and start your life of adventure with Mickey, Minnie, and TONS of chicks . . .* Okay, so I may have paraphrased that a bit, but that was the gist.

The spring semester flew by faster than a magic carpet ride and in August 2004, now completely on my own, I flew down to Orlando with my mother, my brother, and my grandpa to start my life as an autonomous young man. During my first foray into independent living, my mom visited three times, and my dad, my grandpa, and my uncle Rich all stopped in twice. Now a grown-up, my breakfast consisted of oatmeal cookies my grandma Sandy made and would send to me every few weeks in a big Tupperware container, and strawberry applesauce, which I'd suck through a straw to avoid my precarious relationship with spoons. Of course, I'd have this morning meal in my closet, because if I ate the cookies in the common area, my roommates would undoubtedly want some and I decided that, despite what you learn in kindergarten, real adults don't share.

I began my tenure at Epcot as the worst employee that Disney World had ever seen, and that's taking into account that I had a roommate who was fired for drinking malt liquor on the job. I was originally assigned a position selling tickets at the park entrance. Though my boss was quick to commend my ability to upsell the customer from a fifty-five-dollar

One-Day Pass to a Five-Day Park Hopper Family Pack, he also noted that, due to my inability to count or even handle money without dropping it, my register never balanced out. So I was transferred to a position where I wouldn't literally lose the company money.

I was given the title of Park Clearer at the World Showcase, a role that made full use of all of my abilities and disabilities. I'd show up to the offices at Epcot at around four p.m. dressed in my uniform—a red shirt covered with flags from around the world and white pants. I'd grab a walkie-talkie and wander around the Disney version of our planet. Epcot was a place where China was represented by golden dragon statues, Germany had girls in dirndls carrying beer steins, and Canada just had people who were nice. For some reason, Norway sold pinwheels and glow sticks. This might seem culturally insensitive, but I'll note here that the employees who worked there were actually natives of the countries they were helping to stereotype. I'm not sure if that makes it better or worse, but as they say in Morocco, "Who cares? There's a belly dancer!"

Part of my duties was park security, which seemed like an odd fit for a guy who twice had to be reminded not to leave the door to his apartment open with the key stuck in the knob, as his keys were also conveniently attached to his wallet. At Disney, "security" meant that I was basically an audience member for a series of concerts, which is why I can brag that I've seen Chubby Checker twelve times, Taylor Dayne eight times, and the one guy who's not dead from the original Temptations six times. Occasionally, a guest would get dehydrated and need to be handed a bottle of water, but mostly my duties were limited to lifting a rope so that guests could get to the viewing area, letting them know where they could buy beer, and consoling them when they realized beer was seven dollars.

The bulk of my job happened after sunset. Every night before they closed the park, there was an epic water, laser, and fireworks display called IllumiNations, which cost Disney fifty thousand dollars every single night. It was the best spectacle I'd ever seen and I got to see it a hundred times. My official role was to man and police one of the five disabled viewing areas around the park. This was something all park clearers had to do, and those who didn't have their own wheelchairs used the company Segways. You'd think I'd be pretty good at this job since the only responsibilities I had were to, again, lift the rope, and make conversations with guests who had canes, scooters, wheelchairs, and walkers. But the fact that my tenure at Epcot didn't saddle Disney World with several multimillion-dollar lawsuits was my main accomplishment.

As a Disney Cast Member, I was tasked with creating magical moments for the guests whenever possible. The easiest way for me to help them pass the time before the fireworks was to distract them with all the gadgets built into my wheelchair. On several occasions when park goers had small children, I'd even let them sit on my lap while I drove in circles. This seemed to be a universally enjoyed experience for my young riders and the adult onlookers alike.

On one occasion though, a particularly hyper seven-year-old yanked the joystick while I was driving and sent us careening into an older gentleman in a Hawaiian shirt and Mickey ears, the brunt of my three-hundred-pound chair slamming into his knees. He was very gracious about it considering that he already used a crutch and I all but ensured he'd be leaving the park with a souvenir wheelchair of his own. He didn't sue or even file a formal complaint. If he had, he might have saved me from committing my worst offense.

As Christmas neared, park attendance soared. My manager worried about the growing crowds and was concerned that able-bodied guests were sneaking into the disabled viewing areas and hindering visitors with disabilities from having a place to watch the fireworks display. Asking someone directly whether or not they are disabled is legally and socially challenging. My boss theorized that, given my own impairments, I'd be particularly well suited to tastefully navigate this sensitive task.

He said, "Just ask them very politely what their disability is if you think they might be trying to sneak in to get a good spot."

That night, at 8:00 p.m., in the viewing area located in Mexico, I spotted just the type of reprehensible lowlifes my boss had warned me about: a family in the disabled viewing area with no wheelchair, no crutches, not even a stroller in sight. Just a mother, a father, and an eight-year-old son sitting on his dad's lap. After overhearing their conversation I could tell that they were from jolly old England and probably didn't respect the guidelines us Americans had put forth in Mexico. Those limey little bastards!

It was a chilly evening, so the kid had cleverly stuffed his arms inside his short-sleeve shirt to keep warm. I'd gained a reputation for being a pushover, but this threesome from across the pond had crossed the line. I went up and exchanged pleasantries, but then my tone shifted and I asked them point-blank, "Excuse me, what exactly is your disability?" The man was clearly taken aback, probably because I'd just caught him red-handed. Indignant, he asked, "Are you serious?"

"Yeah," I shot back, and as soon as I said this, I realized my mistake. The boy, as it turned out, did not have his arms tucked into his shirt to keep warm, because he had no arms at all. Then, glancing downward, I saw what could only be described as an absence of legs. I had just audaciously demanded that a small boy with zero limbs prove beyond a reasonable doubt that he was, in fact, disabled.

These are just two examples of the plethora of poor judgment I exercised while employed by the House of Mouse. Other shining moments include the two times I fell asleep at the entrance to the World Showcase during the morning shift, only to wake up and realize that a handful of guests were wandering the park unsupervised forty minutes before it was officially open.

There were only a couple of jobs I can actually say I excelled at. One was making the guests I didn't run over or inadvertently discriminate against feel very welcome, and the other was diplomatically telling those same guests at the end of the night when the park was closing to get the hell out and have a magical day. That's the main thing a park clearer does. When the fireworks are over, he or she is responsible for escorting all stragglers to the gates and sending them on their way home. Every night I got the unique experience of seeing Disney World completely empty. I was the one responsible for closing down and locking up the most magical place on Earth.

While I may not have been a star employee while I was on the clock, in my leisure time, I was determined to make some personal strides. The Disney apartment complex was named Vista Way but had gained such a reputation as a hookup mecca that it was nicknamed Vista Lay. Rumors were circulating that there was so much sex going on that people had gotten STDs just from swimming in the pool. Ever the hypochondriac, this unpleasant thought prompted me to call my uncle Rich, a pool chemical salesman, to ask him if you can get AIDS from a swimming pool.

"From fucking in pools you can," he replied.

"Oh," I said, relieved, now certain that I didn't have anything to worry about.

All I knew about sex at the time was that I would like to have some. This was my first chance to play the field without parental supervision or personal aides. Unburdened by the experience of the dearth of experience that was to follow, I was optimistic. Every cute girl felt like an opportunity. I was never again gonna get the chance to score with so many real-life versions of cartoon characters I'd found confusingly hot as a boy, so I resolved to make myself the most accessible Prince Charming I could be.

First, I set my sights on a girl named Cherry, who was Hawaiian but had been deemed Chinese-ish-looking enough to play Mulan. That is, until it was decided she was too short to play a princess and was recast as Stitch. Cherry seemed like a promising lead at first. We set up a movie day to watch *Lilo and Stitch* so that she could tell me everything about the film that offended her culture and heritage.

"They make all the characters have stumpy legs and big noses. We don't ALL look like that!" and she showed me her ankle to illustrate how it was decidedly thinner than the ones on-screen. *An ankle! That's basically like seeing a leg*, I thought, *which is basically like seeing her naked! Vista Lay, here I come…*

Moments later, my optimism toward this Hawaiian, sometimes Chinese princess, sometimes blue space alien, was crushed when she casually remarked, "My boyfriend does look like that surfer dude though. So I guess they got some stuff right." After the movie, we bid each other aloha, and unfortunately never hung out again. I recommitted myself to finding a girl at Disney World who didn't already have a boyfriend.

I found exactly that in Allie, a girl I met as she was hopping off the bus from Pleasure Island, which is not, as it sounds, a Disney-themed strip club but rather a boardwalk with bars and shops where adults can unwind and drink after the parks close. On a Friday night, the people who didn't go to Pleasure Island were comprised of the sizable Mormon population and me, as I was the only one who took the program's zero tolerance underage drinking policy seriously.

I was zooming around the parking lot, waiting for the people who had had fun that night to come home and tell me about it. So when a girl bounced up to me covered in glitter and sweat after a hard night of dancing and matter of factly stated, "You look cool, we should hang out," I was more excited than I had any right to be. As I was wearing shorts, knee-high argyle socks, and Velcro shoes at the time, even I thought her assessment of my coolness was a stretch, but who was I to argue? Allie introduced herself and scrawled her number out on my arm and I called her the next night to see if she wanted to hang out in an environment I considered subtly romantic— a hot tub. Never mind that the hot tub at Vista Way was so heavily chlorinated it could burn the skin off an elephant, because that's a small price to pay for STD protection.

Even though I brush-burned everything from my chin to my testicles getting into the Jacuzzi, it still felt like a sexy place to talk. I was only able to say about three words to Allie before the jets knocked me off balance and I gulped down roughly a gallon of water. When my lungs recovered, I wanted to make sure that I wouldn't be competing with another sculpted expert surfer or anything like that. But I had to be coy about it. I didn't want Allie thinking I only thought she was cool because she was a girl I could potentially hook up with. (If I'm being completely honest, there was about a sixty-forty split between my being a horny teenager and my just wanting to make friends.) So I phrased my question in the most delicate, round-about way I could think of.

"So, uh, my roommate actually came here with his girl-friend, and he really regrets it now 'cause there's so many girls here he'd like to, ya know, explore things with."

"I know," she said, "it's crazy."

Feeling I'd adequately masked my true intentions, I meekly inquired, "Do you have a boyfriend back home?"

She sort of smiled and stayed quiet for a minute. Choosing her words carefully, she began, "We don't know each other very well, but I like you, so I don't have any problem telling you this, but . . ."

Go on . . . , I thought. I felt like I was an Oscar nominee waiting for his name to be called. There were so many things that could have followed that "but."

But . . . I'm really attracted to you.

But . . . I've never had a boyfriend and I want you to be the first.

But . . . I can only climax if my partner is dressed as Chewbacca.

So many ways that that one sentence could open A Whole New World™ of possibility.

But what she actually said was, "I don't have any problem telling you this, but I like women."

It took a second for me to realize that I had just become the Leonardo DiCaprio of the Hot Tub Academy Awards. I wasn't Allie's type of guy because Allie's type of guy didn't exist. I didn't know much about courtship, but what I did know is that you can't bring a Nintendo Wii remote to an Xbox tournament. So Allie and I just stayed friends. And she was almost a hip enough girl to make me regret having a penis.

What I lacked in game I gained in basic life skills. I spent entire days sorting through the intricacies of doing laundry and putting clothes on hangers so they wouldn't wrinkle. I didn't have a fitness regimen at the time, but I worked up a sweat when I spent five hours struggling to put a fitted sheet on my bed. Sure, I could have asked a roommate to help, but I wanted to prove to myself that I could live independently so long as my only responsibilities were to wear clean clothes, make a bed, and shower afterward.

I had gone through my life feeling like the most inept and underprepared human being in the world, but as it turned out, I wasn't even the most inept human being at Disney World. I was encouraged when I saw a twenty-year-old girl with no physical disabilities (and all of her limbs, because I checked for that now) stuffing two months' worth of laundry into one washing machine and dumping half a container of detergent on top of the explosive mess. The washer bucked like a bronco and frothed like a middle school baking soda volcano. Perhaps there were worse things than taking forty-five minutes to fold a shirt. Even if I wasn't maturing sexually, domestically I was making progress.

Vista Way never lived up to its nickname for me, despite several more attempts. I hadn't gotten laid, but at least I hadn't gotten fired. During my short time in Orlando, I was able to fulfill the dream of a twelve-year-old and come into my own as a twenty-year-old with a job, a home, and the ability to ride Rock 'n' Roller Coaster ten times in a row on a single day. I made friends, money, and personal strides that bolstered my confidence about the next chapter I'd be starting at the University of Texas at Austin.

I knew as I was leaving Disney World that I had a long way left to go on the road to adulthood. But unlike in Disney films, you can't just wave a wand or try on a slipper and have your dreams come true. In real life, magic takes time. Sometimes it takes so long, you start to doubt it even exists. Romance, just like a pixie fairy, will die if you don't believe in it.

The decade between the Disney College Program and my next milestone with the Magic Kingdom gave me little reason to hope that Tinker Bell could be resuscitated. And by Tinker Bell, I mean, of course, my love life. Over those ten years, my quest for intimacy led me all the way from the comfort of the Olive Garden to the extreme discomfort of a bathroom floor and a ball shaver. But in the end, my first romantic connection still happened among roller coasters, spinning teacups, and Winnie the Pooh.

✧

Gillian Grassie came into my life the way most meaningful relationships do these days—via Twitter. It was June 15, 2013, and I was gearing up to move to Los Angeles to begin working on *Have a Little Faith*. I sent out a tweet to announce the move and jump-start my social life on the West Coast. Among the replies of "Good Luck!" and "If you ever come back to Austin, we need to hang!" there was one tweet that stood out because it included an invitation to Europe.

Gillian Grassie: *@Zachanner LA's a lucky city—come to Berlin! Love your show, love your humor.*

I had a fan base now that was filled with girls who explicitly stated that they would like to date and/or marry me. Having given up on actual dating, these 140 character propositions made me feel wanted without requiring me to take any emotional risk or even close down my game of Words with Friends. As I did anytime a girl tweeted at me, I clicked on her avatar to see if she was cute and saw a picture of a girl with curly blond hair, a pop of red lipstick, and a pair of piercing brown eyes that were somehow sexy without being cold. She looked kind of like a young Drew Barrymore, the same one who'd graced the cover of the first *Playboy* I ever saw. Jackpot! Her profile only got better from there. Not only was she attractive, but she described herself as an "indie harpist-singer-songwriter, polyglot wannabe, reluctant nomad." I was intrigued both by the harp and by the word "polyglot," which I didn't recognize, so I followed the link to her Web site.

What I saw there—or more accurately, what I heard—made me giddier than a techie geeking out over Apple's new iSandwich on release day. Her music wasn't the Celtic ballads about fair maidens from long ago that I'd expected from a harpist, but instead soulful songs that told stories and made me want to know the person behind them. When she sang about traveling the globe, she made me want to hit the road again; when she sang about death, I was compelled to examine my own mortality; and when she sang about lovers, she made me wish that I was one of them. And then there was her voice itself—sweet and just a touch smoky in a way that was undeniably seductive. I could have listened to this woman sing prefab furniture instructions for hours.

After streaming three songs, I was inspired to do something that only twelve people have done in the past decade—buy music. I downloaded both of her albums and her EP on iTunes and spent the day listening to my new favorite artist on my bedroom floor. By the time I replied to her tweet, I was in complete fan-girl mode.

Zach Anner: *@gilliangrassie Thnx but I'd only go to Berlin if there was an amazing singer/songwriter who played harp & had 3 albums I just got on iTunes.*

Zach Anner: *@gilliangrassie And we BOTH know the chances of that happening are pretty sli . . . yeah, I'll start lookin' at flights.*

We exchanged ten encouraging tweets over the course of twenty-four hours, which is a record for me. I desperately wanted to get to know this girl better without having to type in short, very public bursts. I needed a way to transition off of social media and just become social. If I was going to build a friendship with her, it had to happen organically. So I stalked the shit out of Gillian online, methodically mining for a casual way to continue our correspondence. Fate rewarded my creepiness when, buried in some of her recorded onstage banter, she revealed that she was a Quaker and was possibly single. I was in the middle of preproduction for *Have a Little Faith* and as luck would have it, Quakerism was one of the religions we planned to profile. So I posted this carefully crafted status update on my Facebook fan page: *I'm gonna be a Quaker! I'll explain later . . .*

Then I waited, and waited, and finally she took the bait.

Gillian Grassie: *Wait, really? I'm Quaker, you know, if you need fact-checking for your sketch or what have you.*

With that, we had an excuse to graduate from Twitter and Facebook to Skype. In our first face-to-face video chat, I asked her a few token questions about Quakerism that were designed to make sure she wasn't an Amish person who was saving herself for a carpenter named Eli, because I really didn't know anything about Quakers. The fact that our entire budding friendship was a result of technology should have tipped me off that she wasn't Amish, but I had to double-check. Thankfully, Quakers, as I've come to know them, are more similar to hippies than the Pennsylvania Dutch.

Whenever I Skyped with Gillian over the next few months, the conversations were so natural that it felt like we'd known each other for years. We both loved to travel and meet new people, and shared a sense of wonder and excitement about the world. Other than those things though, we were completely different. She had European sensibilities and the sheer amount of soda I drank made it imperative that I live in a country with free refills. I speak in mostly '90s movie quotes whereas Gillian grew up without a television on a farm in Pennsylvania and misses nearly every pop culture reference I make. Her childhood was filled with books and animals, and my youth was spent playing video games, watching cartoons, and being terrified of all living things. She played in tree houses and I played in couch forts. We came from two different worlds but did our best to meet in the middle. I introduced her to films like *Up* and *It's a Wonderful Life* while she in turn suggested I read Jorge Luis Borges and David Foster Wallace. When I told her that my lazy eye prohibited me from enjoying books, within a few days I had an MP3 of Gillian reading aloud from *The Library of Babel* and *A Supposedly Fun Thing I'll Never Do Again*. All the differences between us made our exchanges more exciting, and we both agreed that we'd love to meet each other in person someday.

Someday came in October, when Gillian returned to the United States for a tour. Conveniently, a date was set for a house concert in the Hollywood Hills, like, *right* below the Hollywood sign. Watching her at that show had me smitten all over again. Unfortunately, she had seventy-five other adoring fans to attend to, so we didn't get to talk much, but she reassured me, "I really wanna hang out with you, but I'm kind of in work mode right now. Are you free at all tomorrow?" We made plans for the next night.

We went out to dinner and I was so comfortable with her that I actually ate two slices of pizza. I still had that rule to never eat when I'm out with anyone other than family and very close friends, but Gillian was special. She felt like a different kind of friend than I'd ever had before. I couldn't exactly put my finger on it. What was this?

I later found out that when I took her to dinner and we ended the evening in a Jacuzzi making plans to someday go to Disneyland together, Gillian had defined this as a very nice first date. However, my ridiculous inner narrative at the time was something more along the lines of *It looks like a date, it feels like a date . . . best not to make a move and find out it isn't a date. I'll just send her along with my USB car charger so her phone doesn't die on the way to San Francisco. That's what gentlemen do!*

Once again, it didn't register that a girl I wanted to be romantically involved with had been flirting with me all night and was waiting for a kiss. All I needed was a subtle hint that she felt the same way I did. But when Gillian stayed in Los Angeles an extra night just so we could spend more time together and suggested we watch a movie on the couch, I thought that was still a little ambiguous. So I took her out for ice cream instead. I didn't put two and two together until Gillian was back in Berlin. I was asking her for dating advice over Skype and she said, "Well, that's kind of tricky because I could probably give you some really good friendly advice—but *I'd* actually really like to date you."

That was all I needed. An explicit declaration that the girl I had a crush on would like to go out with me. I would have preferred it signed and notarized, but I guessed I'd have to take her word for it. Having completely blown my first opportunity, Gillian graciously arranged another trip to LA in February so that we could try again. I spent most of my days leading up to this redo texting or video chatting with her, frantically trying to lower her expectations of my dateability. We talked through every potential disaster scenario and finally, after countless hours of correspondence, I worked up the courage to suggest that Gillian stay with me. I was a little worried about cohabitating with a girl because I spent 90 percent of the time in my apartment in my underwear or less. We didn't really know if we'd have any chemistry, but for once in my life, I thought that it was worth the risk to find out. We both took a leap of faith.

To cut down on the potential awkwardness, we took precautionary measures to ensure that if things fizzled romantically, we'd still have a graceful exit strategy with an opportunity to salvage the friendship: we made sure that we had some work to do in town independent of each other and planned some activities together where it would be almost impossible not to have fun. At the top of both of our lists was going to Disneyland. I'd never been there before, but Gillian had never been to *any* Disney park, and she was twenty-eight. To me, this was almost as unbelievable as my being a twenty-nine-year-old virgin was to her. How could someone who'd traveled around the world with a harp on her back still have never heard of Space Mountain? I reasoned that, much like sex, Disney theme parks are a life experience that everyone should have before thirty.

Before we actually took the drive to Anaheim, we'd had a few days in Southern California to bond over a lot more than Mickey Mouse. Things went so well that we were sleeping in the same bed the first night. The only problem was that the bed folded into a couch by day and was located in my apartment's living room, while Brad slept in the sole bedroom. If I'd known that I'd be having a girl come stay with me for two weeks, I probably wouldn't have agreed to set up my bed in a space with zero privacy, and Brad probably would have gotten some better noise-canceling headphones. So the night before our amusement park adventure, Gillian was as excited to see Disneyland as I was to check into a hotel room at Disneyland with a girl I adored, knowing that the most fun we'd have would be after we left the park.

We giddily sorted through all of Disneyland's attractions, prioritizing them in order of Most Fun all the way down to Haunted Mansion. Gillian naturally gravitated toward the iconic and nostalgic experience that no Disneyland guest can leave the park without doing at least once—hugging a pigmy goat. That's why you see so many people walking around with goat ears, if you've ever wondered. Also, albeit lower on her list, was Splash Mountain, Tower of Terror, the Matterhorn, California Screamin', and the Ferris wheel.

With our itinerary set, we headed out early on a brisk and sunny February morning, fully prepped with contraband snacks stuffed into the back of my wheelchair. It was only a forty-five-minute drive, but it was a special one because, for the first time in twenty-nine years, the person sitting next to me in the driver's seat was my date, holding my hand and wearing my shirt. It wasn't long before we drove my refrigerator masquerading as a minivan to the entrance of the park.

Our first stop was guest services to get our Disability Fast Pass* where we were greeted by the least enthusiastic Disney Cast Member in the history of the Magic Kingdom. He seemed less like an ambassador to the most magical place on Earth and more like a window treatment salesman who had just lost his job. In a downtrodden monotone, he Eeyored his

---

*Rules had gotten much stricter since my time at the College Program because there had been a big scandal where able-bodied guests were hiring disabled people to get them to the front of the lines. I'd express outrage at this, except if I'd been aware of this extra source of income and free trips to Disney, I totally would have exploited myself in a heartbeat.

way through the epic list of wondrous Disney attractions that were currently closed.

"We wanna ride Splash Mountain first!" we enthused.

"Splash Mountain is down for maintenance. Are you still gonna be here on the ninth of March? You could always come back."

"Aww . . . that's okay, we'll just ride Soarin' first," we said, determined not be heartbroken.

"Soarin' is also down for repair."

"What about Thunder Mountain?" I asked, exasperated.

"That's closed too."

I looked at Gillian apologetically, embarrassed that this was her first Disney experience, and said, "Well, at least there's A Small World—that's a classic!"

". . . which is also closed," he said, as if deliberately deflating a small child's last birthday balloon.

"You sonofabitch!" I burst out, only half joking. "Well, what is open?"

He shrugged and then handed us a map and showed us several routes that wouldn't ultimately lead to disappointment.

Even though Splash Mountain was closed, there was still one water attraction that caught Gillian's eye—the Grizzly River Run, a flume meant to simulate white-water rafting in one of those big, round, tire things. I was wearing my red Gillian Grassie merch shirt and as we got settled into our raft, we were surprised to see eight people all wearing red T-shirts ushered in behind us. It was a group of adults with learning disabilities and their caretakers on a field trip. We were all ready to get a little wet and have a great time. But the ride wasn't the light misting I'd anticipated. That raft had it out for Gillian and me. Every dip and turn drenched us, and every man-made waterfall poured buckets of freezing cold, chlorinated water directly on our heads, and only *our* heads. I was soaked from my scalp all the way down to my regrettably suede shoes, while the rest of our bone-dry raft mates giggled and screamed with glee.

As the raft finally slowed and we made our way to the disembarking area, I was laughing but very much ready to end this frigid onslaught and change into the warm, dry clothes I'd neglected to bring. My teeth were chattering, my skin was covered in goose bumps, my T-shirt clung to my skin like body paint, and my nipples were in fight-or-flight mode, ready to jump off my chest. To my horror, the Disney Cast Member on dry land asked, "Do you guys want to go again?" Eight-tenths of our raft shouted, "Yes!"

I was just sitting there shivering like Jack Dawson at the end of *Titanic*, so Gillian asked on my behalf if we could exit the raft before the next round.

"Sorry, the whole group has to either ride or get out."

I looked around at the eager, happy faces awaiting my decision and I couldn't do anything but say yes, I would like to be cold, wet, and miserable for another ten minutes please. So we endured the entire monsoon again, and again no one else on the raft got wet. When the perky Disney employee proposed a third ride, I staunchly caved, ensuring that both Gillian and I would spend the rest of our romantic day at Disneyland as waterlogged human sponges. But borderline hypothermia was no match for the happiness I felt. We made it to Space Mountain, the Tower of Terror, the Matterhorn, and California Screamin'.

The entire day felt like a romantic comedy with the typical gender roles reversed. When I struggled to lift myself into a roller-coaster seat, Gillian was the one to hoist me up and ensure that I didn't ride it backward with my legs in the air. And as she helped me into the passenger seat of the go-cart in Autopia, I tripped her and then fell on top of her in a manner befitting a Meg Ryan and Tom Hanks movie, except my Tom Hanks was way cuter. Even the person who operated the ride couldn't resist giggling with us.

But the best ride of the day was not one I was on, but the one I was giving. In an effort to take advantage of both our Fast Pass and our body heat (since we were both still sopping wet from the Grizzly River Run), Gillian sat on my lap as we zoomed from site to site. In all my years, I'd never had a better companion to an amusement park.

At the end of the day we headed back to the hotel, and because we were still soaking wet, the first thing we did was strip off our clothes, more out of survival than any sexy impulse. This simple disrobing would have sent me into a spiral of self-doubt if I had been with anyone else. But there I was, in my birthday suit, in front of a woman, and it felt like no big deal. We didn't automatically come together in some passionate embrace; instead we just hung out naked and ordered in Thai food, with Gillian only putting on a robe so she could tip the deliveryman. Stretched out on the floor, we had dinner together and just talked about what we were going to do in the park the next day. We had to see those goats! But that night, there were other things we had to do.

To say that I'd been anxious about my inexperience would have been an understatement. For most of my life, my body felt like something that was disguising my true identity, but with Gillian, I was able to accept it as an extension of myself. Gillian knew I was a novice, and a virgin, and she was the first girl I'd felt comfortable enough to speak candidly with about that.

She had to teach me everything, but her advice came with kindness, warmth, and a bit of good-natured humor. There wasn't even the slightest hint of judgment. When we kissed, she gently corrected my technique, whispering, "Just close your mouth a little," which I did, and then we carried on. She didn't laugh at me or storm out of the room, we just worked through it step by step, kiss by kiss.

The first time we had sex presented unexplored territory for both of us. My body did things I never expected it to do and couldn't explain, and, despite making a living as a communicator, all I said for feedback at first was the word "okay," meaning both "slow down, I'm not sure about this" AND "keep going," depending on the context. Gillian encouraged me to employ less ambiguous words like "stop" or "that feels good." I was still nervous about doing almost everything wrong, but somehow, as I tried not to make out with her like a velociraptor eating its prey, I still felt safe enough to be bold.

When it was over, I didn't, as I had always imagined, call Andrew and text all my friends. This wasn't something to brag about or check off a list. It was a first step.

Since I've come into the public eye, the most discouraging sentiment I hear echoed from people with disabilities is that they have given up hope on finding love or a partner. As somebody who has stared into that lonely future and, against all evidence, refused to accept it as inevitable, I can tell you that it doesn't have to be that way.

On that night with Gillian, I realized that the years I'd wasted being too afraid to try things and fail were my only true failing. My mistake had been to label my body a burden rather than a tool. I'd accepted long ago that what I brought to the table was unacceptable. But being with Gillian on that unassuming bed at the Extended Stay America showed me what physical intimacy is really about. It's not about "getting it right" or "doing it well" but rather listening and learning.

I'd operated under the preposterous assumption that since I didn't know anything, I wasn't ready to learn anything. All that had done was ensure that I'd missed out on a sexual education and was consequently figuring out how my own body worked at the same time that my partner was. We had a lot of fun learning together, but my experience that night made me wish that I'd had a whole lot more fun to draw on. I wished I'd taken more chances so that when this beautiful person came into my life, our time together would have been less about navigating through all the emotions and trials of my first relationship and more about growing congruently as a couple. I was extremely grateful that my first time was spent with such an amazing individual, but also thought to myself, *God, I wasted a lot of time being scared of this.*

All the mistakes that I was terrified of making, I made with Gillian, and to my surprise, it felt fine. I always thought that once I had sex, there would be this great change, some sort of enlightenment, but the only thing that became clearer to me afterward was what a fool I'd been for not thinking myself worthy of love before I had it. Rather than describe the evening in some lurid *Fifty Shades of Gimp* detail, I'll just say that it was everything I'd hoped for and nothing I expected. The rest I'll keep for just Gillian and me.

By no grand design, the times when my life has crossed paths with Disney have been less about staying young and more about growing up. Sometimes life surprises us and a trip to Disney World will fall from the sky. But more often, we have to make our own magic, and to get there, we have to be willing to make mistakes. The key to moving forward is not pretending that you've got it all figured out but rather admitting that, like everyone else, you're a work in progress. There are so many things worth leaving Neverland for. Real things. Seeing the world beyond your hometown, taking your first job in which people actually depend on you, and going outside of your comfort zone just to let someone else in, and getting close enough to hear them say, "I love you."

CHAPTER 15

Game Changer

I was a born athlete. It was obvious just by looking at me that I was headed for Olympic gold. Compared to me Tiger Woods was merely a mini-golf master, Michael Jordan would have had better luck if he'd stayed in baseball, and Michael Phelps was like a Labrador retrieving tennis balls in a swamp. Or at least that was the gist of how my adaptive PE teacher, Colleen Fatta, must have felt about me.

In fourth grade the list of things I couldn't do was about a thousand times longer than the list of things I could. If I were just to name a few of my encyclopedic inabilities, they would include such impossible feats as making a sandwich, eating a sandwich without wearing a sandwich, and tying my shoes. Without a doubt, the most embarrassing of my ineptitudes could be summed up by the phrase, "Behind every great man there is a great woman." In my case that great woman was a personal aide holding me up at the urinal, making sure I didn't pee on myself.

Occasionally other boys would come into the bathroom ready to let loose and instead found themselves being quizzed by a forty-five-year-old woman on whether or not they had completed their math homework. I, however, always played it cool and said something like "Hey man, what's up?" as I pulled down my sweatpants, exposing my bare ass to the breeze.

This daily ritual seemed like a better reason than any diagnosed medical ailment to excuse me from participating in athletic activities. Wouldn't it have made sense for a doctor to just write that on a note? *Zach is excused from gym class because he can only urinate with his pants down and a middle-aged lady behind him. P.S. He's also in a wheelchair.*

My other teachers seemed to understand this. In art class, if we were supposed to draw trees, I would inevitably wind up with something that looked like Oscar the Grouch if he'd

stepped on a land mine. I'd struggle to draw the branches and the roots until the masterpiece was finished, which was usually when I dropped my crayons. Instead of alerting the teacher, I simply took it as a sign that art had a life of its own. With five minutes left in class, my art teacher, Mr. Pufpaff, would come around to my desk, see the blobs of colors I called trees, and say something like "Here, let me help you." Without exception, by the end of the period, I'd have a beautiful drawing of a tree that was done by the teacher, but *inspired*, and signed, by me.

This was what it meant to be the first kid with a disability to be mainstreamed into my public school system. Without my parents' relentless insistence, I would have either been placed in special ed classes or sent to another school altogether. The only reason I wasn't held back in special ed kindergarten for another year was my mother's absolute refusal to accept that as her son's only viable academic path. While her fierce advocacy ensured that I would be among the other kids, inclusion was still something nobody had quite figured out.

In music class, while the rest of the students learned to play the recorder, my complete lack of fine motor skills made it impossible for me to master the intricacies of "Hot Cross Buns." So I was outfitted with a triangle instead. Luckily, twenty poorly played recorders can easily drown out the sound of one completely a-rhythmic triangle.

My participation in gym class required an asinine amount of accommodations. I had no depth perception because of a botched eye operation, so I didn't know a ball was being thrown to me until it hit me in the face. At the age of nine, I spoke with a voice so high, it'd make Minnie Mouse sound like Barry White. But if puberty had taken its cue from the countless balls I dropped in gym class, I would've been able to convincingly perform "Old Man River" in some racially oblivious production of *Showboat*.

I have never seen more dumbfounded looks than the ones on the faces of my gym teachers during their futile attempts to include me in the high jump. The height at which I could leap out of my wheelchair was a towering zero inches, so while the rest of the children catapulted themselves over the bar, I was allowed to pass under it while throwing my fists up into the air as if I were breaking tape at a marathon.

When my classmates were required to run around the gym for the period, Mr. Marquardt outfitted me with a whistle to blow at the end of every lap. I exploited this power by blowing into the whistle whenever I wanted to. Sometimes I would purse my lips ever so softly, so that half the class would stop and half would stay in motion. This was what taught me the important life lesson that authority without the skill to back it up is just as fun as (and much easier than) earning your place in the world. However, if I was going to learn anything other than how to be a prick, it was clear that I'd need some help.

Believe it or not, even though I enjoyed being a jerk, I *longed* to play sports and compete like everybody else. I just didn't want to make the necessary effort to do so. Halfway through the year it was determined by my fourth-grade teacher and the man with the big whistle that I needed adaptive PE. This meant that one of my gym classes per week would be spent in an individual setting so that the shame of my wussiness could be scoffed at in private. I was told that we would work on things like shooting baskets, throwing footballs, and even walking so my legs wouldn't look like swizzle sticks.

These were activities I wanted to do in theory, but the

idea of being separated from the rest of the class and having another adult ride my ass was disheartening. I was already an outcast who was taken out of class for physical therapy and occupational therapy throughout the day and now I needed *gym* therapy? Next they were going to tell me that my contribution to "Hot Cross Buns" was not welcome and that my blobs were not trees! And who decided that whistle blowing was not a sport?

So when an energetic, petite, and perky strawberry blond thirtysomething named Mrs. Fatta came up to me dribbling a basketball with each hand and telling me I was going to learn how to shoot baskets, I was suspicious . . . yet intrigued. She said, "Show me how you normally would shoot," and I positioned myself at the three-point line. She raised her eyebrows and said, "You sure you don't want to move a little closer?"

"No, I got it," I insisted, as I lifted my arms over my head and hurled the ball at the basket. Looking up and listening for the swish, I jumped as the ball came crashing down on my feet. With all of my strength and determination at work, the only thing I'd managed to do with a basketball was injure myself and my pride. Nursing my ego and toes, I took her advice and moved a little closer . . . and then a little closer still, until I was directly underneath the basket. If she had been physically able to do so, I'm sure she would've lifted me up onto her shoulders and had me place the ball in the net—just to keep up my morale! I knew I was disabled, but I honestly had no idea that I'd be THAT terrible. I'd seen *dogs* play better basketball. (*Air Bud* is the greatest documentary of all time, amirite?)

It was obvious that this, meaning I, was a lost cause. I would've thrown in the towel if I didn't think it would just get caught in my tires. This humiliation was bad enough shared between two people, but what I didn't know was that Mrs. Fatta would be overseeing ALL of my gym classes and making adjustments so that I could "compete" with my peers.

It was always my goal to never be pitied by anyone and Mrs. Fatta made sure of that. Though my athletic prowess was undeniably pitiful, the special rules she created in an attempt to level the playing field between me and my classmates caused me to be despised rather than pitied.

In basketball, instead of a net, I was allowed to score by tossing the ball into a trash can (which is where I thought it belonged anyway). Typically, the rule in baseball is three strikes and you're out, but in my case it was three strikes and . . . let's give it six more tries. Eventually, Mrs. Fatta would just gently loft the ball onto my bat from three feet away. During football, if the quarterback had mistakenly thrown the ball at me while I was peacefully bird-watching and the pigskin so much as brushed my front wheel, Mrs. Fatta would blow her whistle, rush onto the field, and hand me the ball. She would then proclaim, "It touched his wheelchair, that means he caught it." "Caught what?" I'd ask, noticing a blue jay. "The ball," she'd insist, and then the play would continue as if it were in the realm of possibility for me to actually catch a ball.

Unfortunately for the other team, though every accommodation had been made on MY behalf, none was made on theirs. A reception by me meant that in order to be stopped, I would have to be tackled—a task that would require more brute strength than five sixty-pound fourth graders could muster, since I raced past them not on legs but atop two hundred pounds of electrified steel. When I inevitably zipped into the end zone and my flailing opposition derided me with cries of "motorized fag," I muttered "douche bag" under my breath like a true sportsman, and shrugged off this sham by spiking the ball victoriously. This was a triumph for affirmative action that in no small way changed one fourth-grade class's perception of the disabled from meek and helpless invalids to entitled cheating assholes.

Though Mrs. Fatta and her aggressive support had made it possible for me to be a participant rather than a spectator, her work did little to increase my self-confidence. When she was there, she'd do everything to make sure I could contribute to a team effort, regardless of how embarrassed and emasculated her adaptations made me feel. Hockey was particularly excruciating because I couldn't go five feet without running over the stick. Though I chased after the puck, it wouldn't have done any good even if I'd gotten to it because at no point did my blade ever touch the floor. But without fail, whenever I came anywhere near it, Mrs. Fatta would blow her whistle and make everyone else clear away so that I could either touch the puck for a split second or run over it with my wheelchair.

One day, after a brutally demoralizing match, I couldn't take it anymore. In frustration, I shouted what everybody already knew: "This is ridiculous! I can't play!" I threw the stick on the ground and sat out the rest of the game thinking, *I used to be somebody, I used to have a whistle! That was something I was good at! Whistling, sitting, thinking, and tandem urinating.*

Afterward Mrs. Fatta came up to me and said, "What was that? Haven't you heard the expression, it's not whether you win or lose, it's how you play the game?"

"Well, that's not playing, that's cheating and I still suck! Why should I have to do something I have no chance at being good at?" I sulked.

"Because if you quit, you'll never know if you could be good or not," she countered.

What does she know, I thought. *I'm not an athlete. I didn't decide that; God decided that.* In my mind this woman was so stubborn she would've given Stevie Wonder golfing lessons. I thought I should just quit school and become a mattress tester, or one of those living mannequins in storefronts, or a guy who posed for photos in the 1860s—one movement every fifteen minutes sounded just about right to me!

So the next week when we switched from hockey to handball, I was all but optimistic. I'd been so devalued that it had been decided that any team captain who was foolish enough to pick me would get my best friend, Andrew, as well. I was part of a two-for-one special that no smart shopper would touch. When the choices dwindled, I finally made it onto a team, but I dreaded the certain humiliation Mrs. Fatta had cooked up in her palsy playbook.

But as the game began and I prepared to be dishonored and disgraced, something unexpected happened. A ball was thrown to me and I actually caught it. Not caught in the sense that it was thrown in my general direction and touched my chair—I actually caught it. I'd like to think it was because Mrs. Fatta's speech had struck a chord and awoken a competitive spirit in me, but it's more likely because the ball itself was so big and squishy that a cucumber in a coma could have caught it. Whatever it was, from that moment on, that little bit of encouragement propelled me through the whole game to play harder than I'd ever played.

With two minutes 'til lunch, we found ourselves in a tie game and my friend Andrew tossed me the ball. *Oh my God, I caught it,* I thought, dropping it. I heard a familiar piercing whistle and the rustle of windbreaker pants as Mrs. Fatta came to meet me on the court. *Damn it,* I thought. *I should have left after that first catch. Just taken a bow and quit while I was ahead.* But as she handed me the ball, she told me to do something, "Take a shot," and I noticed that I was directly in front of the goal. I suddenly realized that all those castrating concessions she'd made throughout the year were because she wanted me to meet her halfway and make an effort. So I cocked my arm and launched the ball forward with all the force and fury I could muster.

I didn't see it go in. All I saw was the disgust on the goalie's face as he realized he'd been beaten by quite possibly the worst athlete ever to grace the fourth grade. (I won't name him for fear that, upon reading this and discovering the truth, his wife would leave him and his family would disown him.) My team won the game, but for me it was a much bigger victory; I had won this day because I had chosen to play instead of giving in to my suckiness. And that's what Mrs. Fatta was trying to drive home all along—that the only way to win is to first find any way to put yourself in the game.

Over the next six years, Mrs. Fatta remained my adaptive PE teacher. During our time together, I got to compete in the New York State Games, which are like statewide Special Olympics, where I received eight gold medals (for participation). In honor of the 1996 Summer Olympic Games, Mrs. Fatta had me do a metaphorical trek from Buffalo to Atlanta in my walker over the course of the entire school year, where distance was measured on a peculiar scale of ten miles per lap around the gym. She also took me on several field trips to Holiday Valley for their adaptive downhill skiing program, which I enjoyed so much that I didn't even notice the time my trainer took a spill and I accidentally dragged his tethered body down the slope.

Mrs. Fatta made all of those experiences possible. I appreciated them, but not enough at the time. One day in 2001, after my family had moved districts and I'd dropped out of high school, I got a somber call from Andrew, who told me that he'd learned at school that Mrs. Fatta had been diagnosed with a brain tumor. Her prognosis had been grim and, during an attempt to remove the tumor, she died on the operating table at the age of forty-one.

Her funeral was so beautiful, and the things that were said about her were so lovely, that one of my other teachers absentmindedly referred to it as a wedding. Afterward, there was a reception held at my old high school. I didn't know what to say to her daughter and the only thing I managed to get out to Mrs. Fatta's husband was "I'm so sorry. She always made me feel like I was part of the game."

She had done that for so many people. She was the only adaptive PE teacher in the whole district, after all, and to this day, her impact is not lost on me. In the years since, I haven't gotten any better at sports, but I have gotten a lot better at trying them. On *Rollin' with Zach* I fell off surfboards, flew off water skis, and got yanked up mountains by my balls while rock climbing. Those physical feats were often painted as more successful and inspirational than I was comfortable with, but when I was coming up with ideas for my YouTube channel I found myself in the altogether unlikely role of personal trainer for a comedy fitness and sports show called *Workout Wednesday*. In that series, I'm still fundamentally the same person I was in fourth grade, at least as far as my athletic abilities are concerned. I'm just outfitted with a better attitude now. So I've been able to encourage myself and my audience to be good sports at the sports we're not good at. I've swum, walked, slid off a treadmill, duct-taped my feet to a stationary bike, and even ridden a mechanical bull.

In highlighting everything that made me feel like I was a failure and an outcast in elementary school, I somehow managed to produce my most successful and widely appreciated work to date. The Gregory Brothers even songified one of my episodes into an insanely catchy dance-anthem called "Lo Lo Lo Lo Lohan." Seriously, you can check it out on iTunes! With *Workout Wednesday,* I've finally found a vehicle in which I can be funny, positive, and self-deprecating at the same time. I get as many messages from people laughing at my ridiculous one-liners as I do from viewers who are genuinely inspired to start getting in shape. I'm still the worst player, but that doesn't mean I can't be the best cheerleader.

In one episode, called "Your Best Shot," I try to shoot baskets, missing dozens of times, but moving closer and closer, until I finally find the net, exclaiming to the camera, "See? I told you you could do it!" In the comments section below the video people wrote things like "He makes me feel better" and "No offense, you suck at basketball—Love your winning spirit though!"

It's not that impressive that after shooting hoops for two hours on a hot patch of asphalt, I finally scored two points. What's important is that seeing those attempts helps my audience take people like me off the sidelines. I'm able to encourage others because someone taught me how to appreciate the tiny victories a long time ago. Now I know why Mrs. Fatta rewrote every rule of fourth-grade gym class; it's because she understood that in order for me to succeed in life, I'd have to change the game entirely.

CHAPTER 16

A Wedding, Two Meat Loaves, and a Lobster Funeral

In July 2014, after a decadelong courtship, my childhood friend Kevin was finally getting married to Kate, his high school sweetheart. But enough about them, let's talk about why this wedding was important to me. I'd be settling into several new roles at these nuptials. Along with my best friend Andrew and Kevin's brother-in-law (confusingly, also named Kevin), I was one of three anointed best men. But this would also be the first wedding where I'd have a date who wasn't just a dance partner for the electric slide or a girl friend who'd agreed to come to enjoy the open bar and serve as my wingwoman, but a real live, legit, compound-word girlfriend, who'd come all the way from Germany to Buffalo just to be with me.

For once, when I busted moves at the reception, people wouldn't be asking "Is he drunk?" but rather "Who's that smokin' hot lady dancing with Zach?" Gillian and I had only been a couple for five months and we'd been on separate continents for three of them, but for someone who had absolutely zero prior experience dating, I really felt like I was killing it as a boyfriend. Not to brag or anything, but we'd already managed to exchange "I Love You's," and I'd gotten the prestigious distinction of being the best man Gillian had ever met—her words, not mine. How did I do this, you ask? Well, after years of watching other people's relationships flounder, I knew in my heart that I could be more thoughtful and romantic than any of my friends. Not that I'm saying it's a competition, but if it was, I'd win. This was finally my moment to shine.

Some of my best boyfriend achievements to date included, but were not limited to:

- Oh, she's had a tough day? I'll send flowers with a personal note!
- Oh, she's just finished a tour in Italy? I'll text a series of photos of me holding up signs expressing how proud I am of her!
- Oh, she just organized all her favorite books from childhood into a library at the farmhouse where she grew up? Well, since I can't be there on her birthday, I guess I'll just contact her mom, get a list of those books, purchase a set, and donate them to a children's hospital in her name! Oops, I forgot to get the far superior British editions of Harry Potter . . . wait, no I didn't! *Philosopher's Stone* away, you brave little soldiers . . .
- Well, we both agree that Valentine's Day is overcommercialized, but I still wanna do something thoughtful. Good thing I remember the name of one of her favorite

charities and the fact that she loves animals; so, here you go, African villager in need, take this goat as a token of how much I pay attention to my girlfriend!

- Oh, and what's that? The seminal Joni Mitchell album *Court and Spark* inspired her to be a songwriter? I'll go to the ends of the earth to find a signed copy on vinyl. I don't care how many niche record stores I have to visit. Wait, it's just right here on Amazon. Well, whatever, still counts!

Just so you guys don't feel shitty, I'll admit that I made some mistakes too. After all, this was my first relationship and I was learning on the job. In our first few months together I was getting life lessons all over the place and figuring out not just how to be a better boyfriend but how to be a better person all around. Obviously, there are some things you can only learn from experience. For instance, no matter how hot you think it looks when your girlfriend's mascara runs, you should make her aware of it, because to her, it's not sexy, but unkempt and sloppy. Likewise, if you love absolutely every single outfit your girlfriend tries on, your opinion doesn't hold a lot of weight. And, even if you think the analogy is accurate based on scale alone, you should never refer to one of the country's largest, oldest, and most prestigious greenhouse conservatories as "the Walmart of gardens" because that assessment belittles something that has great sentimental meaning to your girlfriend and her family (okay, so that last one is pretty specific, but just in case it comes up . . .).

I also learned that no matter how nervous you are, subconsciously touching your crotch in public always sends the wrong signals, *especially* if you're at an amusement park surrounded by children. Granted, I should have known that already, but it was nice to have someone in my corner discreetly pointing it out instead of calling the cops.

All in all, even taking these minor missteps into account, I'd still give myself a solid 7.8 as a significant other. I felt like the role of boyfriend was one I was born to play. There's no denying that I'd arrived on the scene pretty late, but remember, Harrison Ford didn't play Han Solo until he was thirty-five. Everything about being somebody's somebody was a new and exciting first for me. First time getting to share meals off the same plate. First time holding hands—gotta set the right speed for my wheelchair so that I don't run into my lady's amazing legs when we're walking!

My mind was blown on a daily basis by even the tiniest revelations. Like, did you guys know that once you've kissed somebody, sharing gum or candy with them doesn't feel gross? It even sounds gross to write it, but in the moment it's like . . . yeah, that totally makes sense! After decades of ignorance, I was finally getting the romantic education I'd always hoped for.

This transatlantic trip to Buffalo was the first time Gillian would be meeting my family. I'd never brought a girl home before, so this was uncharted territory for everyone in my house. When you're in a long-distance relationship and haven't seen each other for three months, the thing you're looking forward to most is privacy. We'd have to make a few minor adjustments to ensure that Gillian felt both welcome and comfortable because in my house privacy is not really a thing.

"Hey, Mom? You know how I haven't had a door on my room for the past two years? Do you think we could put one on before Gillian gets here?"

"You remember the reason you don't have a door, don't

you?" she replied, pointing out that my door was off its hinges because I'd rammed into it so many times with my wheelchair.

"Yeah, but still," I said. "It would make Gillian and me feel a lot better if we had at least some privacy." She gave in to that one, ensuring that everyone who walked to the bathroom wouldn't first be popping their heads into my room to check in on the happy couple.

I was a man to Gillian, but no matter how old I got, I'd always be a son to my parents. For me, growing up with a disability meant that, while my family encouraged my independence, there were nurturing habits that became established routines that I never fully grew out of. Others would call it coddling, but I just knew it as life. This codependent comfort came at the expense of boundaries. It didn't matter what I'd accomplished in my professional or personal life—when I was home, I was someone who was taken care of. I was the one in my family who didn't have to sweat the small stuff because he had the big dreams. So when Gillian came to Buffalo, not only would she be meeting my family and childhood friends for the first time, she'd also be meeting my childhood.

She'd love my family, and who wouldn't? They're warm without being fake, they have a grossly inappropriate sense of humor, and all of us are artistic in different ways. An indie harpist who loves to laugh and adores me should feel right at home. Even so, it would still be weird for her to walk into the bedroom of the man she was considering a future with and find a Kermit the Frog plush toy propped up on the bed staring back at her. We tossed Kermit onto the floor, but the next day, after we'd returned from lunch, we discovered that he'd found his way back to my pillow.

I was not the most obvious match for a woman who'd had numerous relationships, moved to Switzerland when she was fifteen, and traveled around the world by herself. Hell, I didn't even learn the truth about Santa until I was eleven. But we shared an enthusiasm for the little things in life, and that made some of the bigger differences seem less daunting. Gillian attempted to ingratiate herself to my family right away by cooking an exotic breakfast dish called a "frittata" with what she referred to as tah-mah-toes. They ate it, cautiously. I took her to all my favorite Buffalo hangouts, and even though she'd been to palaces in Italy and could whip up croissants from scratch, she was still able to appreciate Lasertron and sponge candy.

Though there was no lack of fun things to do in my hometown, the one thing we couldn't find was the alone time we so desperately needed after three months apart. A private island would have been perfect. Luckily, Gillian had one of those in her back pocket. It was a place called Vinalhaven off the coast of Maine where her grandmother had a summerhouse. Time alone was such a precious commodity that Gillian was willing to drive us the ten hours from Buffalo to Maine—a tall order after having taken a transatlantic flight and an overnight bus ride to get to Buffalo in the first place. Then, after a short ferry ride from the mainland, Gillian could finally relax and I could finally continue relaxing, but with the added bonus of lobster.

This had all the makings of a stress-free romantic getaway. So I hopped into the passenger seat of the van to wait while Gillian struggled to master the vacation Jenga that is packing two suitcases, a wheelchair ramp, a harp, a manual wheelchair, and a particularly squirrelly electric one, into a single vehicle.

She'd focus on the logistical stuff—like packing and driving, and doing everything to get us out the door—and I'd focus on the romantic boyfriend-y stuff, like buying wine I knew nothing about and remembering to bring my Bluetooth speaker in case I needed to set a sexy mood. Since we wouldn't have Internet access on the island, I preloaded my phone with plenty of Michael McDonald. *Whelp, I've done my job!* I thought. But as we pulled out of the driveway, Gillian entrusted me with another responsibility.

"I'm gonna need you to help me navigate."

Since Gillian was doing 100 percent of the driving, this request seemed reasonable, but it still flooded me with fear. My sense of direction is so poor that I can't tell you with confidence which side of the street my own house is on. I'm the person who, when the doorbell rings, will rush down the hall to welcome my guests and mistakenly open the door to find, not my friends, but my shirts, because I've opened a closet instead. I tried to temper her expectations.

"I don't know if I can do that," I said, "but I can trrry?"

"Well, if you're riding shotgun, that's your job."

I refrained from mentioning that I'd once hosted a show called *Riding Shotgun* and had managed to escape this responsibility entirely. But there were three other people with me on that trip who had accepted early on that I couldn't be trusted not to route us to Boston by way of Mexico. Despite my inexperience, I resolved to do my best to honor the faith Gillian was placing in me. After all, how hard could it be to follow a little blue car on your phone and say the names of roads? *Never Eat Shredded Wheat*, I recited to myself, realizing that I didn't know which way was Never and which way was Wheat.

It was on that drive that I got my first whiff of what it's like to be a less than baller boyfriend. My navigation skills were even worse than I'd anticipated.

"Okay, so you're supposed to turn left in point five miles . . . now it's point four miles . . ."

"What's the name of the exit?" Gillian asked.

Confused, I looked down at her phone.

"It doesn't say," I shrugged. "Siri, what is the name of the exit that we're supposed to turn on in point two miles?"

"Just hand it to me," she said, exasperated. "You're not giving me enough warning, I have to merge across four lanes of traffic to make these turns."

By the time we finally got to Maine, her exhaustion from a week of near-constant travel finally caught up with her, and, for me, ten hours of making an already stressful situation worse was also pretty tiring.

The only way from the small town of Rockland, Maine, to the even smaller island of Vinalhaven is via a ferry that goes back and forth from the mainland, six trips a day in summer and a generous two trips in winter. It was the first time I'd ever ridden in a van on a boat. The foghorns bellowed as we pulled into the harbor, and I could see the rocky shores of Vinalhaven poking through the thick mist. It took about ninety seconds to drive through the tiny town center. I saw streets lined with quaint white clapboard houses, a handful of charming storefronts, and a gas station with only a single pump, but two tanks filled with lobsters for sale.

Seven minutes outside of the village, nestled in among the trees and facing the ocean, was Gillian's grandmother's summerhouse. It had the rustic woodsiness of a cabin but the warmth of a home. We were the first people to visit that season, so there was a coating of dust and a fair number of cobwebs inside. Somehow a small tree's worth of dried leaves had blown through during the fall. The pantries were stocked with nonperishables and a surprising number of spices to cook with. The best find though, from that initial inventory, was not only a VCR but a VHS of *You've Got Mail*. When I saw that, I was convinced we had everything we needed for a great week.

The place needed a little TLC before we could relax, so Gillian got right to work cleaning and I offered to help. While Gillian swept the floors, and made the bed, and scrubbed out the fridge, and disinfected the bathroom, and unloaded the car, and set up the wheelchair ramp, and unpacked our bags, I dusted two nightstands. Before you get to thinking that the division of labor was not equal, let it be known that I also dusted the lamps that were on top of those nightstands, or at least the parts I could reach without knocking them over. I also tried to scrub some of the rust off of the radiator, but there aren't enough trees in the rain forest to make enough paper towels for that to be achievable.*

Gillian diligently tackled the housework like a modern-day, feminist Snow White. To complete the picture, there were also five tiny, twin-size beds in the open-floor attic upstairs, but instead of seven dwarves, she had one guy with cerebral palsy and no cheery animals to assist her. Besides, if there were any helpful critters around, they would have been lobsters, and nobody wants to see four lobsters cooperatively fold a duvet. After three hours of housework, we finally settled in.

---

*As we write this, Gillian has just informed me that you cannot wipe rust off with a paper towel, which would have been nice to know before I spent a half an hour attempting to do just that, convinced I was making progress.

Our next order of business was to make a grocery list and plan the menu for the week. We knew we wanted a lot of lobster, but we didn't want to get sick of it, so we had to pace ourselves. Our dinner plans were as follows:

Sunday: Lobster
Monday: Meat loaf
Tuesday: Lobster
Wednesday: Risotto and baby kale salad
Thursday: Lobster
Friday: Quinoa-stuffed bell peppers
Saturday: Leftovers, maybe jazzed up with a little lobster

Though we planned to cook most of the week, we were too exhausted from travel to make anything that evening, so we decided to dine out and celebrate our first night on the island with dinner at Salt, Vinalhaven's newest restaurant. It was an all-out swanky joint that served lobster in a molasses demi-glace. I learned two important things about Vinalhaven during my inaugural dinner there. First, the island was not the most handicap-accessible, as many of the local businesses had steps and stoops; if I was going to explore this place, I'd be doing it mostly in the manual wheelchair. Second, maple lavender ice cream is the best thing I've ever had in my mouth, and I've had a lot of great things in my mouth. (That came out disgusting, but what I'm trying to say is it was delicious.)

That dessert alone was enough for me to warm up to Vinalhaven, which was a good thing, because when we got home we realized there was no hot water. You might think that a cold shower after a long day isn't ideal, but it's not that bad. My cold bath was much worse. It was so frigid and horrible that we couldn't help but laugh.

Over the next several days, Gillian and I settled into our makeshift life together. We snuggled and talked for hours in the mornings, we sat out on the porch and wrote together during the afternoons, and my mighty girlfriend even carried me on her back down to the flooded rock quarry so we could swim.

I also learned how to pee outside without assistance, which was the most harmonious I've ever felt with nature.

As it turned out, one thing that Gillian and I were not harmonious with was lobster. Outside of Vinalhaven, you're nervous when you leave the house that people might rob you. But when you're on Vinalhaven, should someone let themselves into your home, they won't take anything, but there's a good chance they'll leave live lobsters in your fridge. When I saw that rustling plastic bag, I was determined to be chivalrous and plop those beady-eyed cockroaches into the pot so Gillian wouldn't have to do it. But no matter how noble my intentions, I was still the kid who'd been too afraid to pet his cousin's guinea pig, Butterscotch, so you can probably guess how well my manliness held up when faced with crustaceans. Gillian wasn't any less terrified by these innocent creatures we were about to boil alive; she was just braver. I tried to be her cheerleader, but there's no amount of moral support that can relieve the horror of picking up a sentient creature that looks like a miniature version of an alien Godzilla might fight, dropping it into boiling water, and scalding it to death.

After a traumatizing two-day lobster binge, we mutually decided that our next meal would be meat loaf. Meat loaf was comforting. Meat loaf didn't scream while you cooked it. Meat loaf, as it turns out, also comes in deceptively large packages that are in no way appropriately portioned for two people. When Gillian opened the oven, we had two meat loaves that were so massive, they ensured that for the rest of our trip we'd be finding creative ways to include meat loaf in all of our meals and snacks. Thus, our bell peppers were stuffed not with quinoa but meat loaf, and garnished with a side of meat loaf, and our risotto was served with meat I suspect was originally in loaf form. But in between the tender moments we shared and the brutal murders of shellfish, there was something that I didn't see.

Each day, starting from the moment I got out of bed in the morning, I set in motion a mini-cyclone of domestic chaos that I was unaware of, first pulling the sheets and blankets off the bed as I made my way down to the floor, then waiting for morning coffee and a breakfast of homemade apple turnovers, just waiting. Then, I'd play my part in the whole affair and say, "Thank you, that was delicious," happily leaving my lovely girlfriend with the considerable pile of dirty dishes I'd abandoned, not thinking to place them in the sink. This was the routine three meals a day on the days when I didn't spill something. If I'm being generous to myself I'd say that I only spilled things half the time.

Aside from my absentminded mealtime debris, there were

also stray socks and underwear that I helpfully left strewn about any number of rooms. This was an old house and obviously the bathrooms weren't accessible, so every time I had to pee I'd call Gillian in and ask her to help me onto the toilet, just so I wouldn't rip the molding off the windowsill trying to hoist myself up. If we were going into town for a meal to give Gillian a break from the kitchen, I'd often have to use my manual chair, but because I'd lost the footrests long ago, Gillian would have to tip the chair back and balance it so I didn't drag my feet on the ground. I don't care how scrawny I look and how strong Gilly is, carting around 140 pounds of me is not easy for anyone.

The only thing that is worse than being completely oblivious to everything that people do for you in order for you to live your daily life is when you first start to notice it. It's that moment when you look at someone you love and realize you're the thing that is stressing them out. This was supposed to be a fun vacation where a new couple could spend quality time together as boyfriend and girlfriend. There should have been plenty of time for doing what we loved, but instead Gillian had dropped everything in order to become a caretaker for me. Four days into the trip, her harp was still in its case. We'd found time to write a new chapter for my book, but Gillian didn't have any time to be creative with her music because the rest of her day was taken up with the seemingly endless list of things I needed help with. I began to feel like dead weight, as a body and as a boyfriend. Finally, one day as she was clearing my dishes after lunch, Gillian also decided to clear the air.

"You know, if down the line we ever decided to live together, we'd need to figure out how to do this differently."

"Like me helping out with dishes and stuff?" I said.

"It's not so much the housework itself, but more . . . being aware of everything that goes on around you."

I wasn't surprised that we were having this conversation, but I was totally unprepared for it. We talked for four hours straight. I don't remember all of what was said over the course of those four hours, but I definitely did NOT cry, if that's what you're thinking. The gist was that my girlfriend basically clued me in to the reality that I rarely paid attention to the daily tasks in my own life and so my family and friends had to pick up the slack.

From the outset, Gillian was the one responsible for being responsible. I was so out of touch with all the forethought and organization that went into our days together that I had just checked out. It wasn't that I didn't do dishes—I didn't even pack my own bag or know what was in it. If I had just refrained from activities that my disability prohibited me from doing, that would have been understandable. But every little thing from flipping off lights in the bathroom to flipping on and off the brakes of my own wheelchair, I had to be reminded about. Her point was that even though I might always be relegated to the passenger seat, that didn't give me the right to be passive.

Up until this point, everything that kept me rollin' toward my big dreams had been habitually taken care of by the people who loved me. Gillian loved me too, but she also had dreams of her own. For more than a decade she'd poured her heart and soul into making a living and a life as a musician. She'd traveled across the country and the world solo, doing everything from booking tours to self-releasing albums, and had even turned down a major label deal. She was the epitome of an independent artist and an independent person. My job as a good boyfriend was to make sure that Gillian had the tools and the time to pursue her own goals rather than dropping everything so that I could pursue mine. I'd fallen in love with a self-made woman and was inadvertently turning her into an assistant and a maid. All I wanted in the world was for her to be fulfilled both personally and professionally, but my immaturity was undermining my best intentions.

Before I started dating, I thought I'd be good in a relationship because I'd always pay attention to my significant other. But in not paying attention to myself I became my girlfriend's responsibility, and if there's a surefire way to kill your sex life, it's to slowly turn your girlfriend into your mother. That's exactly what was happening here. I'd finally found somebody who could see past my disability and because she saw past it, she didn't excuse my complacency. Her expectations for me were not built on any preconceived notions about disabled people, but were rather based on what she needed from a partner: love, freedom to pursue her own goals, and support, not just in gestures but in deeds. If this relationship was going to work I'd have to figure out how to take care of myself and become someone who another human being could count on.

Gilly felt trapped and I felt profoundly crippled. Both of us were in way over our heads. In attempting to give us some solitude, Gillian had unknowingly placed us in an environment that had set us up to fail. While she had fondly remembered Vinalhaven as a place for reading books by the fire and taking walks along the beach to search for clams, I could do neither of these things. My eyes don't track and my wheels are guaranteed to get stuck in sand. In a city, I can go outside my door and be surrounded by modern conveniences, public transportation, restaurants, elevators, and accessible bathrooms that allow me to both be a part of and contribute to society. Here, I was surrounded by rocks and the ocean. The town was more than a mile away and the road that led to it was raked with gravel and riddled with potholes. There was no dishwasher in the kitchen and no grab bar in the bathroom. That's how a charming summer home becomes a big lobster pot destined to boil over.

In her optimism and inexperience, Gillian had assumed that I was far more self-sufficient than I actually was and that any obstacle we faced would seem small in comparison to the joy of being together. Our relationship required so much work and commitment, just so that we could be on the same continent at the same time, that every incompatibility we uncovered took on the added weight of thousands of miles of distance. There was no getting around the fact that even at twenty-nine, this was my first relationship. By the end of our emotionally exhausting conversation, I didn't even know if I was capable of being a partner to anyone.

The next few days oscillated between heavy conversation contemplating our future and tender moments of love and levity. We watched *You've Got Mail* lying head to toe on a sofa together, and it took me twenty minutes just to figure out how to situate my body so that I could both cuddle and not kick my girlfriend in the face. When Gillian finally did take her harp out, I got a private concert of all my favorite songs. Seeing this incredibly talented woman perform in the living room just for me gave me the sort of luckiest-guy-in-the-world moments I'd only seen in movies.

No matter how confusing and difficult dating was turning out to be, I always knew that dating Gillian was a privilege. She'd been around the globe and landed on me as the guy she wanted to be with. So even if I couldn't get up on the toilet seat in that old house independently, there were times when I still felt pretty badass.

Time, like meat loaf, passed slowly on Vinalhaven. After a week, we were both ready to get back to some semblance of our normal lives where lobsters are too expensive to eat every day and the Internet is everywhere. We were sad to be leaving but desperate to go.

On Saturday morning Gillian packed up the van, laundered the linens, emptied the fridge, swept the floors, took out the trash and recycling, and then, to my surprise, put all the garbage into the van. I still contributed nothing to the effort, but this time, instead of zoning out, I actually noticed all the work it took to get us both on the road. It was a start.

Before we left for the mainland, I got to see another special corner of Vinalhaven—the island dump. There was a smorgasbord of antique televisions in wooden cabinets that suggested the village of Vinalhaven had—after skipping over color TVs, flat screens, and high definition—collectively decided to take the plunge on 3-D. When Gillian got back in the car and headed us toward the ferry terminal, I described a man I'd seen throwing out cans of tuna fish.

"He was wearing a big straw ladies' hat and looked kinda like Richard Attenborough in *Jurassic Park* if he'd given up on breeding dinosaurs and just gotten a cat."

She laughed and it was a small but meaningful reminder of why anyone might want to date me in the first place. I was glad we were ditching some of the emotional baggage we'd collected over the week along with our lobster shells and empty wine bottles.

We drove down to the ferry terminal and Gillian parked

the car to go buy our tickets. When she returned, she seemed very relaxed for someone who had a ten-hour drive ahead of her.

"So, apparently there were some medical emergencies that bumped two ferries this morning. The ticket lady basically told me there's no way we're getting off the island today, so we're stuck here until two o'clock tomorrow afternoon."

We decided to regroup at the island's one and only pizza joint. While we were waiting for our order, we got to eavesdrop on the people who call Vinalhaven home not just for the summers but year-round. I don't want to generalize, but I would describe a lot of Vinalhaven's residents as jolly in a life-threatening, type 2 diabetes kind of way. The gentleman behind us in line was in his midtwenties and roughly four hundred pounds. Most of his right leg was a swollen shade of purple. If this were a war movie, the doctor would have given him a swig of whiskey and something to bite down on, and just started amputating right there and then. But since this was Vinalhaven, no one really seemed to think much of it.

"So how's your leg there, Bobby?" our waitress asked casually.

"Eh," he shrugged, "thing's about to burst. The doctor wanted to slice it open and wrap it up again, but I'll just hit it with the iodine and I think it'll be okay."

"Ah yeah?" the waitress said, unfazed. "You want your usual?"

"Yeah," he said. "Saw your dad the other day. Almost ran him over."

"Ah yeah?" she said, kneading out the dough for our pizza, "with the car or with the truck?"

"Truck," he replied flatly.

I loved being in a place where almost running over some-one's parent and having gangrene was not noteworthy news. This man's leg was about to fall off, but he clearly wasn't in any rush to seek medical attention (which made me wonder what kind of horrific accident would constitute an emergency wor-thy of shutting down transportation to and from the island). But maybe Bobby was onto something. If he could find time to stop and enjoy a slice of pizza on his way to an amputation, then why couldn't we put the anxieties of an uncertain future on hold to appreciate this treasure trove of folksy banter? So that's exactly what we did. I didn't think I'd ever want to go back to Vinalhaven after this trip, but all it took was one four-hundred-pound man with super-diabetes to show me the joys of island living.

I'd spent the majority of that week wishing I was back at home, where I understood things. But while Vinalhaven had the landscape to match, I realized my life in Buffalo was its own sort of island. I'd grown up surrounded by people who only knew one way of life—the way of making things easy for me. It was simple. I could have stayed there forever and just said that the world I knew was all I needed. But it's impossible, once you've looked at the ocean, not to wonder what else is out there. Now I could finally see through the fog that there was some-thing worth swimming toward.

A few days later, back in Buffalo, we watched Kevin and Kate get married at the historic Lafayette Hotel. In our Best Men speech, Andrew and I talked about the decade that these two obnoxiously gorgeous people had spent together. On the surface, they couldn't have been more different. Kate was an English teacher with impeccable grammar and diction while Kevin was an artist whose marriage proposal was a painting that included a comma between the words "will you" and "marry me." They communicate differently but understand each other perfectly. Kevin and Kate had had a decade to figure each other out, grow together, and decide that they were right for each other. It was pretty baller to witness their union.

I didn't know what the future held for Gillian and me. There was really no way to tell where we'd be ten years down the line. What I did know for sure was that I was happy to have someone to dance with. I have no doubt that we strutted our stuff harder and had more fun than just about anyone else at that wedding. She took my hands and expertly twirled her way into my lap, somehow managing to make it look like I was dipping her, even though I was just sitting there watching the magic show that was my girlfriend. After thirtysomething hours of driving over the past few days, she was still up for five hours of dancing, and at the end of the night, I was the guy who got to carry her heels.

I didn't know how I was gonna get there, but the week on Vinalhaven had taught me that I wanted to be more than just a dance partner. I wanted to share someone's life. And when that person looked over at me at the end of the night, I wanted her to see not a child or a boyfriend or someone to take care of, but a person who was willing to take risks and finally put in the work necessary to earn the title of The Best Man.

CHAPTER 17

Grandma: The Musical!

I don't think it's exaggerating to say that I come from a family of musical geniuses. My aunt is a violinist with the London Philharmonic Orchestra, and she's married to the first chair bassoonist. My other aunts and uncles play the flute, the clarinet, and the cello. My father, the trombonist of the family, has musical tastes that are decidedly less refined. Still, he contributed to the Anner legacy with homespun cassette recordings of original songs, including such lo-fi '80s masterworks as "Pam and the Yellow Trans Am" and "Smash It, Crash It." But the leader of the Anner band was my grandma Ruthie, who was a church organist and piano teacher for decades.

As for me? I never inherited any of that musical talent. Zero. When I was four years old and was asked to sing "Twinkle, Twinkle, Little Star," I would sort of sing, mumble, and then trail off as I forgot the words: "Twinkle, Twinkle, Little Star . . . Won't You Come and Play with Me?" In spite of a complete lack of talent, there was still a time when I had high hopes for my music career.

Fall of 1994. Fourth grade. That was the year when all the kids in my class finally got to join orchestra. The music teacher sized us all up and assigned us instruments according to our aptitude. I was excited because I thought I could play the saxophone. Or the sousaphone. Or the tuba. Whatever, as long as it was shiny. I liked the shiny ones. At some point in the fall, my music teachers and my physical therapist had convened without my knowledge and relegated me to percussion. Me. The kid whose very first action in life was to arrive two months early, completely off time. Maybe that kid could keep rhythm!

I remember that upon hearing this horrible news, I went to the teacher to sort out what I was sure was a mistake. Every student was asked to write down their top three instruments and I had clearly stated: saxophone, sousaphone, tuba! I would have settled for a trumpet. How could they possibly confuse blowing into something with banging onto something?! Only drummers think drums are cool. Have you ever gone to a concert that featured a drum solo of any kind? By the end of the solo, *no one* is into it but the guy banging the drums. I might have been able to become the sort of guy who drumrolls the table with his fingers every time Ringo comes in with the chorus of "Hey Jude." But the problem is, I'm horrible at banging on things. I can bang into them. Just not on them. Plus, I knew tuba players got ALLLL the chicks.

Still, I dutifully tried to bond with my instrument, which

was, I was further dismayed to learn, not even a drum but a wooden block with a piece of rubber on it. The practice pad was meant to spare my parents' ears, but my father, a purist, would have none of that. He tried to make the best of a bad situation by giving me a real drum. It looked like it was from the Civil War—the kind of big, booming snare drum that was meant to signify the death of several thousand people. Unfortunately, due to my parents' custody agreement, he would only get to hear this thunderous march one day a week, while my mom would enjoy the other six.

I tried to play that thing—I really did—but after two weeks of my disjointed doomsday booming effectively bringing orchestra practice to a halt, my music teachers came to the conclusion that perhaps it would be better if I received "individual instruction" rather than participating in band. I would now catch an early bus on Tuesdays and Thursdays as my presence was no longer necessary or welcome. It was like musical hospice. They decided there was nothing else they could do for me, so they just sent me home to be comfortable.

There was only one person who steadfastly believed I might have something more to offer the music world than the occasional poorly timed *clunk*—my grandma Ruthie.

I always knew her as the oldest person I knew. She had hair the texture of cobwebs that she swept up into a bun as white as a thousand mothballs. It kind of smelled that way too. Her entire face looked like the tips of fingers that had pruned in the bathtub too long. She didn't own a pair of pants and would wear floral dresses and knit cardigans on ninety-degree days. She once said of Ray Charles, "I don't understand why people like this new music." That was in 2002. But when I was little and she would sit beside me and play "Somewhere over the Rainbow" on the organ after church—pulling out all of the stops and commanding two keyboards, a hundred pipes, and I don't know how many foot pedals—she wasn't just my grandma from a unfathomable time with milkmen and carriages: she was a magician.

For her, music was not just a passion but the means to her family's survival. When her husband died suddenly of an asthma attack, leaving behind only a $10,000 life insurance policy, she taught piano to raise their seven children by herself. By the time I came along, her house was mostly a museum of trinkets and toys left over from the '50s and '60s—Lincoln Logs and original Tonka trucks and Beatles paraphernalia from when the Beatles were just the One Direction of their day. The only thing that didn't seem like a relic in her house was the piano. Whenever we went over there for dinner, I would always ask her if I could sit at the bench and she would inevitably join me. This was the highlight of all my visits.

The lessons were fairly simple—basic scales, that sort of thing. Sometimes she'd play a chord and ask if I could find a note that fit with it, wince when I didn't on my first three tries, and then give a reassuring "Good!" when I finally found a note that wasn't dissonant. To boost my confidence, she'd say, "Just play the black keys." That way I could play something that sounded nice, or, as she'd put it, "Oriental." Then she'd bring out the *My Fair Lady* songbook and play "On the Street Where

You Live." I'd improvise a countermelody and wait for her to stop and teach me the one-finger version of what she was playing.

One time she came over to Dad's house to babysit after I had just gotten an electric Yamaha keyboard for Christmas. I played over the prefab bossa nova beats and pop/rock settings, mimicking the motions I'd seen her do at the piano. It sounded more like a family of squirrels being executed by machine-gun fire than any songs she played, but when I stopped for a second, she just looked at me and said, "Keep playing, Zachary, keep playing your beautiful music," and from what I could tell, she meant it. This was a woman who had a well-earned reputation for being bluntly cruel when she didn't like something. Once, when my cousin was sharing photos of his new girlfriend, she remarked with a smile, "Oh, her sister's much prettier than she is. It's the face that's the problem." But musically, at least, I received nothing but unwavering encouragement from her.

As I got older, my fascination with music grew into a deep appreciation. I discovered jazz and my favorite pianist was Oscar Peterson. While my friends were obsessed with "Thong Song" and that awful graduation/"Pachelbel's Canon" thing, I was diving deep into the Cole Porter and Duke Ellington songbooks. I bought every album of Oscar's I could, and as his lightning fingers flew over the keys with an effortless virtuosity, I would wheel up to the piano in the next room and try to find one or two notes to accompany his rendition of "The Girl from Ipanema." I was too old to delude myself into thinking that I could ever play piano as well as he did, but I still dreamed about it every time I touched the keys. If some genie or *Extreme Makeover—Cripple Edition!* show had given me the choice between fully functional legs or fingers that could confidently navigate through "Sophisticated Lady," I would have chosen having the coordination to play a musical instrument over walking in a heartbeat. Nobody has ever been moved to the point of tears by someone being able to stroll through an aisle and pick up sixty rolls of toilet paper from the top shelf at Costco—but music has soul!

Despite my frustration over my own musical expression, my passion gave my grandmother and me a new language to speak. Our shared love for music overcame a cultural gap spanning seven decades. I had grown up with TV shows like *South Park*, while the only television she watched were things she called "progrims" that were all British, aired on PBS, and had laugh tracks. She canned ketchups and jams, and made chocolate chip cookies using leftover chicken fat. I ate Skittles off the floor after struggling for ten minutes to open the bag. I was a creature of comfort, whereas she was one of survival, shaped by the Great Depression. But all those differences collapsed whenever music brought us together; when we talked about jazz standards, we understood each other.

In 2004, when I was nineteen, my dad told us that our favorite pianist, Oscar Peterson, was going to give a rare performance at the Hummingbird Centre in Toronto. This not only promised to be the concert of a lifetime but one of the few opportunities I'd get to see my grandma genuinely excited about something that was set to happen in the future. At eighty-eight years old, she tended to think of the future as the time when she'd probably be dead. She'd taken to ending all of our visits by cheerfully saying, "I'll see you next time . . . if I'm alive that long!" So it was nice to imagine something on her calendar other than "Prune Apple Tree" and "Plan Funeral."

Oscar Peterson was returning to the stage at the age of seventy-eight. He had suffered a stroke and reportedly couldn't use his left hand at all anymore. After several years of not performing, he'd learned to play again, with the assistance of guitar accompaniment that could fill in the parts previously covered by his left hand. Even if compromised health and old age had drastically reduced his technical ability, I couldn't miss the chance to see one of the performers I admired most with one of the people I admired most. So my dad, my grandma, my friend Kevin, and I all headed up to Toronto on a Saturday afternoon in May.

During the two-and-a-half-hour drive up from Buffalo, the conversation in the car was mainly about whether Oscar would be able to recapture any of his former glory or if it would just be kind of depressing to see an artist who had once been able to light a cigarette for someone in the front row mid-song without missing a beat, reduced to using only five of his ten fingers. The only other thing we talked about in the car was Kevin's lovely new girlfriend, Kate. He brought pictures along from the prom they'd just gone to. Thankfully, upon seeing them, my grandma had the good graces to say that Kate was pretty.

When we finally arrived at the Hummingbird Centre, the only handicapped seating available was in the very back, but it didn't matter—we were just glad to be there. At the front of the theater, we could make out two technicians carefully tuning the grand piano. As the lights went down, Oscar's opener, Oliver Jones, took the stage. We were all surprised and delighted when we realized that although he was a pianist none of us had ever heard of, Oliver Jones was a tremendous talent, playing with almost the same speed and ease that Oscar had on some of his recordings. During Oliver's onstage banter, we found out why. Oliver, like Oscar before him, had gotten piano lessons from Oscar's sister, which prompted us all to wonder how good of a pianist she must have been and ask ourselves why no one was aware of this amazing woman as a solo artist in her own right.

As the audience was let out for the twenty-minute intermission between sets, Kevin, my dad, and I all exchanged excited "That was AMAZING!"s and "Wasn't that awesome?!"s, as though we had contributed to the performance ourselves. My dad, never one for sugarcoating, remarked, "If Oscar's not at a hundred percent, he might kinda suck compared to that!" Even I thought this was a distinct possibility. I'd never seen someone play an instrument so well in my life, so everything to come had the potential to be underwhelming. We all agreed that Oliver Jones would be a tough act to follow.

My grandmother expressed her awe more quietly. The thing she couldn't contain was her appreciation that the piano technicians had returned, and after only an hour of use, they were tuning the piano again, just for Oscar's performance. To see such care and respect given to an instrument was something that affected her so deeply that every single time I saw her after this night until the end of her life, whether we were eating hot dogs or on our way to my aunt's house, if there was a lull in conversation, she'd say, "You remember during the Oscar Peterson concert? What was so interesting to me was that they were TUNING the piano in between performances. My gosh!" as though it was something new to marvel at and remember each time.

As the crowd returned and the lights went down again, none of us was sure if Oscar could live up to his own legend.

Oliver Jones came out to introduce him simply as the world's greatest jazz pianist. After a few moments, a frail and feeble Oscar limped onto the stage with the assistance of an aide and sat at the piano bench, the rest of his quartet already waiting in place. He launched into a song called "Wheatland," a grooving, entirely hypnotic tune he'd composed in the '70s. It wasn't flashy, but it was still the tightest group of musicians I'd ever heard. While he played the lines of his right hand with great fluidity and finesse, his left hand mainly rested on the keys, only playing the occasional chord, while the guitarist filled in most of the accompaniment.

Next, he transitioned into another original called "L'Impossible,"* a tune I'd listened to a hundred times before and that had been, in its recorded version, a prime example of his ambidextrous mastery. It starts with a simple melodic phrase with smooth, rolling chords beneath, and then quickly ramps up to what would be the equivalent of ten fingers in a drag race. Every time I listen to that song, the frenetic energy pulsing through Oscar's hands leaps out of the recording and smacks a smile on my face. I didn't think the age-encumbered live version could possibly elicit the same joyous response, but it did! He wasn't playing as many notes, but he was playing the right ones. All our fears and doubts regarding Oscar's form had faded, replaced by absolute wonder. With only one hand at his disposal, Oscar Peterson had bested the best pianist I'd ever seen live, and he'd done it within ten minutes. Then, another truly extraordinary thing happened.

---

*Despite my intensive research, I have never been able to find the appropriate translation. So the meaning of this title shall remain a mystery.

As he moved through the set, playing a Duke Ellington medley, his left hand began to play, waking up more and more with each tune, like an old friend that just couldn't stand to miss a good party. His brain had told his body that regardless of what it was going through, his spirit as a pianist would not be denied. He had a will and a love so strong that it overcame a brain injury that should have stopped him cold. I was inspired by his resilience.

The next morning, as the rest of us ate breakfast, my grandma sat down at my aunt's piano and played Gershwin. After witnessing the transformative power of music, it didn't matter what limitations I had, I just wanted to be a part of the magic. We may not have seen Oscar Peterson in his prime, but we saw him at his finest—as an irrepressible performer who kept an audience in the palm of his hand, despite only having one that worked! Music wasn't just his living—it was his life. It was the same for Grandma Ruthie too.

At the age of ninety, she became gravely ill and almost died after she lost her position as church organist. It was no secret that she didn't play as well as she once had. During the last few years, she'd often played pieces in whatever key was most pleasing to her ear, even if it didn't match the register of the choir.

Not having purpose gave her little to do, and her health deteriorated over the next three years. She eventually recovered enough to sit at the piano, but my dad expressed genuine concern when he heard her playing "Somewhere over the Rainbow" after dinner one night and noticed her struggling to find the right chord to resolve a song she'd played thousands of times.

During those last few years, we were thankful for the

moments when Grandma Ruthie managed to rally against old age and infirmity to share her prodigious talents. On Christmas Day in 2009, as her children and grandchildren all gathered 'round the piano at my uncle's house with their violins, violas, flutes, and other instruments, she was able to confidently play every carol without a single piece of sheet music. Sadly, the next summer, no amount of passion could keep her from succumbing to a stroke. She died at the age of ninety-four, leaving a rich musical legacy behind in the lives of her family, her students, and her church community.

The last time I saw her before she passed away was three weeks after my Oprah audition video went viral. For once, the woman I'd previously only seen in cardigans and dresses was wearing a SEXIEST OF THE PALSIES T-shirt. Like all other conversations since that night in Toronto, we talked about the Oscar Peterson concert. I told her that I was going to write the story in a book.

That evening at the Hummingbird Centre and the years that followed helped me realize what music truly meant to my grandma—it sustained her. She supported herself and seven children on little more than a garden and a piano, and five of those seven kids went on to have musical careers of their own. Even when music wasn't what put food on the table, it was what nourished her and gave her life purpose.

When something sustains you, no matter what you're up against, you'll find a way to get it. With my first paycheck from my show on the Oprah Network, I immediately went online and bought a collection of piano samples I could compose with on my computer using a MIDI keyboard. These were actual recordings of a Bösendorfer, the same kind of piano that Oscar had played in Toronto.* For the first time, I was able to write music, note by note, the way my grandmother had taught me, except now I could digitally manipulate and edit every mistake and nudge each note until the phrasing was just right. It's a roundabout way to the musical expression I'd always longed for, using technology my grandma couldn't have dreamed of.

While comedy is the medium I use to express myself to the public, music is more like my diary. When I'm working through something emotional that I don't have the words for, I'll put my headphones on and sit down at the keyboard. What comes from these sessions is rarely good, but it's always transportive and ignites my imagination in a way that nothing else does. The best music is a collaboration between the composer and the listener that transcends space and time and can be as much about recalling a memory as it is about living in the moment. In the past few years, I've not only written pieces for the piano, but have also commanded entire synthesized orchestras with my fingertip. I've composed themes for my show *Riding Shotgun* among dozens of other ditties ranging from "pretty good" to "no one can EVER hear this!"

I wish I could tell you that I shared some of my simple tunes with my grandma, but I didn't have the courage to let anyone hear them until after she passed away.

It wasn't until 2012, after a long night of Apples to Apples and a box of Franzia split among my brother and two of our

---

*I like Bösendorfers because they have an extra octave on the bass end that no one ever plays but gives the tone of the piano a deeper resonance. Plus I'm from America and more is always better!

friends, that I finally got up the nerve. Hoping the alcohol would be enough to impair their critical faculties, I plugged in my speakers, opened up iTunes, accepted that if I used iTunes I gave Apple the right to eat my firstborn child, and then pressed Play on a Zach Anner original.

It was the longest two minutes and eleven seconds of my life as Jess and her fiancé Josh listened in silence. It was a sparse piano instrumental, with a wandering and contemplative melody that I composed while reflecting on days at the beach with my aunt Bethany. As my friends listened, I tried to read their faces but couldn't bear to lock gazes. The entire thing felt like a walk to the principal's office. I was preparing for the emotional equivalent of being sat down at an administrator's desk, having him look me dead in the eye, and say, "I just called you in here to tell you that your heart *sucks*. You're horrible at everything you love, and no one loves you." When it was all over, the last sustained note hanging in the air, everyone was quiet. I wondered if I should apologize. But instead, Jess finally spoke, her voice broken up with emotion. "That sounds like the purest expression of love I've ever heard. I want to play it at my wedding."

The only reactions I'd allowed myself to fathom ranged from befuddlement and indifference to vague, patronizing words like "nice" or "interesting." "Beautiful" was not a word I thought my music would ever be called by anyone other than my grandma. Thinking back on it now, I realize that maybe Grandma Ruthie had lied and said that my noises were beautiful just so I would stick with it, until one day my music actually was. "Keep playing, Zachary," she'd say, "just keep playing."

CHAPTER 18

The Wurst and Best of Berlin

Growing up, my mom and my dad had two very different interpretations of the word "vacation." When we went on trips with my mom, vacation meant a hotel with a pool, a bag of bulk candy from the grocery store, and playing bingo with the fifteen-year-old lifeguard at the Knights Inn. When I'd get back from Easter vacation and kids would ask me what I'd done, I'd say, "We went to Baltimore and stayed in this awesome hotel with shields and swords on the walls!" and they'd follow up with "Why were you in Baltimore?" Confused, I'd try to clarify: "We went to a hotel."

For my mother, vacations were about getting away and having someplace to relax. For my father, they were about going somewhere and doing everything. He took us on trips to New York City to see Broadway shows, the Statue of Liberty, and that gigantic piano from the movie *Big*. Though, if I'm being honest, I was disappointed when my four wheels, planted firmly on the keys, didn't cooperate to play chopsticks. On one of our camping trips, my dad disregarded the signs warning that food could attract bears and fried up a steak teriyaki in our tent. Later that night, we heard the hungry and heavy huffing of a very curious black bear just on the other side of the nylon. All vacations with my dad were adventures, but none more so than when we went to Europe for the first time in 1997.

The plan was to spend ten days in England with our aunt Naomi and uncle Gareth and then continue on to France. Upon our arrival in London, my dad made sure to clue us in to the little cultural differences, noting the exposed breasts in shampoo commercials and lamenting that due to the discreet and regal design of English toilets, you can't look back to admire your work when you've taken a great dump. But the biggest culture clash didn't come from the loo.

It only took my brother and me a few days to drive my childless, classical-music-playing aunt and uncle to the brink of madness with our incessant fart jokes. One afternoon, our aunt finally broke. Furious that his sister had scolded his sons, my dad had us board a train in the dead of night and by morning we were on the lam, masquerading as Parisians.

Three years later, now a freshman in high school, I was preparing for a quiet spring break at home when, out of the blue, my dad called to let Brad and me know he'd gotten four-hundred-dollar round-trip flights to Rome and we were going next week. Armed with only a *Frommer's* guide, a tiny Italian phrase book, and a video camera, we ventured across the Atlantic again. It was on this trip that I first became a travel host. I shot segments on my little handicam: in front of the

Spanish Steps, I demanded to be directed to the Spanish Ramp; at the Accademia Gallery, I admitted to having penis envy when gazing upon the glory of the statue *David*; and, when visiting the Pantheon, I gave a heartfelt impromptu eulogy at the tomb of my favorite ninja turtle, Raphael. This is what happens when you try to expose a fifteen-year-old to history.

My manual wheelchair had been sufficient for our previous trip across the pond, but Italy marked my first attempt to travel in Europe with an electric wheelchair. As I bumped over the ancient cobblestones, it occurred to me that perhaps Rome was not handicap-accessible because back when they built it, Roman soldiers would have taken a baby like me and thrown him off a cliff. While history wouldn't have been kind to me, my disability also presented very modern problems.

My dad had packed an adaptor to fit our American electronics into European outlets, but he forgot to bring a transformer to convert the voltage, so we fried the wheelchair charger the first time we plugged it in. After that, my brother and father had to manually push my two-hundred-and-fifty-pound chair through the streets until my dad was able to jerry rig jumper cables that gave my batteries at least a little bit of juice. The blessing I received when I watched Pope John Paul perform stations of the cross at the Vatican fixed neither my legs nor my chair.

My father and brother worked with all the precision of a pit team changing tires at the Indy 500 every time they had to break down my chair to get it on the very wheelchair-unfriendly Italian trains. When we arrived in Pompeii, we were dismayed to find that an ancient city that had been engulfed in volcanic ash had not made appropriate ADA accommodations for differently abled citizens. We had planned to spend the night but couldn't find a single hotel that was accessible, so we boarded the train again, one wheel at a time, and headed back to Roma.

My tumultuous experiences with *bella Italia* would later become the basis of my Oprah pitch for a travelogue that shows you how to have the "perfect" vacation when things don't go as planned. In the fourteen years between our trek through Italy and my next trip to Europe, I'd hosted two travel shows and learned to be more tasteful with my fart jokes.

Going abroad again had always been a goal, but over the past decade and a half, whenever I started to look overseas, something would get in the way—money, timing, Oprah. All through high school and undergrad, whenever I was overloaded with tests and papers, I would run through my list of dream travel destinations where I would go once I had the money and the time: Norway, Australia, Israel, Japan. . . . There was one place though that was never on my worldly to-do list—Germany, especially Berlin.

If you were to say "Berlin" in a word association game, my first responses would be as follows: Wall, War, Holocaust, Heroin, and Wurst. My perception of the capital of Deutschland was a cold, rainy, war-torn place populated by drug addicts eating sausages in the middle of a country known for beer, a beverage I equated with carbonated urine. All it took to transform a place I never wanted to visit into the only place I wanted to be was having a girlfriend who lived there. She had an important concert coming up in September 2014 at Berlin's most prestigious jazz club, the A-Trane. I was heartbroken to have missed her debut there nine months earlier. I'd even looked up flights back in January but then decided that, since we weren't even dating at the time, it might be a smidge too creepy to show up in Germany out of the blue as a superfan. Now, as her boyfriend, I had earned the right to be that creepy superfan. So, after fourteen years of dreaming about it, I finally booked another transatlantic flight. This time, I'd be going solo. I was bound for the homeland of Hasselhoff.

Determined not to repeat the mistakes of previous European vacations, I had ordered a special wheelchair charger that I'd been assured was designed specifically for traveling overseas. I'd been practicing my Pimsleur language tapes for weeks and could competently navigate my way through a conversation about how well I didn't speak German. I had gotten my passport renewed, informed my banks I was traveling, and was finally at peace with the idea of spending eight days in an apartment with three girls and one bathroom. Like some average-size, crippled Napoleon, I felt prepared to rule the world.

But before I could conquer Europe, I had to leave the United States, which proved a more fearsome battle than I'd anticipated. I arrived at JFK airport two hours early with my buddy Kevin tagging along to carry my luggage and push my spare manual wheelchair to the gate. We made our way up to the Air Berlin kiosk and handed the attendant my passport. She typed in my name and then paused, perplexed.

"Huh," she said. "We weren't expecting you to be in a chair."

I thought this was odd because I distinctly remembered clicking the little wheelchair man when I'd bought the ticket online. Rather than argue, I simply asked, "Is that a problem?"

"Possssibly," she mumbled. "Let me make a call." In hushed, concerned tones, she spoke to her superior about the surprise wheelchairs she'd just encountered. When she finally hung up, she let out a long, uncertain sigh and went back to her computer. "I'm gonna have someone come and talk to you."

Forty minutes went by as I impatiently buzzed back and forth in front of her station, waiting for any news. Had I missed a memo? Were people in wheelchairs no longer allowed on planes? Was I gonna have to call Gillian and have a very awkward conversation?

"Yahp, can't make it. Yeah, it's the chair. Well, what can you do? See ya on Skype."

Then, finally, a salt-and-pepper-haired, no-bullshit New Yorker in uniform emerged, extended his hand, and said, "Hi, nice to meet cha. I'm Tom, the director of passenger relations with Air Berlin. We had no idea that a wheelchair was comin' tuhday. Yuh gotta let us know forty-eight hours in advance dat cha have a wheelchair so we can ready the plane. Can I ask yuh some questions?"

"Shoot," I said.

"Are yuh able to walk at all?"

Under normal circumstances, I'd have assumed he was asking if I was able to transfer to my seat independently, without the use of an aisle chair, but in this instance, it seemed more likely that he was asking if we could just ditch my chair at the terminal. I didn't care.

"Well, if someone is stabilizing me, I can take a few steps, yeah."

"Oh-kay, dat's good," he said. "Now, yuh gonna be able to make yuh way to the bathroom and all dat?"

The unabbreviated answer to this was that technically, yes, I could get out of my seat and crawl on all fours up the aisle to the diorama-size toilet and quite possibly heave myself onto it, might even be able to close the door. Given that even when

NOT flying through the air I can lose my balance at all times for any or no reason, I'd probably fall over a bunch, but, yes, I could get there. I'd never *done* it, but it seemed doable. Rather than bore this obviously busy gentleman with the details, I just said, "Yeah, sure."

"Okay, dat's good. Finally, in the event of an emergency, would cha be able tuh assist in evacuating duh plane?"

"Uhmmm . . . ," I said, trying to imagine myself shepherding babies and the elderly through flaming wreckage, our flight crew reduced to sobbing frantic prayers in German. "You mean, like, will I be able to carry other people off the plane and put on oxygen masks and stuff?"

"Well," he backpedaled, "would you be able to assist yourself?"

Not understanding the question, and hyperaware that the international security line was growing exponentially, I just said, "Yeah." That lie, which might possibly endanger the lives of all the other passengers on board, got me a comfy, primo seat on the flight and a jolly flight attendant named Fritz who told me to simply call him if I needed anything. As the landing gear went up and the plane left the ground, I sat back, unpacked the nutritious Rice Krispies Treats my mother had made, and turned on the in-flight entertainment.

By the time we landed, I was already steeped in culture, having watched the latest X-Men film, *Maleficent*, and *Mrs. Doubtfire*. As soon as I got off the plane, I realized that I had never been to a place that felt so simultaneously gloomy and friendly. The men who were responsible for carting my wheelchair to the gate welcomed me to Germany by telling me that I had to try the beer as soon as possible. It was 7:45 in the morning, local time.

"Which one should I try?" I asked.

"All of zem are good, *ja*. Drink all ze *bier*. Zat's how you get zis!" He laughed, cradling his considerable belly. "Zis is called a *bierbauch*, and when you drink ze *bier*, you raise your glass and say, '*Prost!*' Zat's all of ze German you need to know. Don't bother learning ze rest of it, it's a complicated language."

Five minutes in Germany and I'd already gotten permission from the natives to be a drunk and obnoxious American who demands everyone speak English. But after not sleeping for almost twenty-four hours, I didn't need to be drunk. Exhausted, I hugged my girlfriend (at least, I think it was her).

Gillian was determined to help me overcome jet lag by forcing me to stay awake until a locally appropriate bedtime. This had the side effect of giving me an approximation of what it might be like to trip on psychotropic drugs without actually having to try them. My first day in Berlin was a blur of markets, pastries, schnitzels, and a singing walrus in a unitard. I don't remember how I got to Gillian's apartment, but I woke up in her bed the next morning refreshed and ready to spend a relaxing two days together before all her free time would be eaten up with rehearsals and preparations for the upcoming gig. Then I looked out the window and saw nothing but gray and drizzly skies.

Gillian loves and thrives in dreary weather, whereas I require sunshine and Popsicles to feel content, and, at least for my first few days in Berlin, the sun never came out. My vacation seemed to take its cues from the clouds. I had just gotten there and desperately needed to recharge my spirit and my wheelchair. But when my girlfriend plugged my specially obtained, ultrasafe, European battery charger into the wall, I got just the spark I didn't need. As it turned out, my charger was not actually equipped to handle European voltage. History was repeating itself and that left both me and my wheelchair fried and depleted. Who could have thought that Germany of all places would turn out to be so depressing?

I was downtrodden in Deutschland, but my faithful fräulein was still determined for me to see the best in Berlin. I knew from experience that fixing a wheelchair charger in a foreign country was not easy. Luckily, everyone in Berlin spoke perfect English. Everyone, that is, except wheelchair repairmen. Gillian had a whole year of German under her belt and had been preparing for such a complicated conversation about complex electrical engineering by reading the German editions of the Harry Potter books. As long as everything wrong with my wheelchair could be described in terms of horcruxes, I'd be up and running in no time. To my amazement, Gilly was able to piece together enough coherent German to communicate our problem to a very patient electrician, who promised to fix what the Dementors had done to my chair.

We left the shop in a manual chair on loan. The setback was an inconvenience, but at least Berlin's public transport system was top-notch and in large part accessible. Unfortunately, when we returned the next day, we discovered that the U-Bahn station's elevator had broken overnight. If we continued the three stops to the next accessible station, we risked missing our chance to retrieve my chair before the shop closed promptly, as most businesses that sell necessary medical equipment do, at 11:00 a.m. So Zach and Gill plunked up the stairs to fetch a working wheelchair.

By the time I was finally mobile again, the two days' respite we'd planned to spend together before Gillian's intense concert prep kicked in had evaporated. For the remainder of the week, while she was busy working, I'd be wandering. But the only thing I'd actually planned to do in Berlin was get there. To the average tourist, it might seem like a waste to be in a vibrant city filled with famous landmarks, museums, and *biergartens* without so much as an inkling of what they wanted to do or see. But for me, this trip was primarily an opportunity to simply exist on my own in the world.

I zoomed around the neighborhood of Prenzlauer Berg in my chair, up to the shopping center on Shönehauser Allee, then took the U-Bahn to Alexanderplatz. I went to an electronics store and envied their entire floor of espresso machines, and stopped by the H&M to buy two shirts. I got lost and found myself at closed comedy clubs boasting shows in all English, and I happened upon typewriter boutiques and haberdasheries that were just old and quaint enough to ensure there'd be a six-inch stoop out front that would keep me from doing anything other than window-shopping. For the most part, I was cold and unhappy, but still somehow proud because even if I was bored, I was bored in Berlin. I was *in Berlin*. I felt like a man making his way through the world like everyone else. That foreign sensation was more valuable to me than any tourist's top ten list.

One day, I sat in a café for five hours. I had two espressos and half an almond croissant, but I also had the chance to reflect on how long of a journey it had been to get to this beautifully mundane moment. Long before I ever hosted a travel show, all the way back to my Cindy Crawford–chasing days, I had the deep-seated desire not just to travel but to escape. Even when I was at home, life came with baggage that I couldn't shed. I was dependent, disabled, treated differently. By my early twenties, my mind wanted to mature, but my body made it next to impossible for me to be seen as anything other than a child.

There's a lyric in one of Gillian's songs that has always spoken to me. In the third verse of "The Hinterhaus," she sings, "I know what it is to be half-transformed / still burdened with the evidence / of what you were before." From my perspective, that feels like a pretty poignant description of what it can be like to go through life with a disability. I've often felt like a half-transformed man, someone who could be truly great if he didn't have so many bullshit problems. I sometimes fantasize about what might be different if I were unencumbered by my condition, the places I'd go if I didn't have the chair, the art I would make if my body would cooperate, and the person I'd be if the simple things weren't so complicated. It's like that magic mirror Harry Potter stares into to see what his life would have been like if his parents were still alive. In my darkest moments, the "what-if"s bury me and the "if only"s keep me from enjoying what *is*.

This faulty thinking led to an oppressive low when I was twenty-three. In 2008 I was living in Austin off Social Security with no money, no job, and no direction. I was stuck. I thought that if I could just get away from my environment, I could find out who I actually was, independent of my problems. It was in the midst of this quarter-life crisis that my aunt Marian passed away. We'd always shared a special connection, but I was still surprised when she left me a modest inheritance. I planned to save most of it but also saw an opportunity to finally have an autonomous adventure, hit the Reset button, and chart a new course. My dad told me to invest the money until I figured out what I wanted to do with it, so in September of that year I followed his advice and placed all of my inheritance in mutual funds. One month later, on October 6, the stock market crashed and my nest egg was immediately cut by more than half.

I was luckier than some in that I didn't have a mortgage or a family to support, but judging from all the job interviews I'd ever had, society had also deemed me unemployable and there was no indication I would ever find a career. The generous gift from my aunt also meant that I'd lost my Social Security benefits. As my bank account dwindled, I realized that the money, along with the newfound sense of freedom it had brought, would completely vanish in a few months. Rather than just watch myself slowly go broke, I wanted to do something that could have a lasting impact on my perspective. I couldn't afford to go to Europe anymore, but I needed to go somewhere.

So I hatched a plan that was devoid of any planning. I wouldn't tell my parents, my brother, his girlfriend, or my roommate that I was leaving until I was already gone. I'd pack a bag, bungee my charger to the back of my chair, and take a cab to the airport in the middle of the night. When I got there, I'd have one directive for the ticket agent—"Send me anywhere." Now, naturally, I assumed that they might have follow-up questions, like "How much can you spend?" "Window or aisle?" and, noting my urgency, "You didn't just murder somebody, did you?" I wouldn't know where I was going, but it didn't really matter. Any place I ended up—Tallahassee, Omaha, Tucson—would be new to me and I'd be new to it. I wouldn't put any pressure on what I was supposed to do or how I was supposed to feel; I'd just take the experience for what it was.

So while my roommate was on a date and my brother was in his adjacent apartment with his girlfriend, I started packing, knowing that if I was going to leave unseen, I'd have to move faster than I'd ever moved in my life. I stuffed underwear, socks, and other clothing into the bag, unable to fold them. I was just about to call a cab when my brother walked through the front door and caught me red-handed. I froze.

"Uh, Tenielle just wanted me to stop by and get the pickles we left here. You goin' somewhere?"

"Yeah," I said, and, not wanting to lie, told him what I was doing.

"Well, first, don't order a taxi—I can take ya; cabs are expensive. I like your idea, but it's gonna cost a fortune if you just show up without a ticket. Let me talk to Tenielle. Her mom has airline miles and travels a lot. She might have some advice so you don't waste all your money."

And just like that, my spontaneous, incognito getaway morphed into vacation by committee: a budget-conscious and sensible four-day sabbatical in Boulder, Colorado. At Tenielle's suggestion, I had pointed to five different locations on a US map and then she looked up flights and told me which was cheapest. I'd no longer be flying away in the middle of the night but was scheduled to leave at eight in the morning the following Thursday.

"I'll e-mail you a list of hotels in the area," Tenielle said. "I know you want this to just be time for you, and your brother and I both totally support that. Just text me when you get there and we'll see you when you get back."

"I think it's great that you're doing this. Should be a really positive thing," my roommate Jesse assured me the night before I left.

I was now required to have a life-affirming, transformative experience. I was still excited to go to Colorado, sure, but everyone else was excited for me too. They had expectations, opinions, and suggestions. I hoped that when I got there I'd be able to block out all the noise and find something for myself. It was overwhelming. *But at least I'm going*, I thought. And then, I didn't go.

As we pulled up alongside the departures curb at the airport and I got into my wheelchair, a look of panic came over my brother's face.

"Um," he said, "I don't think your bag is here."

"What?" I said, horrified.

"I don't know how this happened, but I think we just left your bag outside the van back at the apartment. Let me see how fast I can run back and get it."

There was less than an hour until my tightly scheduled flight. I knew that there was no way he'd make it back in time. On the surface, it seemed like this catastrophe was perfectly in line with the spirit in which I'd conceived the expedition. But there was one problem. My wheelchair charger was in that bag. I would have been fine buying a whole new wardrobe of souvenir T-shirts with either the Rocky Mountains or cannabis on them, but even I had to accept that if I'd be immobile once I got to Colorado, there was really no point in flying there.

As my brother made the futile race home to retrieve my luggage (which was hopefully still standing in the parking lot), I tried to convince the ticket agent that my wheelchair was malfunctioning so that she would rebook my flight without charging me the two-hundred-dollar change fee. But I wouldn't be able to get to Boulder that day, or even the next day. Rather than stay true to my own mantra and just roll with it, I simply gave up.

I went home defeated and spent the next few days in my bedroom banging my head against the wall. I felt like my identity was comprised solely of the echoes of a world that assumed I couldn't or wouldn't amount to much. To their credit, my family and friends never gave up on me, but there were years when their faith clung to the abstract of my potential, in the absence of any hard evidence that I would succeed.

And now, here I was in Germany, with a croissant's worth of crumbs in my lap and no one to tell me I was putting too much sugar in my espresso. *Wunderbar.* I'd gone from being nobody to being somebody, and for the first time I felt I could be anonymous without being invisible. As the week progressed, I started to warm up to Berlin when I stopped blaming it for how cold and gloomy it was. I made a conscious decision to find things about Berlin I appreciated, without necessarily having to like the city. For one thing, the fact that I could stare out a window for five hours in a café and not be hustled out the door was an approach to hospitality I admired.

Contrary to the assumptions I'd made before arriving, Berlin is a very relaxed place, now that all the Nazis, Communists, and citywide walls are gone. The entire population, including the dogs, are free to roam the streets and not be bothered. Normally, if you told me there was a city where four-legged friends walk beside humans as equals, tethered not by leashes but by trust and devotion, I would have laughed at you and then immediately been terrified of being attacked and eaten by a pack of wild dogs. (It only takes one Cujo to spoil the bunch.) But these pups were civilized. The dogs in Berlin do not have owners, they have partners. Every canine confidently trots beside its human counterpart, sharing an unspoken agreement.

I love you, but zis is a bond zat ve've built on mutual respect and admiration for each other. I vill vait for you outside ze shop vhile you get your cigarettes, but I do not approve of your choices. Vhy is it zat you can put cancer in your body, but I cannot eat a shoe, ja?

On the rare occasion that someone like me who's not yet found their doggie soul mate can steal their focus, it is only for a fleeting moment.

Ja, guten Tag! How are you? Ja, I love you, but not as much as I love zat man. He's ze best man in zeh vorld. He seems to be rounding the corner now, so I'm afraid ve must cut zis affectionate exchange short. Auf Wiedersehen!

And just like that, they're bolting down the street and out of your life, determined to get back to the one they truly love above all others. Like its dogs, Berlin's humans were friendly without being nosy. They were accommodating but not patronizing. But what really won me over about Berlin was not the people, or the dogs, but the McDonald's.

I found my way to the golden arches after what had been a generally crappy morning. I'd lost my ticket for the U-Bahn and couldn't find the street market Gillian had given me detailed directions to before she'd rushed off to yet another rehearsal. It was raining, again, and to top it off, I really had to pee. I went inside the shopping mall at Shönehauser Allee, found my way to the bathroom, didn't tip the bathroom attendant because I didn't know that was a thing, and then, as I was getting onto the toilet, the seat moved, and I slipped, submerging my arm in the water. Even I could admit this was funny, but you can only fall in so many toilets before it starts to weigh on your self-esteem. I said to myself, *You know what? I'm not very happy, but I am very hungry.* So I found the most American solution to both problems and went to McDonald's for a Happy Meal.

I could write an entire chapter of this book on how extraordinary German McDonald's are. In the US, the only art you see at Mickey D's is generally either crayon-based or penis-shaped. People who aren't in middle school don't enjoy themselves. In America, you go to McDonald's as an adult because everything else is closed, you're stoned, or you just finalized the divorce and your husband is getting the boat (or in my case, you've just fallen into a toilet). But in Germany, McDonald's is THE destination for amazing service and culture. I'm not kidding you! There were pieces of art on the wall. There was a whole series of Jack Vettriano reproductions, and it wouldn't have felt out of place to have fountains with doves and an on-staff masseuse who'd rub your back with french fry oil.

I didn't get some crappy plastic toy with my Happy Meal, I got a BOOK! Not a pamphlet, but an actual hardcover book with full-color illustrations called *SUPER TIER* about the world's most amazing animals. *I'm lookin' at art, learnin' about nature, and eatin' organic chicken McNuggets! I'm lovin' it!* I thought, *Oh, that's where that comes from! They were referring to the GERMAN McDonald's!* All it took was one trip to the golden arches and I was completely convinced that I had to come back to Berlin. That, plus the bonus of my girlfriend living there.

Now that I was ready to experience Germany with an open heart and an open mind, I needed somebody to show me a more authentic side of the city. And since my girlfriend was busy, who better than my girlfriend's roommate's boyfriend to take me out on the town? Carl was every bit the girlfriend Gillian is. We made the most of our sausage fest by getting bratwurst, and in Germany, bratwurst is sold on every corner. Every time I turned away for a moment, as soon as I glanced back Carl would be munching on a new one. Since it was Oktoberfest and neither of us was a big drinker, we shared a *bier*, and then continued the day at the two most romantic spots in Berlin: the Brandenburg Gate and the Jewish History Museum. All in all, it was a pretty solid first date.

On top of that, I still had Gillian to come home to. I loved listening to stories of her rehearsals and showing her the pictures of Carl and me kissing in front of the gate. I liked living my own life and having my own stories to tell. But what I treasured most were the tiny moments that were too boring to share with anyone else. These were the types of vacations I liked to have. I wasn't as brashly cavalier as my dad or as laid back as my mom; I was a guy who took big chances so that he could enjoy small things.

On the night of Gillian's concert, I was one of the first people to arrive because I came with the star of the show. I wheeled up to my VIP seating at a tiny round bar table beside the stage. In the hour leading up to the show, I watched as the small club became packed with a hundred people whose collective body heat managed to raise the temperature twenty degrees by the time Gillian and her trio took the stage. Finally, the room went dark and a hush came over the audience.

I recognized the woman who settled in behind her harp, but it was hard to imagine that this picture of poise in black jeans and high heels was the same person I'd seen nearly fall asleep in her salad after ten-hour rehearsals over the previous week. From the first plucked note I reverted back to the same starstruck fan who had sent her that initial tweet over a year earlier. I'd said then that her music would bring me to Germany and now it finally had.

Over the course of two sets, Gillian was able to not just share an experience with her audience but also shepherd them through an emotional journey. She had them cheering along with drinking songs, stunned to silence after darkly provocative ballads, and hypnotized by the soothing drone of lullabies. Whatever the mood, the crowd moved with her and was moved by her.

Just as the songs had been born from moments of relentless introspection, entrenched struggle, and wistful memory, this beautiful night had arrived by way of chaos, practice, and sleep deprivation, and at the expense of regular showers. As I watched her up there, rocking her harp back and forth like it was an extension of herself, I recognized an artist who knew exactly who she was, what she wanted to say, and how to say it. I was proud, enamored, and a little turned on, to be honest.

The evening was even more special because my aunt Naomi and uncle Gareth had come all the way from London just to see the concert. For the first time, we were able to see one another away from the context of big family gatherings. During Gillian's rendition of Irving Berlin's "What'll I Do?" I looked across the table and saw my uncle—who wouldn't look out of place in a pith helmet standing with a musket beside a dead Siberian tiger—with tears running into his bushy white handlebar mustache. The last time I'd seen them in Europe, we had been worlds apart. But that night, as we listened to my girlfriend perform a standard even my grandma Ruthie would have appreciated, we were just three people sharing a wonderful experience.

I could tell that Naomi and Gareth saw me in a new light. I was an adult now, a man who flew across the ocean, made a living doing what he loved, and was dating the prettiest, most talented girl in the room. I felt different too, like I was no longer the wandering and weary traveler in my own life. The solitude I'd had in Berlin had given me the time, not just by myself, but as myself that I'd been searching for for so long. Berlin made me realize that I didn't need to go anywhere anymore. I had already arrived. I was a traveler who finally knew that no matter where I was in the world, I had found my place in it.

Thirty Candles

When I was six years old, a fifth grader was the oldest human being I could ever imagine turning into. At Lindbergh Elementary, every first grader was paired with an upper-class mentor. Once a week, the mighty fifth graders would march down the stairs to the first floor and pile into our tiny classroom like giants, their Reebok pumps and LED sneakers creaking the generously lacquered floorboards. They'd loom above us and then sit down with us, and we'd read to each other. My paired reading partner, Alex, read me chapter books like *Scary Stories to Tell in the Dark*, while I would sound out and stammer my way through *Little Bear*.

I remember looking up at those ten-year-olds who so confidently wore jeans and sports jerseys and had mousse in their hair, and thinking, *I can't wait to be a grown-up like that! I wonder if my mom would buy me mousse. . . . Is this purple sweat suit with the glitter and abstract art printed on it something adults would wear?* For one hour every Thursday, I came face-to-face with my future and it seemed exciting but so distant that I thought I would never get there.

But in November 2014, I woke up to find that I was nearly three fifth graders old! My purple bedazzled sweat suits had been replaced by lavender button-downs and my flashing LED sneakers had been upgraded to the exact same pair of brown suede loafers my grandfather wears. I'd gone through my entire twenty-ninth year being asked what I was going to do for my thirtieth birthday and how it felt to officially be an old man. The truth is, I had no idea how I was supposed to feel or why this birthday was so important to everyone else. I felt a lot of pressure to have an epiphany that would give me some profound perspective on the meaning of my existence, like I'd be blowing out my birthday candles surrounded by friends and as I plunged the knife into the first slice of cake and made a wish, it would all become clear. I'd exclaim, "I get it! My life has been about shoes this whole time!" and head off into the mountains to live out the rest of my days as a cobbler.

But in the months leading up to the big Three-O, I actually felt anxious that no life-altering lightbulb had gone off in my head. I didn't feel like I was at a pivotal moment at all. I'd worked hard and had great friends, an amazing family, a girl-friend I loved, and a career I was proud of. *This isn't gonna make a good story!* I thought, *Hopefully, something will go wrong.* I racked my brain to find a celebration that had the potential to be a disaster. After all, failure had been the catalyst for most of the meaning in my life, and because I hoped to live to at least ninety, this birthday was meant to be the climactic cliffhanger ending to the first part of my life's trilogy.

It wasn't until September that I finally called Chris Demarais with an idea.

"Hey," I said, excitedly, "I'm turning thirty in two months and I know what I wanna do for my birthday."

"Oh yeah?" he said, intrigued.

"Yup. I wanna rent out a theater at the Alamo Drafthouse and screen the last three episodes of *The Wingmen*. Can we finish them?"

Silence. One of those twelve-month pregnant silences that only Chris Demarais does.

"Uh . . . ," Chris wondered aloud. "I like the *idea*, and I know we can get episodes eight and nine done, but I have no clue about ten."

"Can I book the theater then?" I asked.

"Maaaybe?" he guessed. "Actually, why don't you go ahead and book it. No, wait, give Aaron and me until Monday to look over the footage. No, don't book anything yet. But maybe."

This is as close as Chris Demarais ever gets to making a commitment, so I was hopeful that my college comedy troupe's long-abandoned Web series might finally get the ending it deserved and that my thirtieth birthday would see me closing out an important chapter in both my personal and my professional life. It could also be a train wreck, which was equally appealing.

Me and the four other members of our group, Lark the Beard, started *The Wingmen* way back in 2008, when we were still undergrads at the University of Texas. *The Wingmen* tells the story of four hosts of a dating advice radio show who are being followed around for a documentary. Their romantic wisdom includes such gems as "Do one little thing every day to make your girlfriend sad," "A man is better than a raft," and my personal favorite, "Take her to Olive Garden!" In the first episode Chris's character flies off the handle on air, spouting profanity when he discovers that his girlfriend is cheating on him. After being fired from their show and fined $15,000 by the Federal Communications Commission, they decide to start a dating service where, instead of matching clients up, they go out on all the dates themselves in order to meet women and make money. The entire show was improvised and shot in the mockumentary style of *The Office*.

We released the first seven episodes online and it went so well that we got the attention of FOX television, wrote a treatment for them, did five versions of a trailer, got a fancy LA agent to tell us that we were about to make millions of dollars, and then . . . nothing happened. Everything stalled and, disheartened, the final three episodes were never released or even finished.

In the seven years since *The Wingmen* fizzled, three of the five Wingmen had gotten jobs at a digital media company called Rooster Teeth, several of the principal cast members had gotten married, Aaron had gotten ceremoniously engaged and unceremoniously disengaged, and I'd had time to win and lose a show from Oprah, make an Internet travel series, move out to LA for two seasons of *Have a Little Faith*, and wind up back in Texas where it all started. I didn't have a network contract or a large sum of money to throw in front of my friends as incentive to complete a project we had all moved on from—all I had was my thirtieth birthday and the fact that I'd already told anyone who would listen that the last three episodes would finally be released.

On the day before my birthday everything was going so

smoothly, I almost felt disappointed. When I left to pick up Gillian from the airport, the final *Wingmen* videos were already exporting, our RSVP list for the Drafthouse screening was overflowing, and my stomach was strangely calm. With no conflicts, catastrophes, or crises to address, I felt like I could rest easy, so Gillian and I snuggled up on the mattress on the floor of my rented Downtown Austin apartment and I fell asleep, for the last time, as a twentysomething.

I was not awoken by an earthquake or even a mariachi band, and they're everywhere in Texas! No, I just woke up well rested and happy, barely noticing that I'd entered a whole new decade of my life. The rest of the day was uneventfully lovely. Well, there were events, there just weren't any problems. The worst thing I had to deal with was that it was a little nippy out when Gillian sent me off to go get hair conditioner, but when I returned, she surprised me with homemade Olive Garden breadsticks she'd shaped into letters that read, "H-A-P-P-Y B-D-A-Y Z-A-C-H." She'd even remembered to spell my name with an "H."

I checked in with Chris and Aaron and everything was going swimmingly on their end too. They didn't need my help. Heck, even when I'd stopped by a few nights earlier to edit, I found that 90 percent of the work had already been done. There just were a few stray pickup shots we needed to get, and so we found ourselves running down to the lobby of Aaron's apartment and acting in roles we hadn't inhabited since 2009. But our *Wingmen* characters came back to us as naturally as riding a bike because we all played idiots.

"Try and fit as many nuts in your mouth as possible," I shouted at Chris from behind the camera. "You're always funnier when you're eating."

"Raise your voice up half an octave and add about fifty percent more dumb," Aaron suggested.

Our group had developed such a shorthand that "more dumb" and "more nuts" were all the direction any of us needed. When we started making *The Wingmen*, we had no idea what we were doing. Now, shooting scenes on the fly was a reflex. It was invigorating to be working on a deadline with my best friends again.

Back in our UT days, everything was always down to the wire. Sheer lack of time, sleep, and experience was what motivated us to get stuff done. I remember one night, three days before an episode's premiere, Brad, Chris, and I were all working late at my place during finals week. Chris still had half an hour of footage to color-correct and we didn't have a minute to spare because in those days, exporting thirty minutes of video took the computer two days and there was no guarantee it wouldn't crash during the process.

At four a.m., after three hours of staring at a screen trying to get a fondue pot to look less blown out, Chris begged me, "Zach, I just need to sleep for fifteen minutes, just maybe half an hour . . ." His eyeballs were so bloodshot that he could have easily gotten excused from class for pinkeye, and the bags underneath his eyes were so dark and pronounced that they looked like folds of rhinoceros skin. I said, "Sure, you can take a nap, but it can ONLY be half an hour. We really need to get this to Aaron so that he can start the final export." As soon as Chris hit the mattress in my bedroom, he was out cold. Brad and I knew that we couldn't afford this nap, so we did what any responsible producers would do. We went through my apartment and set all of the clocks forward two hours. We even stealthily changed the time on Chris's phone, swiping it from the bedside table. Ten minutes later, I roused Chris from a deep sleep.

"Dude, you gotta get up! It's already past six!"

"What?" he said, still in a daze.

"Yeah, you slept for like an hour and a half, two hours. We gotta get back to work!"

"I don't know why I still feel so tired!" he moaned. "I feel like I've only been asleep for like five minutes!"

"You want me to make some coffee?" asked Brad.

"Yeah, I guess I need it. I gotta get to class by nine. Why didn't you guys wake me up sooner?"

"I thought it was important that you get your rest," I said. "Clearly I was right!"

After we'd convinced him that he didn't have the right to be anything other than wide-awake, Chris trudged through the rest of his work. By the time he thought it was eight thirty a.m., there was only one scene left to finish.

"There's no way I'm gonna get this done before class. Man, I thought the sun would be up by now. I guess the days are getting really short, huh? I better call Aaron to see if he can come over and finish this."

"No, you've got time," I said. And then I let him know just how horrible a friend I actually was. Chris, being one of the most affable humans I know, found the whole thing hysterical.

Now the clocks had moved forward seven years, and my imminent birthday party brought back a drive and camaraderie we hadn't shared since college. When I'd called up our former cast mates Marshall and Jordan, who were both living in LA, and told them about the screening, they immediately began organizing a road trip to Austin. Even though work would only allow them to be in Texas for twenty-four hours, they wouldn't miss the chance to see their most fondly abandoned labor of love completed.

The stars had aligned and all of our ducks were in a row. All five wingmen would be there to witness their work projected on the big screen and a lot of other important people would be in the audience too: cast members we hadn't seen since we'd filmed with them, several of Chris's and Aaron's ex-girlfriends and my ex-crushes, and students who'd volunteered as crew. The night promised to be a merging of worlds between friends old and new. All I had to do for this magical event to transpire was turn thirty and show up.

We had an eighty-seat theater and Chris and I were worried that, like our ill-fated Salsa Dancing and Christmas Sweater Party in 2008, many would RSVP but, in the end, no one would come. But as soon as we got to the theater, familiar faces began filtering in. They were even showing up early, before our scheduled retrospective preshow DVD had started playing. I guess the call of late-aught nostalgia had proven irresistible for everyone.

I got more birthday hugs in a twenty-minute window than I'd gotten over my last five birthdays combined. I also got the long-overdue pleasure of introducing someone as my girlfriend to the people who had so gallantly tried and failed to get me one. There were no glitches, no hitches, and when the lights finally went down, the theater was packed and the crowd was ready to blow the Alamo Drafthouse food and beverage minimum out of the water and enjoy a three-hour marathon of a Web series—mostly shot by volunteers who were using cameras for the first time—on a big screen.

I sat back in the dark and watched scene after scene of my friends making terrible dating choices, like the one where

Chris picks up his date on a tandem bike and takes her to Boston Market, or when Jordan assumes a double date just means going out with two girls at once. I watched us have a sleepover together in the same TV station where I'd had all my *That's Awesome!* meetings, and I saw the fictional version of Zach getting kicked out of the same Olive Garden where I'd taken Holly for dinner. That scene had actually been filmed three times at three different Olive Gardens, which is the reason I'm now only welcome at one branch in the Austin area. Luckily, it's the Olive Garden across the street from my current apartment. Each episode was like a time capsule of places, people, and experiences that were important to me.

While all the other main characters in *The Wingmen* found themselves conveniently coupled up at the end of the series, I was always adamant that my character should not have a happy ending. Instead, Wingmen Zach meets a girl he thinks he has chemistry with, goes on a few dates with her, and ends up getting his heart broken. He realizes they have no romantic future when she asks him to be in an antidrug PSA she's producing and he finds out that she wants him to play a severely mentally handicapped cautionary tale whose only job is to drool applesauce on himself.

I felt obligated to shoot this story because I'd actually lived through it. I remembered how painful it was to feel as though I was making a connection with someone, only to discover that I'd been reduced to every stereotype I'd tried so hard to overcome. To this day it's the most common type of role I'm offered. I still get e-mails from people saying "I've got this part you'd be perfect for!" with an attached script that features a character who wears a bike helmet and a diaper all the time.

When the applesauce scene played at the Drafthouse, there

were audible gasps from the audience. No one laughed, except Jordan, who could see the pitch-black humor in such a brutal scenario. I always knew that this had to be the way my character's arc in the show ended. In 2008, when we had filmed it, I didn't know how to write a happy ending for a fictionalized version of myself because I didn't know if one was actually in the cards for me. What I did know was how to remain hopeful in the face of great failure, pain, and dismissal. So in *The Wingmen*, I closed out with hope, because that's all I knew for sure was true.

In the final episode, the wingmen pay off their fine and get their radio show back, and my character is the last one to speak directly to the camera. Reflecting to our fake documentary crew, I impart the wisdom that "I may not be the right guy for everyone, but I'm the right guy for someone. Sure, I've got the wheelchair and the lazy eye, and I may have really long balls that flush in the toilet when I'm using the bathroom, but beneath those balls is a heart that loves. So keep that in mind while you're judging my balls!"

That's basically the end of *The Wingmen* and that was how I closed out my thirtieth birthday—by acknowledging my most glaring imperfections and then declaring that I deserved to be loved anyway. As my parting words of optimism were said on-screen, I heard them in the real world, while sitting next to my girlfriend and holding hands in the dark.

When it was all over, my former cast mates and I went up and thanked everyone for coming. I gushed about how much I loved the assholes standing beside me because they were the best friends that anybody could have. I looked out at my friends, my girlfriend, my brother, and my colleagues gathered together in the theater, and at Aaron's insistence they all sang "Happy Birthday" to me. I felt grateful and lucky, but I didn't have much perspective on what I'd actually done to get to this picture-perfect moment. It wasn't until about a month later when I came home to Buffalo for Christmas that I was able to find meaning in the happiness I felt that night. I was content at thirty, proud of myself even, and that sense of accomplishment gave me the courage to confront a time in my life that I'd largely tried to forget.

When I was sixteen, I spent my days as an isolated and sick high school dropout, only leaving the house for doctors' appointments. Most of the time I was too weak to leave my bed even to pee, opting instead for a plastic urinal held by my mom. I had shut down physically and was so despondent that I became a stranger to myself. Even now, it feels bizarre to recount this period of my life in the first person.

During those hazy years when I was housebound and bed-ridden, the one thing that saved me from being a Hamlet-level Debbie Downer was writing. Even when I was laid up, too infirm to go to school or see friends, I had a typist come over and work with me on my first screenplay. Somehow, at a time when I felt like my entire life had stalled, I managed to finish a 157-page movie script. On one particularly ambitious February day in 2001, I also wrote out a list of goals for the distant and unforeseen future of 2003. I outlined my biggest dreams and personal aspirations in the boldest rainbow bubble font I could find in Microsoft WordArt. These proclamations were designed to inspire and challenge me. I printed them out, framed them, and displayed them prominently in my room so that I'd be held accountable for my own destiny. But as time passed and I realized that my lofty ambitions were beyond my reach, I took down the list and turned it to the wall in shame.

At the end of 2014, I was almost twelve years past my self-imposed deadline for personal success. I never forgot about the list, but I avoided rereading it over the years, first out of guilt for not accomplishing anything I'd dreamed of and then later, as I got older, out of fear of embarrassment. I worried that everything I'd hoped for was so naive and juvenile that I'd lose all respect for myself and would never be able to look in the mirror again without seeing that pathetic sixteen-year-old staring back.

But now, at thirty, I was finally old enough and, more important, mature enough to be compassionate and forgiving toward that younger and greener version of myself. As I was rooting through my bedroom closet over Christmas, I asked my mom if she still had that list of goals I'd written, and, without even pausing to think, she knew exactly where it was. I was surprised by this because a recent perusal of my baby book had revealed that in the chaos of my birth, nobody had even thought to write down the time I was born, let alone get my footprints. But this list was something she'd been compelled to save. When I flipped over the frame, my eyes were assaulted by the color scheme and I was somewhat disappointed in the lack of font consistency. Then I started reading the idealistic future I'd envisioned for myself over a decade ago. It started with three simple words—"Go For It!"—followed by the bombastic heading: ZACH'S GOALS TO BE ACCOMPLISHED BY FEBRUARY 28th, 2003.

Keep in mind, I'd only given myself two years to complete these things because, much like my six-year-old self, my sixteen-year-old self thought two years was an eternity. As I read through the list, I was surprised to find that despite having written this document when my life showed very little promise, my hopes for myself were boundlessly optimistic and as bold as the magenta and aquamarine ink they were typed out in. Some of them were short-term goals, like "Finish my screenplay and send it to competitions," which came with the parenthetical insight "(judges are generally bitter about their sexual inadequacies; weigh their advice and quickly move on)." While I didn't achieve the Academy Award(s) I was hoping for by 2004 or 2005, I was pleased to find that at thirty, I had actually completed or exceeded many of my planned achievements. Here, for example, are numbers three through seven on the list:

3. Set smaller goals so that you become more physically independent. (You can't have family do everything; be your own man.)
4. Exercise! (To match the rest of you, be strong physically.)
5. Make contacts in the film industry. (Your personality will help you out.)
6. Get a good SAT score. (Prove that sometimes people don't go to school because they don't need it.)
7. Get accepted into film school. (If you believe it'll help your career.)

But even at my most grandiose, my teenage-oracle self still couldn't imagine the wild, oftentimes extraordinary path my life would actually end up taking. There's no mention of Oprah in these goals, nor of the friends I'd make at the University of Texas, or the travel shows I'd host, or that somebody with no college degrees would be speaking at colleges around the country and motivating people around the world through humor.

Goals nine, ten, and eleven, while not specific, at least hint at that higher trajectory:

9. Distance yourself. (To fulfill your potential, you must change your environment.)
10. Be a positive role model. (You can inspire people.)
11. After you succeed, help those who are less fortunate. (You can still make a difference *before* you have huge success.)

There's only one mention of dating in that document, a special bonus goal, which reads, "BONUS: Take 10 girls on dream dates. (They're beautiful people and they deserve absolute beauty.)"

This is the only one on the list that makes me cringe and say, *What an asshole!* to myself about myself, and I'm glad that time and experience have rendered this goal null and void, because I've realized that instead of taking ten girls on one dream date, I'd rather take one dream girl on ten.

I was admittedly shocked by this list, but not in the way I thought I would be. I remembered the time I composed that document as the most hopeless and fatalistic I'd ever felt in my life, but here in my hands was proof that even in my darkest days, I couldn't resist being optimistic. As random as these thirty years had been, hope was one of the few constants in my life—hope, and a family ready to dust off my dreams if I should ever need to be reminded of them.

My stomach problems were never cured. You already know that if you've read this book in order and haven't put it on shuffle. I didn't get better at being better; I just got better at coping. I started taking an antidepressant that also combated my acid reflux and I began a love/hate relationship with Imodium. I gained confidence that even if my body sabotaged me, I had the strategies and tools to make it through. Slowly, I started feeling like myself again. With the support of my family and friends, I got out of my head, out of my bed, out of Buffalo, and never really looked back until this moment, holding that plastic frame from Michaels with all my Technicolor aspirations in it.

My first three decades hadn't gone exactly as I'd planned, but I think planning them so ambitiously might have made them richer and better. As my left eye finally made its way down to the end of the page while the right drifted off and kept tabs on my lamp in the corner, I read my last, and aptly named, ultimate goal for myself:

ULTIMATE GOAL

NO MATTER WHAT HAPPENS IN YOUR LIFE,
ALWAYS HAVE A DREAM. ALWAYS REMEMBER
YOUR PURPOSE AND MAINTAIN A PASSION FOR
LIVING. (YOU'RE ONE LUCKY BASTARD :O) .)

I can't say that I've gotten everything right up 'til now or that I'll get everything right after this point. In fact, I hope to have another thirty years of mistakes ahead of me, and, depending on how this book sells, I might have to cram them into the next five just to hit a deadline. But whatever stories of failure and success I have left to tell, I'll try to remember what I wrote to myself when I was sixteen, because no matter how old I get, good advice is good advice.

Acknowledgments

While this book recounts my first three decades, its pages also reflect a year of beautiful partnership and collaboration. Gillian Grassie and I have spent over five hundred hours working together on this book. Whenever I struggled, she was always right there on Skype and Google Docs helping me find a more descriptive verb, write a tighter sentence, build a stronger paragraph, craft a better narrative, tell a funnier joke, and imploring me to dig deeper. Gilly, thank you for so selflessly giving me the tools, the courage, and sometimes even the words, to be a better writer and a better person. For me, this has been the most rewarding chapter of a life filled with great stories that now, thanks in large part to you, have been told well.

Emi Ikkanda, thanks for believing in this book from the very beginning, having a vision when mine was still hazy, and ruthlessly cutting away unnecessary blabber. Your faith and fortitude kept me from going insane on multiple occasions.

Anna Sproul-Latimer, you are a rock star who single-handedly restored my faith in agents. Thanks for staying with me for two years while I circled around the idea of writing this book. Having you in my corner has been the best thing to ever happen to my career. Even more than that, I'm so happy to call you a friend.

Massive thanks to everyone at Henry Holt for championing the book so fervently and lending me your many talents.

Mom, thanks for never giving up on me, being my most dedicated advocate, and giving me my creative spark. Remember that birthday card I gave you when I was seven that said, "I think I'm starting to like you"? Well, I can now confirm in writing that I love you, Mom. Thanks for giving me everything.

Dad, thank you for your love, support, and ingenuity, which have allowed me to thrive in the world rather than be bogged down by my problems. You are the Leonardo da Vinci of adaptive technology and the reason I'm a man of the world. (For future reference, if I ever bring a girl home for the first time again, maybe don't show her the shower seat you made for me that doubles as a bidet right off the bat?)

Brad, you're the most selfless and patient brother on the face of the planet, not to mention the funniest and most original person I know. You're also my most consistent collaborator and the only reason people see most of my work. Your staunch resolve to never pay more than twelve dollars for a haircut is an inspiration to me every day.

Greg McGill, you're like a hilarious older brother who also sleeps with my mom. I owe you many nickels for all the jokes and awkward phrases I've stolen from you over the years.

Thanks for teaching me that getting older is inevitable but growing up is optional.

Andrew Martina, you are my moral compass and a shining yet hairy example of what it means to be a best friend. The twenty-three years I've known you have been the best twenty-three years of my life so far. Growing up with you has been the privilege of a lifetime. So glad to see that we're both kicking ass and chewing bubble gum.

Kevin Scarborough, thank you for these incredible illustrations and for being a consistent inspiration and creative cheerleader. Hot beverage? Kate, thanks for letting me crash at your place and being the most gracious hostess. I resolve to squabble over the check for every dinner.

Chris Demarais, my friendship with you is what kept me in Austin. No matter the project, you've always been there to help. Sadly, you were also my first kiss. That's for another book. For now, I'll just say, thanks for the memories and the muffins.

Aaron Marquis, most of the things I just said about Chris also apply to you, so instead of saying them again, I'm just gonna gloat about how I finished a book before you. Suck it, Aaron, I'm an author!

J. Dillon Flanagan, you are a dreamboat who will stop at nothing in pursuit of truth and honor—a great war hero, a great person, and a much better actor and comedian than you ever give yourself credit for. You are the moon of my life, my sun and stars.

Marshall Rimmer, thanks for your friendship, all of your help with my videos over the years, and for those two days we spent at Mocha Joe's banging out the first draft of the Cindy Crawford story.

Jordan Crowder, my all-American French-Canadian friend,

thanks for the countless shoots you helped out with and your impeccable deadpan delivery.

Josh Tate, your assistance has meant a lot through the years, but even more so your filmmaking has shined a light on disability issues in a way that I never could. Thanks for fighting the good fight.

Dave Phillips, thanks for being my first wingman and introducing me to Mel Brooks's comedy.

Mark, my gratitude to you is boundless. Thank you for helping me find my path.

John and Janet Pierson, thank you both for your continued support and advice, and for always shooting straight. It is an honor to call you both friends and mentors.

Kristina, Philip, Luka, Matea, and Han, thank you for being my family on the West Coast.

Papa, I love you as a grandpa, but I admire you as a man. Thank you for always putting family first, letting me raid your closet, and introducing me to strawberry milk shakes.

Grandma Sandy, you fill my life with great memories and meals. Thanks for infusing me with some of that Greek passion, even though I don't have the heritage to back it up!

Thanks to my aunt Bethany, who fought harder to live and enjoy life than anyone I've ever known and could make me pee my pants every time we got together because I laughed so hard.

Grandma Ginny, that was true for you too. Thanks for always being a kid with me and turning me into the goofy sugar freak who always cheats at Yahtzee that I am today.

Grandma Ruthie, thank you for the music, the cookies, and the caramels.

Uncle Rich, I know I promised to describe you as a Brad Pitt type who's married to a Bea Arthur doppelgänger, but I didn't find a way for it to naturally fit in the book. Thank you and Aunt Terri for all the great advice, awesome summers, and confidence boosters (anaconda!), and for always forgiving me when I forget to call.

Corey and Travis, I can think of no better people to be ridiculous with. Laughing with you makes every experience better.

Aunt Naomi and Uncle Gareth, thanks for coming all the way to Berlin to add a special memory to our family's already considerable collection.

To the Anners, the Becks, the Marriotts, and the Rubins, I can't possibly name all of you, but thank you for the huge family gatherings and your generous spirit.

The Hodges, thank you for welcoming this proud Yankee to the South with open arms and a jug of sweet tea.

Babette, Jim, Billy, Rashmini, and Maisy, thank you for welcoming me into the family and being so accommodating and warm.

Alexis Ohanian, thanks for helping me navigate through this crazy digital world and for all the things you do to give guys like me a fighting chance.

Redditors, you guys are the best online community. Thanks for being the loudest voices to make sure that my best stuff gets seen. Your support through the years has been instrumental in every big break that I've had. I'll never forget it. I love you. Upvote!

My friends at SoulPancake, thanks for showing me that good people doing good work can make great things happen.

My friends at Rooster Teeth, thanks for always making me feel like I'm part of the team even though I'm not officially employed by you. (Can I still get dental insurance?)

John Mayer, I'll never be able to write you a song, so this'll have to do: thanks for being a truly decent guy to a complete stranger.

To Oprah and everyone at OWN: thanks for giving me a shot and remaining supportive. I'm forever grateful.

To Mark Burnett Productions and the Your OWN Show team: thanks for making the accommodations so that I could excel. You went above and beyond to ensure I felt respected and valued—two words I never expected to associate with the experience of being on reality TV!

The *Rollin' with Zach* road crew: thanks for embracing the unexpected with me and for sharing so many crazy adventures!

To everyone involved in the YouTube Creator Innovation program, thanks for taking a chance on a cool idea.

Thanks to the University of Texas at Austin: once a Longhorn, always a Longhorn. I know I never finished Spanish, but I'm still banking on an honorary degree from you!

Special thanks also to my generous teachers and therapists at Lindbergh Elementary, Kenmore Middle, and Kenmore West High School, the Tomorrow's Youth Today tutors, and my fifth-grade teacher Mrs. Nabozny for giving up her planning period twice a week so I could write my first play.

I'd like to thank David Sedaris, whose books comprise 93 percent of my personal library, and Stephen King, whose memoir *On Writing* gave me newfound respect for the process and made me regret every adverb.

Finally, thank you to every YouTube subscriber, Twitter follower, and Facebook friend who's ever sent me a message, shared a video, or posted an encouraging comment. I hope to keep making you laugh for years to come.

About the Author

ZACH ANNER is an award-winning comedian, show host, and public speaker. In 2011, he won his own travel show on the Oprah Winfrey Network, *Rollin' with Zach*. He hosted the Web series *Have a Little Faith* for Rainn Wilson's media company SoulPancake, and *Riding Shotgun* and *Workout Wednesday* on his YouTube channel, which has over fourteen million hits. Zach lives in Buffalo, New York, and Austin, Texas, and spends most of his spare time in his underwear, thinking about how he can change the world. If you'd like to know more about Zach, consult the book you are currently holding.

Zach would love to hear your thoughts on the book, or at least get an awkward photo of you caressing it, so feel free to tweet him @zachanner or visit his Web site, www.zachanner.com.

About the Illustrator

KEVIN SCARBOROUGH is an animation artist who has worked on projects for Fisher-Price, the Syfy channel, the History Channel, and Sesame Workshop's Emmy-nominated TV series *Pinky Dinky Doo*. Originally from Buffalo, New York, Kevin currently lives in New York City.

Printed in the USA
CPSIA information can be obtained
at www.ICGtesting.com
LVHW042127040823
754239LV00003B/292